Hands-On Vision and Behavior for Self-Driving Cars

Explore visual perception, lane detection, and object classification with Python 3 and OpenCV 4

Luca Venturi

Krishtof Korda

BIRMINGHAM—MUMBAI

Hands-On Vision and Behavior for Self-Driving Cars

Copyright © 2020 Packt Publishing

All rights reserved. No part of this book may be reproduced, stored in a retrieval system, or transmitted in any form or by any means, without the prior written permission of the publisher, except in the case of brief quotations embedded in critical articles or reviews.

Every effort has been made in the preparation of this book to ensure the accuracy of the information presented. However, the information contained in this book is sold without warranty, either express or implied. Neither the authors, nor Packt Publishing or its dealers and distributors, will be held liable for any damages caused or alleged to have been caused directly or indirectly by this book.

Packt Publishing has endeavored to provide trademark information about all of the companies and products mentioned in this book by the appropriate use of capitals. However, Packt Publishing cannot guarantee the accuracy of this information.

Commissioning Editor: Kunal Chaudhari
Acquisition Editor: Karan Gupta
Senior Editor: Rohit Singh
Content Development Editor: Tiksha Lad
Technical Editor: Pradeep Sahu
Copy Editor: Safis Editing
Project Coordinator: Francy Puthiry
Proofreader: Safis Editing
Indexer: Pratik Shirodkar
Production Designer: Nilesh Mohite

First published: October 2020
Production reference: 1221020

Published by Packt Publishing Ltd.
Livery Place
35 Livery Street
Birmingham
B3 2PB, UK.

ISBN 978-1-80020-358-7

www.packt.com

To my dear wife,

Thank you for your patience and your endless support. I know it is challenging to be a mother and a scientist, while being married to me. I can only hope that our son will be lucky enough to meet a woman like you.

To my co-author,

Thank you so much for joining me on this adventure. This book could become a reality only because you accepted to take care of the most difficult chapters. I knew you were a real doer, and you demonstrated it once again. It has been a pleasure to see your chapters taking shape, filled with your experiences. I am certain the readers will enjoy reading them.

-Luca Venturi

To my lovely wife,

Thank you for being so supportive throughout the writing of this book. Your care, attention, and support were invaluable. You believed in me when all I had was doubt. You kept me motivated through my darkest thoughts. You were my 3-star Michelin chef when I forgot to eat. You brought me fruit and tea to keep my energy high. You truly are the only reason I could have ever contributed to this book. You are my sunshine, my water, my air. You are my everything, forever and two weeks. This book is dedicated to you! Kocham Cię!

To my co-author,

I can't thank you enough for reaching out to me to help with this book. I don't think I would have ever been able to do something like this without your help and consideration. I really appreciate you bringing me onboard and allowing me to make my mark on this book. I am extremely impressed with your hard work and dedication and will use it as inspiration for my future endeavors. I never thought I would actually be a published author, but thanks to you we are!

-Krishtof Korda

Packt.com

Subscribe to our online digital library for full access to over 7,000 books and videos, as well as industry leading tools to help you plan your personal development and advance your career. For more information, please visit our website.

Why subscribe?

- Spend less time learning and more time coding with practical eBooks and Videos from over 4,000 industry professionals
- Improve your learning with Skill Plans built especially for you
- Get a free eBook or video every month
- Fully searchable for easy access to vital information
- Copy and paste, print, and bookmark content

Did you know that Packt offers eBook versions of every book published, with PDF and ePub files available? You can upgrade to the eBook version at packt.com and as a print book customer, you are entitled to a discount on the eBook copy. Get in touch with us at customercare@packtpub.com for more details.

At www.packt.com, you can also read a collection of free technical articles, sign up for a range of free newsletters, and receive exclusive discounts and offers on Packt books and eBooks.

Contributors

About the authors

Luca Venturi has extensive experience as a programmer with world-class companies, including Ferrari and Opera Software. He has also worked for some start-ups, including Activetainment (maker of the world's first smart bike), Futurehome (a provider of smart home solutions), and CompanyBook (whose offerings apply artificial intelligence to sales). He worked on the Data Platform team at Tapad (Telenor Group), making petabytes of data accessible to the rest of the company, and is now the lead engineer of Piano Software's analytical database.

Krishtof Korda grew up in a mountainside home over which the US Navy's Blue Angels flew during the Reno Air Races each year. A graduate from the University of Southern California and the USMC Officer Candidate School, he set the Marine Corps obstacle course record of 51 seconds. He took his love of aviation to the USAF, flying aboard the C-5M Super Galaxy as a flight test engineer for 5 years, and engineered installations of airborne experiments for the USAF Test Pilot School for 4 years. Later, he transitioned to designing sensor integrations for autonomous cars at Lyft Level 5. Now he works as an applications engineer for Ouster, integrating LIDAR sensors in the fields of robotics, AVs, drones, and mining, and loves racing Enduro mountain bikes.

About the reviewer

Choo Wilson is a data scientist from Malaysia. He applies computer vision, deep learning, and robotics techniques in projects for his clients. He builds and fine-tunes custom deep learning models from different deep learning frameworks and deploys them on different systems. Additionally, he carries out research on state-of-the-art deep learning models and performs model migration, optimization, and deployment on edge devices, and local and cloud servers. He also trains engineers in the industry though deep learning courses. Choo Wilson is currently building a YouTube channel based on robotics and autonomy using a robot powered by Jetson Nano.

Packt is searching for authors like you

If you're interested in becoming an author for Packt, please visit authors.packtpub.com and apply today. We have worked with thousands of developers and tech professionals, just like you, to help them share their insight with the global tech community. You can make a general application, apply for a specific hot topic that we are recruiting an author for, or submit your own idea.

Table of Contents

Preface

Section 1: OpenCV and Sensors and Signals

1
OpenCV Basics and Camera Calibration

Technical requirements	4	Drawing rectangles and text	15
Introduction to OpenCV and NumPy	4	Pedestrian detection using HOG	15
OpenCV and NumPy	4	Sliding window	16
Image size	5	Using HOG with OpenCV	16
Grayscale images	5	Introduction to the camera	18
RGB images	6	Camera terminology	18
		The components of a camera	25
Working with image files	7	Considerations for choosing a camera	26
Working with video files	9	Strengths and weaknesses of cameras	27
Working with webcams	10	Camera calibration with OpenCV	28
Manipulating images	10	Distortion detection	29
Flipping an image	10	Calibration	30
Blurring an image	11	Summary	31
Changing contrast, brightness, and gamma	13	Questions	32

… Table of Contents

2
Understanding and Working with Signals

Technical requirements	34	Framed-based serial protocols	50
Understanding signal types	34	Understanding CAN	51
Analog versus digital	34	Ethernet and internet protocols	55
Serial versus parallel	36	Understanding UDP	56
Universal Asynchronous Receive and Transmit (UART)	38	Understanding TCP	59
Differential versus single-ended	41	Summary	62
I2C	44	Questions	63
SPI	48	Further reading	63
		Open source protocol tools	63

3
Lane Detection

Technical requirements	66	Combined threshold	77
How to perform thresholding	66	Finding the lanes using histograms	78
How thresholding works on different color spaces	67	The sliding window algorithm	79
RGB/BGR	67	Initialization	80
HLS	69	Coordinates of the sliding windows	81
HSV	70	Polynomial fitting	82
LAB	70	Enhancing a video	84
YCbCr	71	Partial histogram	84
Our choice	71		
Perspective correction	72	Rolling average	84
Edge detection	74	Summary	85
Interpolated threshold	76	Questions	86

Section 2:
Improving How the Self-Driving Car Works with Deep Learning and Neural Networks

4
Deep Learning with Neural Networks

Technical requirements	90	Detecting MNIST handwritten digits	99
Understanding machine learning and neural networks	90	What did we just load?	100
Neural networks	91	Training samples and labels	100
Neurons	92	One-hot encoding	102
Parameters	94	Training and testing datasets	102
The success of deep learning	94	Defining the model of the neural network	103
Learning about convolutional neural networks	95	LeNet	103
Convolutions	95	The code	104
Why are convolutions so great?	97	The architecture	105
		Training a neural network	107
Getting started with Keras and TensorFlow	98	CIFAR-10	111
Requirements	98	Summary	116
		Questions	117
		Further reading	117

5
Deep Learning Workflow

Technical requirements	120	The model	129
Obtaining the dataset	120	Tuning convolutional layers	131
Datasets in the Keras module	121	Tuning MaxPooling	134
Existing datasets	121	Tuning the dense layer	135
Your custom dataset	123	How to train the network	137
		Random initialization	138
Understanding the three datasets	123	Overfitting and underfitting	139
Splitting the dataset	124	Visualizing the activations	141
Understanding classifiers	125	Inference	145
Creating a real-world dataset	126	Retraining	146
Data augmentation	127	Summary	146
		Questions	147

6
Improving Your Neural Network

Technical requirements	150	Early stopping	164
A bigger model	150	Improving the dataset with data augmentation	165
The starting point	151		
Improving the speed	152	Improving the validation accuracy with dropout	168
Increasing the depth	153		
A more efficient network	156	Applying the model to MNIST	174
Building a smarter network with batch normalization	160	Now it's your turn!	175
		Summary	175
Choosing the right batch size	164	Questions	176

7
Detecting Pedestrians and Traffic Lights

Technical requirements	178	Understanding transfer learning	194
Detecting pedestrians, vehicles, and traffic lights with SSD	178	Getting to know ImageNet	195
		Discovering AlexNet	197
Collecting some images with Carla	179	Using Inception for image classification	200
Understanding SSD	185	Using Inception for transfer learning	201
Discovering the TensorFlow detection model zoo	186	Feeding our dataset to Inception	204
Downloading and loading SSD	187	Performance with transfer learning	205
Running SSD	188	Improving transfer learning	206
Annotating the image	190	Recognizing traffic lights and their colors	209
Detecting the color of a traffic light	191	Summary	211
		Questions	212
Creating a traffic light dataset	192	Further reading	212

8
Behavioral Cloning

Technical requirements	214	Introducing DAVE-2	215
Teaching a neural network how to drive with behavioral cloning	214	Getting to know manual_control.py	216
		Recording one video stream	219

Modeling the neural network	228	Training bigger datasets using generators	246
Training a neural network for regression	229	Augmenting data the hard way	248
Visualizing the saliency maps	232	**Summary**	**248**
Integrating the neural network with Carla	**239**	**Questions**	**249**
Self-driving!	**244**	**Further reading**	**249**

9
Semantic Segmentation

Technical requirements	**252**	Adapting DenseNet for semantic segmentation	264
Introducing semantic segmentation	**252**	Coding the blocks of FC-DenseNet	265
Defining our goal	254	Putting all the pieces together	267
Collecting the dataset	255	Feeding the network	269
Modifying synchronous_mode.py	256	Running the neural network	273
Understanding DenseNet for classification	**258**	Improving bad semantic segmentation	276
DenseNet from a bird's-eye view	259	**Summary**	**277**
Understanding the dense blocks	259	**Questions**	**278**
Segmenting images with CNN	**263**	**Further reading**	**278**

Section 3:
Mapping and Controls

10
Steering, Throttle, and Brake Control

Technical requirements	**282**	MPC	289
Why do you need controls?	**282**	**Implementing PID in CARLA**	**293**
What is a controller?	283	Installing CARLA	293
Types of controllers	**283**	Cloning Packt-Town04-PID.py	294
PID	284		

Walking through your Packt-Town04-PID.py control script	295	An example MPC in C++	304
		Summary	308
PIDLongitudinalController	298	Questions	309
PIDLateralController	300	Further reading	309
Running the script	303		

11
Mapping Our Environments

Technical requirements	312	SLAM with an Ouster lidar and Google Cartographer	319
Why you need maps and localization	312	Ouster sensor	320
Maps	312	The repo	320
Localization	313	Getting started with cartographer_ros	320
Types of mapping and localization	314	Cartographer_ros configuration	320
		Docker image	328
Simultaneous localization and mapping (SLAM)	315	Summary	335
		Questions	335
Open source mapping tools	319	Further reading	335

Assessments

Chapter 1	337	Chapter 7	339
Chapter 2	337	Chapter 8	340
Chapter 3	338	Chapter 9	340
Chapter 4	338	Chapter 10	341
Chapter 5	339	Chapter 11	341
Chapter 6	339		

Other Books You May Enjoy

Index

Preface

Self-driving cars will soon be among us. The improvements seen in this field have been nothing short of extraordinary. The first time I heard about self-driving cars, it was in 2010, when I tried one in the Toyota showroom in Tokyo. The ride cost around a dollar. The car was going very slowly, and it was apparently dependent on sensors embedded in the road.

Fast forward a few years, lidar and advancements in computer vision and deep learning have made that technology look primitive and unnecessarily invasive and expensive.

In the course of this book, we will use OpenCV for a variety of tasks, including pedestrian detection and lane detection; you will discover deep learning and learn how to leverage it for image classification, object detection, and semantic segmentation, using it to identify pedestrians, cars, roads, sidewalks, and crossing lights, while learning about some of the most influential neural networks.

You will get comfortable using the CARLA simulator, which you will use to control a car using behavioral cloning and a PID controller; you will learn about network protocols, sensors, cameras, and how to use lidar to map the world around you and to find your position.

But before diving into these amazing technologies, please take a moment and try to imagine the future in 20 years. What are the cars like? They can drive by themselves. But can they also fly? Are there still crossing lights? How fast, heavy, and expensive are those cars? How do we use them, and how often? What about self-driving buses and trucks?

We cannot know the future, but it is conceivable that self-driving cars, and self-driving things in general, will shape our daily lives and our cities in new and exciting ways.

Do you want to play an active role in defining this future? If so, keep reading. This book can be the first step of your journey.

Who this book is for

The book covers several aspects of what is necessary to build a self-driving car and is intended for programmers with a basic knowledge of any programming language, preferably Python. No previous experience with deep learning is required; however, to fully understand the most advanced chapters, it might be useful to take a look at some of the suggested reading. The optional source code associated with *Chapter 11, Mapping Our Environments*, is in C++.

What this book covers

Chapter 1, OpenCV Basics and Camera Calibration, is an introduction to OpenCV and NumPy; you will learn how to manipulate images and videos, and how to detect pedestrians using OpenCV; in addition, it explains how a camera works and how OpenCV can be used to calibrate it.

Chapter 2, Understanding and Working with Signals, describes the different types of signals: serial, parallel, digital, analog, single-ended, and differential, and explains some very important protocols: CAN, Ethernet, TCP, and UDP.

Chapter 3, Lane Detection, teaches you everything you need to know to detect the lanes in a road using OpenCV. It covers color spaces, perspective correction, edge detection, histograms, the sliding window technique, and the filtering required to get the best detection.

Chapter 4, Deep Learning with Neural Networks, is a practical introduction to neural networks, designed to quickly teach how to write a neural network. It describes neural networks in general and convolutional neural networks in particular. It introduces Keras, a deep learning module, and it shows how to use it to detect handwritten digits and to classify some images.

Chapter 5, Deep Learning Workflow, ideally complements *Chapter 4, Deep Learning with Neural Networks*, as it describes the theory of neural networks and the steps required in a typical workflow: obtaining or creating a dataset, splitting it into training, validation, and test sets, data augmentation, the main layers used in a classifier, and how to train, do inference, and retrain. The chapter also covers underfitting and overfitting and explains how to visualize the activations of the convolutional layers.

Chapter 6, Improving Your Neural Network, explains how to optimize a neural network, reducing its parameters, and how to improve its accuracy using batch normalization, early stopping, data augmentation, and dropout.

Chapter 7, *Detecting Pedestrians and Traffic Lights*, introduces you to CARLA, a self-driving car simulator, which we will use to create a dataset of traffic lights. Using a pre-trained neural network called SSD, we will detect pedestrians, cars, and traffic lights, and we will use a powerful technique called transfer learning to train a neural network to classify the traffic lights according to their colors.

Chapter 8, *Behavioral Cloning*, explains how to train a neural network to drive CARLA. It explains what behavioral cloning is, how to build a driving dataset using CARLA, how to create a network that's suitable for this task, and how to train it. We will use saliency maps to get an understanding of what the network is learning, and we will integrate it with CARLA to help it self-drive!

Chapter 9, *Semantic Segmentation*, is the final and most advanced chapter about deep learning, and it explains what semantic segmentation is. It details an extremely interesting architecture called DenseNet, and it shows how to adapt it to semantic segmentation.

Chapter 10, *Steering, Throttle, and Brake Control*, is about controlling a self-driving car. It explains what a controller is, focusing on PID controllers and covering the basics of MPC controllers. Finally, we will implement a PID controller in CARLA.

Chapter 11, *Mapping Our Environments*, is the final chapter. It discusses maps, localization, and lidar, and it describes some open source mapping tools. You will learn what Simultaneous Localization and Mapping (SLAM) is and how to implement it using the Ouster lidar and Google Cartographer.

To get the most out of this book

We assume that you have basic knowledge of Python and that you are familiar with the shell of your operating system. You should install Python and possibly use a virtual environment to match the versions of the software used in the book. It is recommended to use a GPU, as training can be very demanding without one. Docker will be helpful for *Chapter 11*, *Mapping Our Environments*.

Refer to the following table for the software used in the book:

Software/Hardware covered in the book	OS Requirements
Python 3.7	Any
TensorFlow 2.2	Any
Keras 2.3	Any
CARLA 0.9.9.2	Any

If you are using the digital version of this book, we advise you to type the code yourself or access the code via the GitHub repository (link available in the next section). Doing so will help you avoid any potential errors related to the copying and pasting of code.

Download the example code files

You can download the example code files for this book from GitHub at `https://github.com/PacktPublishing/Hands-On-Vision-and-Behavior-for-Self-Driving-Cars`. In case there's an update to the code, it will be updated on the existing GitHub repository.

We also have other code bundles from our rich catalog of books and videos available at `https://github.com/PacktPublishing/`. Check them out!

Code in Action

Code in Action videos for this book can be viewed at `https://bit.ly/2FeZ5dQ`.

Download the color images

We also provide a PDF file that has color images of the screenshots/diagrams used in this book. You can download it here:

`https://static.packt-cdn.com/downloads/9781800203587_ColorImages.pdf`

Conventions used

There are a number of text conventions used throughout this book.

`Code in text`: Indicates code words in text, database table names, folder names, filenames, file extensions, pathnames, dummy URLs, user input, and Twitter handles. Here is an example: "Keras offers a method in the model to get the probability, `predict()`, and one to get the label, `predict_classes()`."

A block of code is set as follows:

```
img_threshold = np.zeros_like(channel)
img_threshold [(channel >= 180)] = 255
```

When we wish to draw your attention to a particular part of a code block, the relevant lines or items are set in bold:

```
[default]
exten => s,1,Dial(Zap/1|30)
exten => s,2,Voicemail(u100)
exten => s,102,Voicemail(b100)
exten => i,1,Voicemail(s0)
```

Any command-line input or output is written as follows:

```
/opt/carla-simulator/
```

Bold: Indicates a new term, an important word, or words that you see onscreen. For example, words in menus or dialog boxes appear in the text like this. Here is an example: "The **reference trajectory** is the desired trajectory of the controlled variable; for example, the lateral position of the vehicle in the lane."

> Tips or important notes
> Appear like this.

Get in touch

Feedback from our readers is always welcome.

General feedback: If you have questions about any aspect of this book, mention the book title in the subject of your message and email us at customercare@packtpub.com.

Errata: Although we have taken every care to ensure the accuracy of our content, mistakes do happen. If you have found a mistake in this book, we would be grateful if you would report this to us. Please visit www.packtpub.com/support/errata, selecting your book, clicking on the Errata Submission Form link, and entering the details.

Piracy: If you come across any illegal copies of our works in any form on the Internet, we would be grateful if you would provide us with the location address or website name. Please contact us at copyright@packt.com with a link to the material.

If you are interested in becoming an author: If there is a topic that you have expertise in and you are interested in either writing or contributing to a book, please visit authors.packtpub.com.

Reviews

Please leave a review. Once you have read and used this book, why not leave a review on the site that you purchased it from? Potential readers can then see and use your unbiased opinion to make purchase decisions, we at Packt can understand what you think about our products, and our authors can see your feedback on their book. Thank you!

For more information about Packt, please visit `packt.com`.

Section 1: OpenCV and Sensors and Signals

This section will focus on what can be achieved with OpenCV, and how it can be useful in the context of self-driving cars.

This section comprises the following chapters:

- *Chapter 1, OpenCV Basics and Camera Calibration*
- *Chapter 2, Understanding and Working with Signals*
- *Chapter 3, Lane Detection*

1
OpenCV Basics and Camera Calibration

This chapter is an introduction to OpenCV and how to use it in the initial phases of a self-driving car pipeline, to ingest a video stream, and prepare it for the next phases. We will discuss the characteristics of a camera from the point of view of a self-driving car and how to improve the quality of what we get out of it. We will also study how to manipulate the videos and we will try one of the most famous features of OpenCV, object detection, which we will use to detect pedestrians.

With this chapter, you will build a solid foundation on how to use OpenCV and NumPy, which will be very useful later.

In this chapter, we will cover the following topics:

- OpenCV and NumPy basics
- Reading, manipulating, and saving images
- Reading, manipulating, and saving videos
- Manipulating images
- How to detect pedestrians with HOG
- Characteristics of a camera
- How to perform the camera calibration

Technical requirements

For the instructions and code in this chapter, you need the following:

- Python 3.7
- The opencv-Python module
- The NumPy module

The code for the chapter can be found here:

https://github.com/PacktPublishing/Hands-On-Vision-and-Behavior-for-Self-Driving-Cars/tree/master/Chapter1

The Code in Action videos for this chapter can be found here:

https://bit.ly/2TdfsL7

Introduction to OpenCV and NumPy

OpenCV is a computer vision and machine learning library that has been developed for more than 20 years and provides an impressive number of functionalities. Despite some inconsistencies in the API, its simplicity and the remarkable number of algorithms implemented make it an extremely popular library and an excellent choice for many situations.

OpenCV is written in C++, but there are bindings for Python, Java, and Android.

In this book, we will focus on OpenCV for Python, with all the code tested using OpenCV 4.2.

OpenCV in Python is provided by `opencv-python`, which can be installed using the following command:

```
pip install opencv-python
```

OpenCV can take advantage of hardware acceleration, but to get the best performance, you might need to build it from the source code, with different flags than the default, to optimize it for your target hardware.

OpenCV and NumPy

The Python bindings use NumPy, which increases the flexibility and makes it compatible with many other libraries. As an OpenCV image is a NumPy array, you can use normal NumPy operations to get information about the image. A good understanding of NumPy can improve the performance and reduce the length of your code.

Let's dive right in with some quick examples of what you can do with NumPy in OpenCV.

Image size

The size of the image can be retrieved using the `shape` attribute:

```
print("Image size: ", image.shape)
```

For a grayscale image of 50x50, `image.shape()` would return the tuple (50, 50), while for an RGB image, the result would be (50, 50, 3).

> **False friends**
>
> In NumPy, the attribute size is the size in bytes of the array; for a 50x50 gray image, it would be 2,500, while for the same image in RGB, it would be 7,500. It's the `shape` attribute that contains the size of the image – (50, 50) and (50, 50, 3), respectively.

Grayscale images

Grayscale images are represented by a two-dimensional NumPy array. The first index affects the rows (*y* coordinate) and the second index the columns (*x* coordinate). The *y* coordinates have their origin in the top corner of the image and *x* coordinates have their origin in the left corner of the image.

It is possible to create a black image using `np.zeros()`, which initializes all the pixels to 0:

```
black = np.zeros([100,100],dtype=np.uint8)   # Creates a black image
```

The previous code creates a grayscale image with size (100, 100), composed of 10,000 unsigned bytes (`dtype=np.uint8`).

To create an image with pixels with a different value than 0, you can use the `full()` method:

```
white = np.full([50, 50], 255, dtype=np.uint8)
```

To change the color of all the pixels at once, it's possible to use the `[:]` notation:

```
img[:] = 64          # Change the pixels color to dark gray
```

To affect only some rows, it is enough to provide a range of rows in the first index:

```
img[10:20] = 192    # Paints 10 rows with light gray
```

The previous code changes the color of rows 10-20, including row 10, but excluding row 20.

The same mechanism works for columns; you just need to specify the range in the second index. To instruct NumPy to include a full index, we use the `[:]` notation that we already encountered:

```
img[:, 10:20] = 64 # Paints 10 columns with dark gray
```

You can also combine operations on rows and columns, selecting a rectangular area:

```
img[90:100, 90:100] = 0    # Paints a 10x10 area with black
```

It is, of course, possible to operate on a single pixel, as you would do on a normal array:

```
img[50, 50] = 0    # Paints one pixel with black
```

It is possible to use NumPy to select a part of an image, also called the **Region Of Interest (ROI)**. For example, the following code copies a 10x10 **ROI** from the position (90, 90) to the position (80, 80):

```
roi = img[90:100, 90:100]
img[80:90, 80:90] = roi
```

The following is the result of the previous operations:

Figure 1.1 – Some manipulation of images using NumPy slicing

To make a copy of an image, you can simply use the `copy()` method:

```
image2 = image.copy()
```

RGB images

RGB images differ from grayscale because they are three-dimensional, with the third index representing the three channels. Please note that OpenCV stores the images in BGR format, not RGB, so channel 0 is blue, channel 1 is green, and channel 2 is red.

> **Important note**
> OpenCV stores the images as BGR, not RGB. In the rest of the book, when talking about RGB images, it will only mean that it is a 24-bit color image, but the internal representation will usually be BGR.

To create an RGB image, we need to provide three sizes:

```
rgb = np.zeros([100, 100, 3],dtype=np.uint8)
```

If you were going to run the same code previously used on the grayscale image with the new RGB image (skipping the third index), you would get the same result. This is because NumPy would apply the same color to all the three channels, which results in a shade of gray.

To select a color, it is enough to provide the third index:

```
rgb[:, :, 2] = 255         # Makes the image red
```

In NumPy, it is also possible to select rows, columns, or channels that are not contiguous. You can do this by simply providing a tuple with the required indexes. To make the image magenta, you need to set the blue and red channels to 255, which can be achieved with the following code:

```
rgb[:, :, (0, 2)] = 255   # Makes the image magenta
```

You can convert an RGB image into grayscale using `cvtColor()`:

```
gray = cv2.cvtColor(original, cv2.COLOR_BGR2GRAY)
```

Working with image files

OpenCV provides a very simple way to load images, using `imread()`:

```
import cv2
image = cv2.imread('test.jpg')
```

To show the image, you can use `imshow()`, which accepts two parameters:

- The name to write on the caption of the window that will show the image
- The image to be shown

Unfortunately, its behavior is counterintuitive, as it will not show an image unless it is followed by a call to `waitKey()`:

```
cv2.imshow("Image", image)
cv2.waitKey(0)
```

The call to `waitKey()` after `imshow()` will have two effects:

- It will actually allow OpenCV to show the image provided to `imshow()`.
- It will wait for the specified amount of milliseconds, or until a key is pressed if the amount of milliseconds passed is <=0. It will wait indefinitely.

An image can be saved on disk using the `imwrite()` method, which accepts three parameters:

- The name of the file
- The image
- An optional format-dependent parameter:

```
cv2.imwrite("out.jpg", image)
```

Sometimes, it can be very useful to combine multiple pictures by putting them next to each other. Some examples in this book will use this feature extensively to compare images.

OpenCV provides two methods for this purpose: `hconcat()` to concatenate the pictures horizontally and `vconcat()` to concatenate them vertically, both accepting as a parameter a list of images. Take the following example:

```
black = np.zeros([50, 50], dtype=np.uint8)
white = np.full([50, 50], 255, dtype=np.uint8)
cv2.imwrite("horizontal.jpg", cv2.hconcat([white, black]))
cv2.imwrite("vertical.jpg", cv2.vconcat([white, black]))
```

Here's the result:

Figure 1.2 – Horizontal concatenation with hconcat() and vertical concatenation with vconcat()

We could use these two methods to create a chequerboard pattern:

```
row1 = cv2.hconcat([white, black])
row2 = cv2.hconcat([black, white])
cv2.imwrite("chess.jpg", cv2.vconcat([row1, row2]))
```

You will see the following chequerboard:

Figure 1.3 – A chequerboard pattern created using hconcat() in combination with vconcat()

After having worked with images, it's time we work with videos.

Working with video files

Using videos in OpenCV is very simple; in fact, every frame is an image and can be manipulated with the methods that we have already analyzed.

To open a video in OpenCV, you need to call the `VideoCapture()` method:

```
cap = cv2.VideoCapture("video.mp4")
```

After that, you can call `read()`, typically in a loop, to retrieve a single frame. The method returns a tuple with two values:

- A Boolean value that is false when the video is finished
- The next frame:

```
ret, frame = cap.read()
```

To save a video, there is the `VideoWriter` object; its constructor accepts four parameters:

- The filename
- A FOURCC (four-character code) of the video code
- The number of frames per second
- The resolution

Take the following example:

```
mp4 = cv2.VideoWriter_fourcc(*'MP4V')
writer = cv2.VideoWriter('video-out.mp4', mp4, 15, (640, 480))
```

Once `VideoWriter` has been created, the `write()` method can be used to add a frame to the video file:

```
writer.write(image)
```

When you have finished using the `VideoCapture` and `VideoWriter` objects, you should call their release method:

```
cap.release()
writer.release()
```

Working with webcams

Webcams are handled similarly to a video in OpenCV; you just need to provide a different parameter to `VideoCapture`, which is the 0-based index identifying the webcam:

```
cap = cv2.VideoCapture(0)
```

The previous code opens the first webcam; if you need to use a different one, you can specify a different index.

Now, let's try manipulating some images.

Manipulating images

As part of a computer vision pipeline for a self-driving car, with or without deep learning, you might need to process the video stream to make other algorithms work better as part of a preprocessing step.

This section will provide you with a solid foundation to preprocess any video stream.

Flipping an image

OpenCV provides the `flip()` method to flip an image, and it accepts two parameters:

- The image
- A number that can be 1 (horizontal flip), 0 (vertical flip), or -1 (both horizontal and vertical flip)

Let's see a sample code:

```
flipH = cv2.flip(img, 1)
flipV = cv2.flip(img, 0)
flip = cv2.flip(img, -1)
```

This will produce the following result:

Figure 1.4 – Original image, horizontally flipped, vertically flipped, and both

As you can see, the first image is our original image, which was flipped horizontally and vertically, and then both, horizontally and vertically together.

Blurring an image

Sometimes, an image can be too noisy, possibly because of some processing steps that you have done. OpenCV provides several methods to blur an image, which can help in these situations. Most likely, you will have to take into consideration not only the quality of the blur but also the speed of execution.

The simplest method is `blur()`, which applies a low-pass filter to the image and requires at least two parameters:

- The image
- The kernel size (a bigger kernel means more blur):

```
blurred = cv2.blur(image, (15, 15))
```

Another option is to use `GaussianBlur()`, which offers more control and requires at least three parameters:

- The image
- The kernel size
- `sigmaX`, which is the standard deviation on X

It is recommended to specify both `sigmaX` and `sigmaY` (standard deviation on Y, the forth parameter):

```
gaussian = cv2.GaussianBlur(image, (15, 15), sigmaX=15,
sigmaY=15)
```

An interesting blurring method is `medianBlur()`, which computes the median and therefore has the characteristic of emitting only pixels with colors present in the image (which does not necessarily happen with the previous method). It is effective at reducing "salt and pepper" noise and has two mandatory parameters:

- The image
- The kernel size (an odd integer greater than 1):

```
median = cv2.medianBlur(image, 15)
```

There is also a more complex filter, `bilateralFilter()`, which is effective at removing noise while keeping the edge sharp. It is the slowest of the filters, and it requires at least four parameters:

- The image
- The diameter of each pixel neighborhood
- `sigmaColor`: Filters sigma in the color space, affecting how much the different colors are mixed together, inside the pixel neighborhood
- `sigmaSpace`: Filters sigma in the coordinate space, affecting how distant pixels affect each other, if their colors are closer than `sigmaColor`:

```
bilateral = cv2.bilateralFilter(image, 15, 50, 50)
```

Choosing the best filter will probably require some experiments. You might also need to consider the speed. To give you some ballpark estimations based on my tests, and considering that the performance is dependent on the parameters supplied, note the following:

- `blur()` is the fastest.
- `GaussianBlur()` is similar, but it can be 2x slower than `blur()`.
- `medianBlur()` can easily be 20x slower than `blur()`.
- `BilateralFilter()` is the slowest and can be 45x slower than `blur()`.

Here are the resultant images:

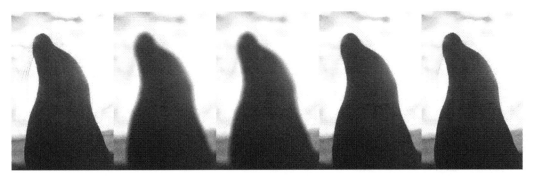

Figure 1.5 – Original, blur(), GaussianBlur(), medianBlur(), and BilateralFilter(), with the parameters used in the code samples

Changing contrast, brightness, and gamma

A very useful function is `convertScaleAbs()`, which executes several operations on all the values of the array:

- It multiplies them by the scaling parameter, `alpha`.
- It adds to them the delta parameter, `beta`.
- If the result is above 255, it is set to 255.
- The result is converted into an unsigned 8-bit int.

The function accepts four parameters:

- The source image
- The destination (optional)
- The `alpha` parameter used for the scaling
- The `beta` delta parameter

`convertScaleAbs()` can be used to affect the contrast, as an `alpha` scaling factor above 1 increases the contrast (amplifying the color difference between pixels), while a scaling factor below one reduces it (decreasing the color difference between pixels):

```
cv2.convertScaleAbs(image, more_contrast, 2, 0)
cv2.convertScaleAbs(image, less_contrast, 0.5, 0)
```

It can also be used to affect the brightness, as the `beta` delta factor can be used to increase the value of all the pixels (increasing the brightness) or to reduce them (decreasing the brightness):

```
cv2.convertScaleAbs(image, more_brightness, 1, 64)
cv2.convertScaleAbs(image, less_brightness, 1, -64)
```

Let's see the resulting images:

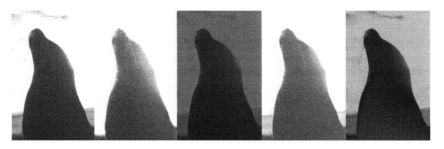

Figure 1.6 – Original, more contrast (2x), less contrast (0.5x), more brightness (+64), and less brightness (-64)

A more sophisticated method to change the brightness is to apply gamma correction. This can be done with a simple calculation using NumPy. A gamma value above 1 will increase the brightness, and a gamma value below 1 will reduce it:

```
Gamma = 1.5
g_1_5 = np.array(255 * (image / 255) ** (1 / Gamma), dtype='uint8')
Gamma = 0.7
g_0_7 = np.array(255 * (image / 255) ** (1 / Gamma), dtype='uint8')
```

The following images will be produced:

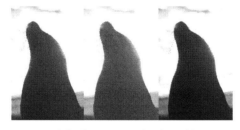

Figure 1.7 – Original, higher gamma (1.5), and lower gamma (0.7)

You can see the effect of different gamma values in the middle and right images.

Drawing rectangles and text

When working on object detection tasks, it is a common need to highlight an area to see what has been detected. OpenCV provides the `rectangle()` function, accepting at least the following parameters:

- The image
- The upper-left corner of the rectangle
- The lower-right corner of the rectangle
- The color to use
- (Optional) The thickness:

```
cv2.rectangle(image, (x, y), (x + w, y + h), (255, 255, 255), 2)
```

To write some text in the image, you can use the `putText()` method, accepting at least six parameters:

- The image
- The text to print
- The coordinates of the bottom-left corner
- The font face
- The scale factor, to change the size
- The color:

```
cv2.putText(image, 'Text', (x, y), cv2.FONT_HERSHEY_PLAIN, 2, clr)
```

Pedestrian detection using HOG

The **Histogram of Oriented Gradients** (**HOG**) is an object detection technique implemented by OpenCV. In simple cases, it can be used to see whether there is a certain object present in the image, where it is, and how big it is.

OpenCV includes a detector trained for pedestrians, and you are going to use it. It might not be enough for a real-life situation, but it is useful to learn how to use it. You could also train another one with more images to see whether it performs better. Later in the book, you will see how to use deep learning to detect not only pedestrians but also cars and traffic lights.

Sliding window

The HOG pedestrian detector in OpenCV is trained with a model that is 48x96 pixels, and therefore it is not able to detect objects smaller than that (or, better, it could, but the box will be 48x96).

At the core of the HOG detector, there is a mechanism able to tell whether a given 48x96 image is a pedestrian. As this is not terribly useful, OpenCV implements a sliding window mechanism, where the detector is applied many times, on slightly different positions; the "image window" under consideration slides a bit. Once it has analyzed the whole image, the image window is increased in size (scaled) and the detector is applied again, to be able to detect bigger objects. Therefore, the detector is applied hundreds or even thousands of times for each image, which can be slow.

Using HOG with OpenCV

First, you need to initialize the detector and specify that you want to use the detector for pedestrians:

```
hog = cv2.HOGDescriptor()
det = cv2.HOGDescriptor_getDefaultPeopleDetector()
hog.setSVMDetector(det)
```

Then, it is just a matter of calling `detectMultiScale()`:

```
(boxes, weights) = hog.detectMultiScale(image, winStride=(1, 1), padding=(0, 0), scale=1.05)
```

The parameters that we used require some explanation, and they are as follows:

- The image
- `winStride`, the window stride, which specifies how much the sliding window moves every time
- Padding, which can add some padding pixels at the border of the image (useful to detect pedestrians close to the border)
- Scale, which specifies how much to increase the window image every time

You should consider that **decreasing** `winSize` can improve the accuracy (as more positions are considered), but it has a big impact on performance. For example, a stride of (4, 4) can be up to 16 times faster than a stride of (1, 1), though in practice, the performance difference is a bit less, maybe 10 times.

In general, **decreasing the scale** also improves the precision and decreases the performance, though the impact is not dramatic.

Improving the precision means detecting more pedestrians, but this can also increase the false positives. `detectMultiScale()` has a couple of advanced parameters that can be used for this:

- `hitThreshold`, which changes the distance required from the **Support Vector Machine (SVM)** plane. A higher threshold means than the detector is more confident with the result.
- `finalThreshold`, which is related to the number of detections in the same area.

Tuning these parameters requires some experiments, but in general, a higher `hitThreshold` value (typically in the range 0–1.0) should reduce the false positives.

A higher `finalThreshold` value (such as 10) will also reduce the false positives.

We will use `detectMultiScale()` on an image with pedestrians generated by Carla:

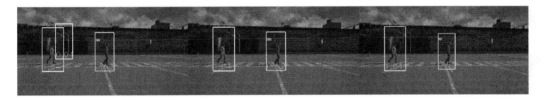

Figure 1.8 – HOG detection, winStride=(1, 2), scale=1.05, padding=(0, 0)
Left: hitThreshold = 0, finalThreshold = 1; Center: hitThreshold = 0, finalThreshold = 3;
Right: hitThreshold = 0.2, finalThreshold = 1

As you can see, we have pedestrians being detected in the image. Using a low hit threshold and a low final threshold can result in false positives, as in the left image. Your goal is to find the right balance, detecting the pedestrians but without having too many false positives.

Introduction to the camera

The camera is probably one of the most ubiquitous sensors in our modern world. They are used in everyday life in our mobile phones, laptops, surveillance systems, and of course, photography. They provide rich, high-resolution imagery containing extensive information about the environment, including spatial, color, and temporal information.

It is no surprise that they are heavily used in self-driving technologies. One reason why the camera is so popular is that it mirrors the functionality of the human eye. For this reason, we are very comfortable using them as we connect on a deep level with their functionality, limitations, and strengths.

In this section, you will learn about the following:

- Camera terminology
- The components of a camera
- Strengths and weaknesses
- Choosing the right camera for self-driving

Let's discuss each in detail.

Camera terminology

Before you learn about the components of a camera and its strengths and weaknesses, you need to know some basic terminology. These terms will be important when evaluating and ultimately choosing your camera for your self-driving application.

Field of View (FoV)

This is the vertical and horizontal angular portion of the environment (scene) that is visible to the sensor. In self-driving cars, you typically want to balance the FoV with the resolution of the sensor to ensure we see as much of the environment as possible with the least number of cameras. There is a trade space related to FoV. Larger FoV usually means more lens distortion, which you will need to compensate for in your camera calibration (see the section on camera calibration):

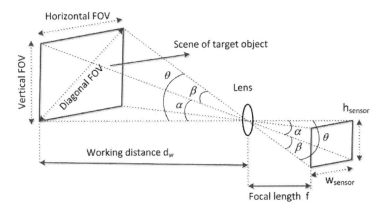

Figure 1.9 – Field of View, credit: https://www.researchgate.net/figure/Illustration-of-camera-lenss-field-of-view-FOV_fig4_335011596

Resolution

This is the total number of pixels in the horizontal and vertical directions on the sensor. This parameter is often discussed using the term **megapixels (MP)**. For example, a 5 MP camera, such as the FLIR Blackfly, has a sensor with 2448 × 2048 pixels, which equates to 5,013,504 pixels.

Higher resolutions allow you to use a lens with a wider FoV but still provide the detail needed for running your computer vision algorithms. This means you can use fewer cameras to cover the environment and thereby lower the cost.

The Blackfly, in all its different flavors, is a common camera used in self-driving vehicles thanks to its cost, small form, reliability, robustness, and ease of integration:

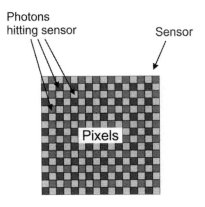

Figure 1.10 – Pixel resolution

Focal length

This is the length from the lens optical center to the sensor. The focal length is best thought of as the zoom of the camera. A longer focal length means you will be zoomed in closer to objects in the environment. In your self-driving car, you may choose different focal lengths based on what you need to see in the environment. For example, you might choose a relatively long focal length of 100 mm to ensure enough resolution for your classifier algorithm to detect a traffic signal at a distance far enough to allow the car to react with smooth and safe stopping:

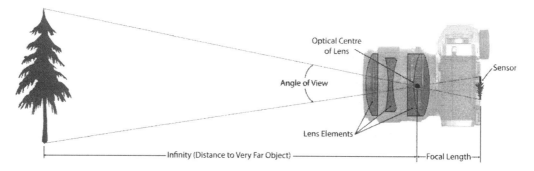

Figure 1.11 – Focal length, credit: `https://photographylife.com/what-is-focal-length-in-photography`

Aperture and f-stop

This is the opening through which light passes to shine on the sensor. The unit that is commonly used to describe the size of the opening is the f-stop, which refers to the ratio of the focal length over the aperture size. For example, a lens with a 50 mm focal length and an aperture diameter of 35 mm will equate to an f-stop of f/1.4. The following figure illustrates different aperture diameters and their f-stop values on a 50 mm focal length lens. Aperture size is very important in your self-driving car as it is directly correlated with the **Depth of Field** (**DoF**). Large apertures also allow the camera to be tolerant of obscurants (for example, bugs) that may be on the lens. Larger apertures allow light to pass around the bug and still make it to the sensor:

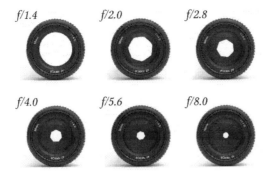

Figure 1.12 – Aperture, credit: `https://en.wikipedia.org/wiki/Aperture#/media/File:Lenses_with_different_apertures.jpg`

Depth of field (DoF)

This is the distance range in the environment that will be in focus. This is directly correlated to the size of the aperture. Generally, in self-driving cars, you will want a deep DoF so that everything in the FoV is in focus for your computer vision algorithms. The problem is that deep DoF is achieved with a small aperture, which means less light impacting the sensor. So, you will need to balance DoF with dynamic range and ISO to ensure you see everything you need to in your environment.

The following figure depicts the relationship between DoF and aperture:

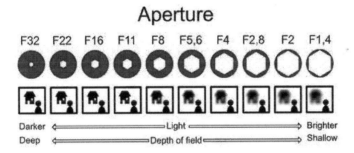

Figure 1.13 – DoF versus aperture, credit: `https://thumbs.dreamstime.com/z/aperture-infographic-explaining-depth-field-corresponding-values-their-effect-blur-light-75823732.jpg`

Dynamic range

This is a property of the sensor that indicates its contrast ratio or the ratio of the brightest over the darkest subjects that it can resolve. This may be referred to using the unit dB (for example, 78 dB) or contrast ratio (for example, 2,000,000/1).

Self-driving cars need to operate both during the day and at night. This means that the sensor needs to be sensitive enough to provide useful detail in dark conditions while not oversaturating when driving in bright sunlight. Another reason for **High Dynamic Range (HDR)** is the example of driving when the sun is low on the horizon. I am sure you have experienced this while driving yourself to work in the morning and the sun is right in your face and you can barely see the environment in front of you because it is saturating your eyes. HDR means that the sensor will be able to see the environment even in the face of direct sunlight. The following figure illustrates these conditions:

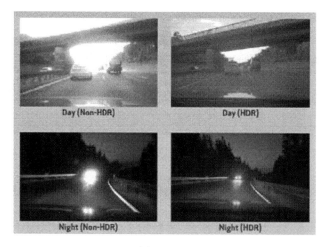

Figure 1.14 – Example HDR, credit: `https://petapixel.com/2011/05/02/use-iso-numbers-that-are-multiples-of-160-when-shooting-dslr-video/`

> **Your dream dynamic range**
>
> If you could make a wish and have whatever dynamic range you wanted in your sensor, what would it be?

International Organization for Standardization (ISO) sensitivity

This is the sensitivity of the pixels to incoming photons.

Wait a minute, you say, *do you have your acronym mixed up?* It looks like it, but the International Organization for Standardization decided to standardize even their acronym since it would be different in every language otherwise. Thanks, ISO!

The standardized ISO values can range from 100 to upward of 10,000. Lower ISO values correspond to a lower sensitivity of the sensor. Now you may ask, "why wouldn't I want the highest sensitivity?" Well, sensitivity comes at a cost...NOISE. The higher the ISO, the more noise you will see in your images. This added noise may cause trouble for your computer vision algorithms when trying to classify objects. In the following figure, you can see the effect of higher ISO values on noise in an image. These images are all taken with the lens cap on (fully dark). As you increase the ISO value, random noise starts to creep in:

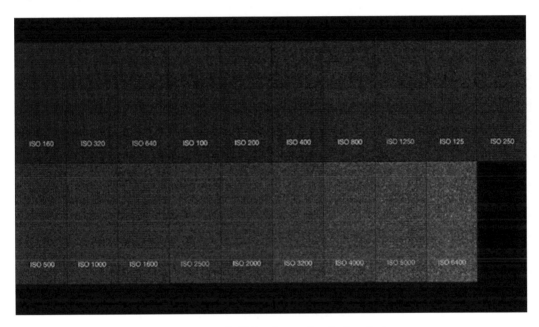

Figure 1.15 – Example ISO values and noise in a dark room

Frame rate (FPS)

This is the rate at which the sensor can obtain consecutive images, usually expressed in Hz or **Frames Per Second** (**FPS**). Generally speaking, you want to have the fastest frame rate so that fast-moving objects are not blurry in your scene. The main trade-off here is latency: the time from a real event happening until your computer vision algorithm detects it. The higher the frame rate that must be processed, the higher the latency. In the following figure, you can see the effect of frame rate on motion blur.

Blur is not the only reason for choosing a higher frame rate. Depending on the speed of your vehicle, you will need a frame rate that will allow the vehicle to react if an object suddenly appears in its FoV. If your frame rate is too slow, by the time the vehicle sees something, it may be too late to react:

Figure 1.16 – 120 Hz versus 60 Hz frame rate, credit: `https://gadgetstouse.com/blog/2020/03/18/difference-between-60hz-90hz-120hz-displays/`

Lens flare

These are the artifacts of light from an object that impact pixels on the sensor that do not correlate with the position of the object in the environment. You have likely experienced this driving at night when you see oncoming headlights. That starry effect is due to light scattered in the lens of your eye (or camera), due to imperfections, leading some of the photons to impact "pixels" that do not correlate with where the photons came from – that is, the headlights. The following figure shows what that effect looks like. You can see that the starburst makes it very difficult to see the actual object, the car!

Figure 1.17 – Lens flare from oncoming headlights, credit: `https://s.blogcdn.com/cars.aol.co.uk/media/2011/02/headlights-450-a-g.jpg`

Lens distortion

This is the difference between the rectilinear or real scene to what your camera image sees. If you have ever seen action camera footage, you probably recognized the "fish-eye" lens effect. The following figure shows an extreme example of the distortion from a wide-angle lens. You will learn to correct this distortion with OpenCV:

Figure 1.18 – Lens distortion, credit: `https://www.slacker.xyz/post/what-lens-should-i-get`

The components of a camera

Like the eye, a camera is made up of a light-sensitive array, an aperture, and a lens.

Light sensitive array – CMOS sensor (the camera's retina)

The light-sensitive array, in most consumer cameras, is called a CMOS active-pixel sensor (or just a sensor). Its basic function is to convert incident photons into an electrical current that can be digitized based on the color wavelength of the photon.

The aperture (the camera's iris)

The aperture or iris of a camera is the opening through which light can pass on its way to the sensor. This can be variable or fixed depending on the type of camera you are using. The aperture is used to control parameters such as depth of field and the amount of light hitting the sensor.

The lens (the camera's lens)

The lens or optics are the components of the camera that focus the light from the environment onto the sensor. The lens primarily determines the **FoV** of the camera through its focal length. In self-driving applications, the FoV is very important since it determines how much of the environment the car can see with a single camera. The optics of a camera are often some of the most expensive parts and have a large impact on image quality and lens flare.

Considerations for choosing a camera

Now that you have learned all the basics of what a camera is and the relevant terminology, it is time to learn how to choose a camera for your self-driving application. The following is a list of the primary factors that you will need to balance when choosing a camera:

- Resolution
- FoV
- Dynamic range
- Cost
- Size
- Ingress protection (IP rating)

> **The perfect camera**
> If you could design the ideal camera, what would it be?

My perfect self-driving camera would be able to see in all directions (spherical FoV, 360° HFoV x 360° VFoV). It would have infinite resolution and dynamic range, so you could digitally resolve objects at any distance in any lighting condition. It would be the size of a grain of rice, completely water- and dustproof, and would cost $5! Obviously, this is not possible. So, we must make some careful trade-offs for what we need.

The best place to start is with your budget for cameras. This will give you an idea of what models and specifications to look for.

Next, consider what you need to see for your application:

- Do you need to be able to see a child from 200 m away while traveling at 100 km/h?
- What coverage around the vehicle do you need, and can you tolerate any blind spots on the side of the vehicle?
- Do you need to see at night and during the day?

Lastly, consider how much room you have to integrate these cameras. You probably don't want your vehicle to look like this:

Figure 1.19 – Camera art, credit: `https://www.flickr.com/photos/laughingsquid/1645856255/`

This may be very overwhelming, but it is important when thinking about how to design your computer vision system. A good camera to start with that is very popular is the FLIR Blackfly S series. They strike an excellent balance of resolution, FPS, and cost. Next, pair it with a lens that meets your FoV needs. There are some helpful FoV calculators available on the internet, such as the one from `http://www.bobatkins.com/photography/technical/field_of_view.html`.

Strengths and weaknesses of cameras

Now, no sensor is perfect, and even your beloved camera will have its pros and cons. Let's go over some of them now.

Let's look at the strengths first:

- **High-resolution**: Relative to other sensor types, such as radar, lidar, and sonar, cameras have an excellent resolution for picking out objects in your scene. You can easily find cameras with 5 MP resolution quite cheaply.
- **Texture, color, and contrast information**: Cameras provide very rich information about the environment that other sensor types just can't. This is because of a variety of wavelengths that cameras sense.
- **Cost**: Cameras are one of the cheapest sensors you can find, especially for the quality of data they provide.

- **Size**: CMOS technology and modern ASICs have made cameras incredibly small, many less than 30 mm cubed.
- **Range**: This is really thanks to the high resolution and passive nature of the sensor.

Next, here are the weaknesses:

- **A large amount of data to process for object detection**: With high resolution comes a lot of data. Such is the price we pay for such accurate and detailed imagery.
- **Passive**: A camera requires an external illumination source, such as the sun, headlights, and so on.
- **Obscurants (such as bugs, raindrops, heavy fog, dust, or snow)**: A camera is not particularly good at seeing through heavy rain, fog, dust, or snow. Radars are typically better suited for this.
- **Lack native depth/velocity information**: A camera image alone doesn't give you any information on an object's speed or distance.

    Photogrammetry is helping to bolster this weakness but costs valuable processing resources (GPU, CPU, latency, and so on.) It is also less accurate than a radar or lidar sensor, which produce this information natively.

Now that you have a good understanding of how a camera works, as well as its basic parts and terminology, it's time to get your hands dirty and start calibrating a camera with OpenCV.

Camera calibration with OpenCV

In this section, you will learn how to take objects with a known pattern and use them to correct lens distortion using OpenCV.

Remember the lens distortion we talked about in the previous section? You need to correct this to ensure you accurately locate where objects are relative to your vehicle. It does you no good to see an object if you don't know whether it is in front of you or next to you. Even good lenses can distort the image, and this is particularly true for wide-angle lenses. Luckily, OpenCV provides a mechanism to detect this distortion and correct it!

The idea is to take pictures of a chessboard, so OpenCV can use this high-contrast pattern to detect the position of the points and compute the distortion based on the difference between the expected image and the recorded one.

You need to provide several pictures at different orientations. It might take some experiments to find a good set of pictures, but 10 to 20 images should be enough. If you use a printed chessboard, take care to have the paper as flat as possible so as to not compromise the measurements:

Figure 1.20 – Some examples of pictures that can be used for calibration

As you can see, the central image clearly shows some barrel distortion.

Distortion detection

OpenCV tries to map a series of three-dimensional points to the two-dimensional coordinates of the camera. OpenCV will then use this information to correct the distortion.

The first thing to do is to initialize some structures:

```
image_points = []    # 2D points
object_points = []   # 3D points

coords = np.zeros((1, nX * nY, 3), np.float32)
coords[0,:,:2] = np.mgrid[0:nY, 0:nX].T.reshape(-1, 2)
```

Please note nX and nY, which are the number of points to find in the chessboard on the x and y axes,, respectively. In practice, this is the number of squares minus 1.

Then, we need to call findChessboardCorners():

```
found, corners = cv2.findChessboardCorners(image, (nY, nX),
    None)
```

found is true if OpenCV found the points, and corners will contain the points found.

In our code, we will assume that the image has been converted into grayscale, but you can calibrate using an RGB picture as well.

OpenCV provides a nice image depicting the corners found, ensuring that the algorithm is working properly:

```
out = cv2.drawChessboardCorners(image, (nY, nX), corners, True)
object_points.append(coords)    # Save 3d points
image_points.append(corners)    # Save corresponding 2d points
```

Let's see the resulting image:

Figure 1.21 – Corners of the calibration image found by OpenCV

Calibration

After finding the corners in several images, we are finally ready to generate the calibration data using `calibrateCamera()`:

```
ret, mtx, dist, rvecs, tvecs = cv2.calibrateCamera(object_
points, image_points, shape[::-1], None, None)
```

Now, we are ready to correct our images, using `undistort()`:

```
dst = cv2.undistort(image, mtx, dist, None, mtx)
```

Let's see the result:

Figure 1.22 – Original image and calibrated image

We can see that the second image has less barrel distortion, but it is not great. We probably need more and better calibration samples.

But we can also try to get more precision from the same calibration images by looking for **sub-pixel precision** when looking for the corners. This can be done by calling `cornerSubPix()` after `findChessboardCorners()`:

```
corners = cv2.cornerSubPix(image, corners, (11, 11), (-1,
-1), (cv2.TERM_CRITERIA_EPS + cv2.TERM_CRITERIA_MAX_ITER, 30,
0.001))
```

The following is the resulting image:

Figure 1.23 – Image calibrated with sub-pixel precision

As the complete code is a bit long, I recommend checking out the full source code on GitHub.

Summary

Well, you have had a great start to your computer vision journey toward making a real self-driving car.

You learned about a very useful toolset called OpenCV with bindings for Python and NumPy. With these tools, you are now able to create and import images using methods such as `imread()`, `imshow()`, `hconcat()`, and `vconcat()`. You learned how to import and create video files, as well as capturing video from a webcam with methods such as `VideoCapture()` and `VideoWriter()`. Watch out Spielberg, there is a new movie-maker in town!

It was wonderful to be able to import images, but how do you start manipulating them to help your computer vision algorithms learn what features matter? You learned how to do this through methods such as `flip()`, `blur()`, `GaussianBlur()`, `medianBlur()`, `bilateralFilter()`, and `convertScaleAbs()`. Then, you learned how to annotate images for human consumption with methods such as `rectangle()` and `putText()`.

Then came the real magic, where you learned how to take the images and do your first piece of real computer vision using HOG to detect pedestrians. You learned how to apply a sliding window to scan the detector over an image in various sized windows using the `detectMultiScale()` method, with parameters such as `winStride`, `padding`, `scale`, `hitThreshold`, and `finalThreshold`.

You had a lot of fun with all the new tools you learned for working with images. But there was something missing. How do I get these images on my self-driving car? To answer this, you learned about the camera and its basic terminology, such as **resolution**, **FoV**, **focal length**, **aperture**, **DoF**, **dynamic range**, **ISO**, **frame rate**, **lens flare**, and finally, **lens distortion**. Then, you learned the basic components that comprise a camera, namely the lens, aperture, and light-sensitive arrays. With these basics, you moved on to some considerations for choosing a camera for your application by learning about the strengths and weaknesses of a camera.

Armed with this knowledge, you boldly began to remove one of these weaknesses, lens distortion, with the tools you learned in OpenCV for distortion correction. You used methods such as `findChessboardCorners()`, `calibrateCamera()`, `undistort()`, and `cornerSubPix()` for this.

Wow, you are really on your way to being able to perceive the world in your self-driving application. You should take a moment and be proud of what you have learned so far. Maybe you can celebrate with a selfie and apply some of what you learned!

In the next chapter, you are going to learn about some of the basic signal types and protocols you are likely to encounter when trying to integrate sensors in your self-driving application.

Questions

1. Can OpenCV take advantage of hardware acceleration?
2. What's the best blurring method if CPU power is not a problem?
3. Which detector can be used to find pedestrians in an image?
4. How can you read the video stream from a webcam?
5. What is the trade-off between aperture and depth of field?
6. When do you need a high ISO?
7. Is it worth computing sub-pixel precision for camera calibration?

2
Understanding and Working with Signals

In this chapter, you will learn about several different signal types that you are likely to see when integrating the sensors that you have chosen for your project. You will also learn about the various signal architectures, and the chapter will help you choose the one that is most appropriate for your application. Each has its pitfalls, protocols, and prescriptions.

In this chapter, we will cover the following topics:

- Signal types
- Analog verus digital
- Serial data
- CAN
- UDP
- TCP

By the end of this chapter, you will be able to apply your understanding of each protocol. You will be able to decode the serial data of various protocols by hand to aid in debugging signals. Most importantly, you will have the knowledge required to help you apply open source tools to do the heavy lifting for you.

Technical requirements

To execute the instructions in this chapter, you need the following:

- Basic electrical circuit knowledge (about voltage, current, and resistance)
- Binary, hexadecimal, and ASCII programming knowledge
- Oscilloscope experience for probing sensor signals

The code for the chapter can be found at:

`https://github.com/PacktPublishing/Hands-On-Vision-and-Behavior-for-Self-Driving-Cars/tree/master/Chapter2`

The Code in Action videos for this chapter can be found here:

`https://bit.ly/2HpFqZa`

Understanding signal types

You will encounter many different signal types when integrating sensors, actuators, and controllers for a self-driving car. You will need an understanding of the strengths and weaknesses of each type to help you select the correct devices to integrate. The next few sections will cover all the details regarding each signal type and arm you with the knowledge to make the right choices.

Here are the basic signal types that you will encounter in robotics and self-driving cars:

- Serial
- Parallel
- Analog
- Digital
- Single-ended
- Differential

In the next section, you will learn the difference between analog and digital signals.

Analog versus digital

The first thing to remember is that we live in an analog world. Nothing is instantaneous and everything is continuous. This is the reason why we can't teleport, sadly!

Similarly, analog signals are continuous and everchanging; they don't jump instantaneously but instead smoothly transition from one state to another. A prime example of an analog signal is the old **Amplitude Modulation (AM)** radio. You can see in the following figure how the smooth data signal is modulated onto a smooth carrier wave to create the smooth AM signal. Here, the pitch is represented by how quickly the amplitude is changing and the volume is represented by how great the amplitude is:

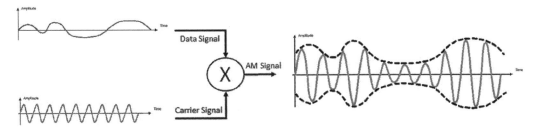

Figure 2.1 – Analog signal example

In contrast, a digital signal is one that is sampled at known points in time. When the signal is sampled, it is checked to see whether it is above or below a certain threshold, which will determine whether it is a logic 0 or 1. You can see an example of this in the following figure:

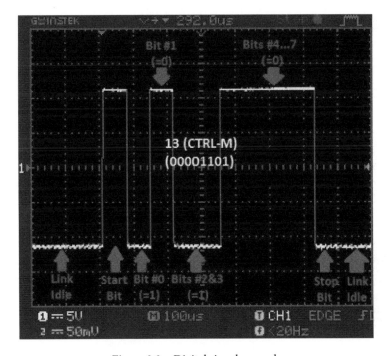

Figure 2.2 – Digital signal example

> **Analog hides in the digital**
>
> Although we talk about digital as jumping from one state to another, it really isn't. It is just changing very quickly but in an analog fashion. We simply choose to sample it in the middle of a pulse. The world is always analog, but sometimes we interpret it digitally.

If you look carefully at the following figure, you see the analog nature that hides in the corners!

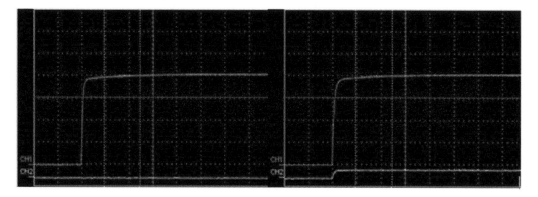

Figure 2.3 – Digital signal oscilloscope – before and after signal has run

Do you see it? Although this is supposed to be a sharp transition between voltages, you can see the rounding of what should be square corners. This is due to the fact that nothing in nature is instantaneous and everything transitions smoothly from one state to another.

In the next section, you will learn the difference between serial and parallel data transfer.

Serial versus parallel

Serial data is probably the most ubiquitous type of data transfer. It is how we as humans are accustomed to communicating. You are doing it right now as you read this. Serial communication simply means that data is transmitted and received one unit at a time (as opposed to several units of data being transmitted in parallel).

In the case of reading this book, your eyes are processing each word by scanning each line of text from left to right, then proceeding back to the beginning of the next line and continuing. You are processing a serial stream of words that are used to communicate some thoughts and ideas. Conversely, imagine if you could read the book several lines at a time. This would be considered parallel data transfer and it would be awesome!

The unit of data that is used in computing is the bit, which is a binary representation for on or off, more commonly 1 or 0.

Parallel data transfer was popular in the early years of computing since it allowed the simultaneous transfer of bits across multiple (usually 8) wires, which greatly increased data transfer speeds. This speed comes at several costs. More wires mean more weight, cost, and noise. Since the multiple wires are usually next to each other, you get a lot of noise induced on adjacent wires, known as crosstalk. This noise leads to shorter distances of transmission. The following figure illustrates how 8 bits are transferred serially versus in parallel:

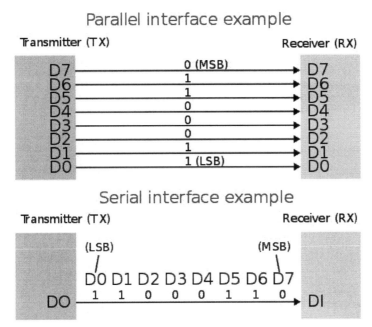

Figure 2.4 – Serial versus parallel

Now you can see a single wire is dedicated to each bit. This was fine in early computing when 8 bits were being sent, but you can imagine how quickly this becomes unmanageable when you consider 32- and 64-bit data. Thankfully, once protocol speeds increased, it became clear that serial transfer was far cheaper and simpler to integrate. That is not to say that parallel data transfer doesn't still exist; it does in applications where speed is paramount.

There are several types of serial data protocols, such as UART, I2C, SPI, Ethernet, and CAN. You will get an introduction to each of them in the next few sections.

Universal Asynchronous Receive and Transmit (UART)

UART is a very common protocol, thanks to its simplicity and cost. Many low data rate applications will use it to transmit and receive data. A common application of UART that you will see in self-driving applications is time synchronization to GPS. A message from a GPS receiver containing all the position and time information will be sent to a lidar, camera, radar, or other sensor to synchronize them to **Coordinated Universal Time (UTC)**.

> **Pardon me, I think your acronym is mixed up**
>
> The French and the English couldn't agree on the acronym, so rather than CUT in English or **TUC** (**Temps Universel Coordonné**) in French, they mixed it up for both to not favor either language. If I can't have it my way, neither can you! Voilà, UTC is born!

Okay, so what does UART look like? The first thing you need to understand is that the protocol is asynchronous, meaning that a clock signal (wire) is not needed. Instead, the two devices must each have pretty good internal clocks to keep time for themselves. Right, so no clock wire needed; but what wires do you need? You only need two wires: one to transmit and one to receive. As such, the two devices need to agree on some ground rules before they start the game:

1. **Baud rate**: This sets the number of bits per second that will be exchanged between the devices. In other words, it is the duration of the bit count. Common baud rates are 9,600, 19,200, 38,400, 57,600, 115,200, 128,000, and 256,000.
2. **Data bits**: This sets the number of bits in a data frame for the payload (data).
3. **Parity**: This sets whether you will have a parity bit in the packet. This can be used to verify the integrity of the message received. This is done by counting the number of 1s in the data frame and setting the parity bit to 0 for an even number of 1s or 1 for an odd number of 1s.
4. **Stop bits**: This sets the number of stop bits signifying the end of a packet.
5. **Flow control**: This sets whether you will be using hardware flow control. This is not as common since it requires two additional wires for **Ready To Send** (**RTS**) and **Clear To Send** (**CTS**).

Great, we have the ground rules. Now let's see what a packet looks like and then decode one.

The following figure illustrates the structure of a packet for a UART message. You can see we start with exactly one start bit (low), followed by 5 to 9 data bits, followed by the parity bit if one is in the rules, and finally the stop bit(s) (1 to 2, high). The idle state is often the high voltage state representing a 1 with the active state usually low, representing a 0. This is a normal polarity. You can reverse the polarity if needed, as long as you lay the ground rules ahead of time:

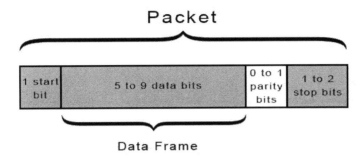

Figure 2.5 – UART packet structure

The following is an example signal trace showing how to decode the bits with eight data bits, no parity, and one stop bit. We begin in the idle (high) state, then the packet begins with a low voltage position. This signifies that the following eight bits are the data. Next, we see five counts of high voltage, signifying five 1 bits, followed by three counts of low voltage, signifying three 0 bits. You should know that UART messages are sent with the least significant bit first, meaning the lowest binary value or 2^0 position, followed by the 2^1 position, then the 2^2 position, and so on. So, if you reorder them into a human-readable format, your data message is 0 0 0 1 1 1 1 1; translated into decimal, that would be 31 or 1F in hexadecimal. There is a great resource at https://www.mathsisfun.com/binary-decimal-hexadecimal.html for different base number systems, such as binary, decimal, and hexadecimal. There is another handy resource for decoding ASCII characters from binary at http://www.asciitable.com/:

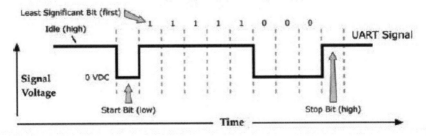

Figure 2.6 – UART example bits

> **Easter Egg**
>
> Take out your decoder ring. It's time to learn the meaning of life, the universe, and everything...

Excellent, now you know how to decode UART serial messages.

Okay, so you may ask, *UART is so simple, why would I use anything else?* Let's go over some pros and cons of UART.

The pros are as follows:

- Cheap
- Full duplex (send and receive at the same time)
- Asynchronous (no clock line)
- Simple, with only two wires between each device
- Parity for error checking
- Widely used

The cons are as follows:

- Maximum bits per frame of nine bits.
- Device clocks must be within 10% of each other.
- It is slow by modern standards, with standard bit rates ranging from 9,600-230,400 bits per second.
- Requires a direct connection between each device rather than a bus architecture.
- Some overhead with start and stop bits, demanding complex hardware for transmitting and receiving.

If you would like to gain experience with UART and Python, the simplest device for you to test UART communication on, will be an Arduino. If you have one, great! You can then jump directly to the documentation on PySerial and start communicating with your Arduino. If you don't have an Arduino, you can find an example emulator code for practicing in the book's repository, in the `Chapter 2` folder:

`https://github.com/PacktPublishing/Hands-On-Vision-and-Behavior-for-Self-Driving-Cars/tree/master/Chapter2`

Next, you will learn about two different standards that use UART messages.

Differential versus single-ended

UART signals can be transmitted in a few different ways. The two most common are **Recommended Standard 232 (RS-232)** and **Recommended Standard 422 (RS-422)**.

RS-232 is a single-ended signal, meaning that its voltage is compared directly to the electrical ground of the system (0 V). The following figure depicts a single-ended signal:

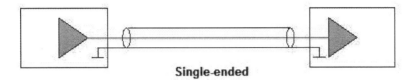

Figure 2.7 – Single-ended line

In contrast, RS-422 is a differential signal, meaning the voltage is compared across the two wires independent of the electrical ground of the system:

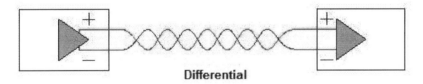

Figure 2.8 – Differential line

Now for storytime…

Once upon a time, the signal was born, with one mission: to take messages from its senders to the far-off lands where receivers live. The world is full of goblins and ghosts that are conspiring against our hero signals. These goblins and ghosts trip and mangle our poor friend the signal. The longer the signal travels on its journey, the more these bad actors will sneak in and wreak havoc. Generally, on short sojourns, the signal is unaffected and passes through the enchanted forest relatively undisturbed. However, the longer the journey, the more the signal needs to find tricks, friends, and guardians to get to its receiver safely.

So, who are these ghosts and goblins? They are electromagnetic fields and induced currents. You see, any time a ghost electromagnetic field moves near the signal's path (wire), it spawns a goblin (current) on the path. This goblin in turn uses its magical powers to stretch and shrink the signal's arms until it arrives at its destination, where the receiver sees the signal's arms as shorter or longer than they should be.

But have no fear – the tricks, friends, and guardians are here! The signal has a great little trick to thwart the ghosts and goblins, but first it must spawn a doppelganger: we'll call it the langis (that's *signal* backward). The langis and the signal twist around each other on their way to the receiver. This confuses the ghosts and causes them to spawn two equal but opposite goblins that unwittingly smash into each other and vanish before they can use their magical powers.

The other trick the langis and the signal have is that they promise to always hold hands and move together on their journey no matter what goblins strike them. So, when they arrive at their destination, the receiver just measures the distance between the langis and the signal to get the message!

Okay, so what does this fairy tale look like in real life? Rather than having only one transmit wire, you instead use two wires. You then set one wire to be your high voltage (V+) and the other to be your low voltage (V-). Now when comparing the signals on the receiver side, you measure the voltage difference between V+ and V- to determine whether you have a high or low signal. The following figure shows a single-ended signal (1a) and a differential signal (1b):

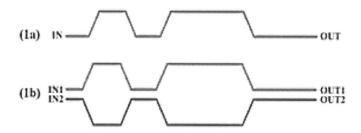

Figure 1. (1a) Single-ended signal waveform; (1b) differential signal waveform.

Figure 2.9 – Single-ended versus differential signal

This has the wonderful effect of having any induced noise affect both V+ and V- similarly, so that when you measure the difference between V+ and V-, it is unchanged from how it was when it was sent. The following figure illustrates what this looks like:

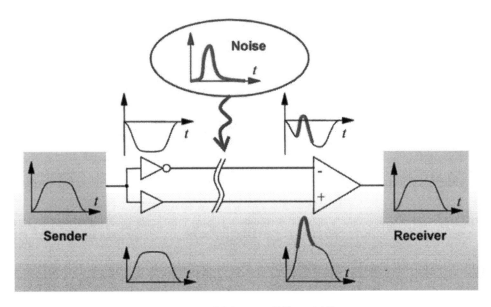

Figure 2.10 – Noise on a differential line

The other trick was to twist the two wires of a differential pair around each other. This has the effect of canceling any induced currents in the wires. The following illustration shows the difference between straight cables and twisted pair cable currents. You can see that at each twist, the wires switch sides, so the noise current is alternating at each twist, effectively canceling itself out:

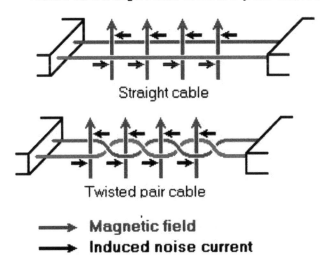

Figure 2.11 – Noise cancellation on differential twisted pair cable

So, what does this all mean for you when choosing between single-ended and differential? Here is a comparison table to help:

	Single-ended	Differential
Max cable length	15 meters	1,220 meters
Number of wires	One per signal + common ground	Two per signal + common ground
Max speed	256 kbps	10 Mbps
Cost	Cheaper	More expensive

Table 2.1

In the next section, you will learn about another form of serial communication that speeds things up a bit, along with some other very handy benefits.

I2C

I2C, or I²C, is short for **Inter-Integrated Circuit** and is another serial data transfer protocol with a few cool new features. More on those in a bit. I2C is commonly used to communicate between components on a single **Printed Circuit Board (PCB)**. It boasts data rates of 100-400 kHz, which is generally supported, and the specification even has room for up to 5 MHz communication, although this is not commonly supported on many devices.

You may ask, "Why use I2C? UART is already very simple and easy." Well, I2C adds some very cool features that you don't have with UART. Recall that UART requires two wires connected between each device, which means you need a connector for each device that you want to communicate with. This quickly spins an unmanageable web of wires when you want several devices interconnected. You also don't have the concept of master or slave in UART, since devices talk directly to each other on separate Tx and Rx lines. You can see an example of a fully connected UART architecture in the following figure:

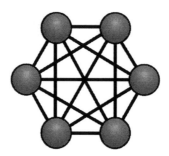

Figure 2.12 – Fully connected UART network

I2C to the rescue! I2C also uses only two wires: a **Serial Clock Wire (SCL)** and a **Serial Data Wire (SDA)** – more on how these work later. It uses these two wires to set up a new architecture between devices, a bus. A bus is simply a set of shared wires that transmits a signal to all devices attached to them. The following illustration will help us understand this better:

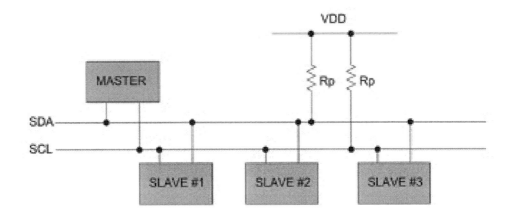

Figure 2.13 – I2C bus architecture

This allows multiple devices to talk to each other without requiring dedicated lines from each device to every other device it needs to talk with.

You might be thinking, *How can everyone be talking on the same lines and understand anything?* The I2C protocol implements the concept of master and slave devices. A master controls the flow of communication by announcing to everyone, *Hey, listen up everyone, I am talking to RasPi1, please acknowledge you are there, then send me data!* The master then gives control to RasPi1, who quickly shouts, *I'm here and have understood the request! Here is the data you requested; please acknowledge you received it.* The master then says, *Got it!* Then the process starts over. The following figure is a timing diagram of an I2C exchange:

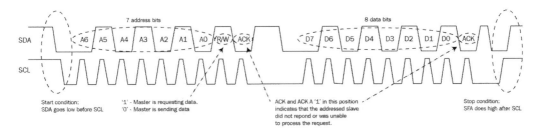

Figure 2.14 – I2C timing diagram

Let's walk through a communication sequence. The sequence begins with the master pulling the SDA line low followed by pulling the SCL line low. This signifies the start condition. The next series of 7-10 bits (depending on your settings) is the address of the slave that is being spoken to. The next bit, the R/W bit, instructs the slave to either write to (logical 0) or read from (logical 1) its memory register. The bit that follows the R/W is the acknowledge (ACK) bit. This is set by the slave that is being addressed if it heard, understood, acknowledged, and will respond to the request. The master will then continue generating pulses on the SCL line while either the slave or the master starts placing data on the eight data bits on the SDA.

> **Bigger bits first**
> Contrary to UART, bits are transmitted MSB first in I2C.

For example, if the R/W bit was set to 0, the slave would receive the data being placed on the SDA and write it to memory. Immediately following the eight data bits, the slave will pull the SDA line low for one clock count to acknowledge that it received the data, stored it, and is ready to give back control of the SDA line to the master. At this point, the master pulls the SDA back low. Finally, to stop the sequence, the master will release the SCL followed by the SDA.

When so many devices can be talking on the bus at the same time, it is important to have some rules to ensure that there is no clashing. I2C achieves this by using an *open-drain* system, which simply means that any master or slave can only pull the line to ground. The idle states of the SCL and SDA are held in the high voltage state through pull-up resistors. This can be seen in *Figure 2.13* with the resistors connected to VDD. When a master or slave wants to send data, they pull the line to ground (or open the drain). This ensures that you will never have one device driving the line high while another is driving it low.

Another interesting feature of the I2C protocol is that not only can there be multiple slave devices on the bus, but there can also be multiple masters. Here, you'll ask, *But wait, you said the master controls the flow. How will we know who is in control?* The genius in this architecture is that every device is connected to the same lines (bus), so they can all see what is happening at any given time. So, if two masters are trying to control the bus at nearly the same time, the first one to pull the SDA line low wins! The other master backs off and becomes a temporary slave. There is a case when two masters pull low at the exact same time and it is unclear who has control. In this case, arbitration begins. The first master to release to high on the SDA loses arbitration and becomes a slave.

> **Easter Egg**
> If a hen and a half lay an egg and a half in a day and a half, how many eggs will half a dozen hens lay in half a dozen days? Decode the following signal for the answer!

Here is a summary of the benefits and disadvantages of I2C.

These are the benefits:

- A multiple-master, multiple-slave architecture, up to 1,024 devices in 10-bit address mode
- Bus-based with only two wires (SCL and SDA) required
- Speeds of up to 5 MHz
- Inexpensive
- Message acknowledgment

These are the disadvantages:

- Half-duplex, cannot transmit and receive at the same time.
- Overhead of start, stop, and acknowledge conditions reduces throughput.
- The pull-up resistors limit clock speed, eat up PCB space, and increase power dissipation.
- Short maximum wire lengths (1 cm–2 m) dependent on capacitance, resistance, and speed.

You have learned a lot about I2C, which has armed you with even more knowledge about dealing with serial data. In the next section, you will learn about yet another serial communication protocol with a bit more spunk but traded for something else.

SPI

Serial Peripheral Interface (SPI) is a serial transmission link used primarily in microcontrollers to link peripherals such as USB, memory, and onboard sensors. Its main advantage is its speed and the simplicity of is implementation. SPI is not commonly used for sensors that you will be using in your self-driving car applications, but it is worth knowing a bit about in case you come across it. It is a full-duplex link with four wires used: SCLK, MOSI, MISO, and SS. The following illustration will help as we talk through their functions:

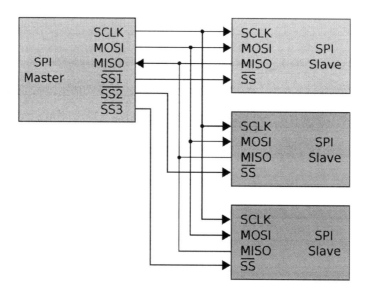

Figure 2.15 – SPI connection diagram

SPI is a synchronous serial link that uses a master clock signal (SCLK), much like what you learned about in I2C. The clock rate is typically in the region of 6-12.5 MHz, which is also its bit rate. The data is passed between devices on the **Master Out Slave In (MOSI)** and **Master In Slave Out (MISO)** lines. MOSI, MISO, and SCLK can be used as a bus architecture, much like I2C. The final wire is the **Slave Select (SS)** wire. This is pulled low to notify the slave connected to it that it should listen to the coming message.

This contrasts with I2C, which sent the slave address the information about which slave to listen for. As you can see in *Figure 2.15*, a separate wire and pin must be dedicated to each slave that is added to the system (denoted by *SS1*, *SS2*, and *SS3* in the figure). The hardware used to implement SPI is quite simple and usually relies on shift-registers. *What is a shift-register?* you say. Well, this is a simple memory register that holds a certain number of bits, say, eight. Each time a new bit is brought in from one side, a bit from the other side is pushed out. The following figure illustrates how this works in SPI:

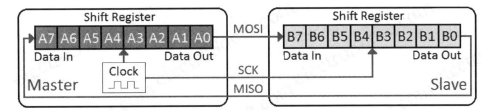

Figure 2.16 – SPI shift register

SPI data transfer is very simple since there is only one master allowed on the bus. The following figure helps to illustrate how SCK, MOSI, MISO, and SS are used to conduct the transfer of data in full duplex:

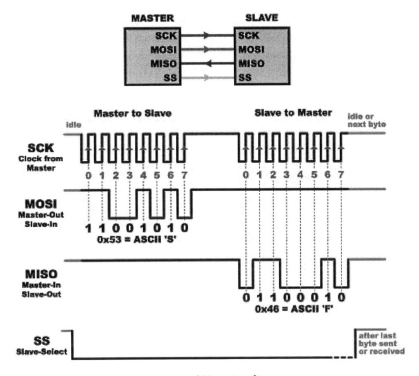

Figure 2.17 – SPI timing diagram

The master pulls the SS line low, which lets the target slave know, *Hey, SS1, this message is for you, please be ready to receive*. Then the master sends clock pulses on the SCK line that tell the slave when they should sample the data coming on MOSI. If it has been predetermined that the slave should send something back, the master then follows with SCK pulses for when the slave should send data on the MISO line. Since there are two lines, MISO and MOSI, these two transactions can happen at the same time using shift-register format.

SPI is not standardized like UART or I2C in terms of protocol. Because of this, you will need to consult the interface control documents for the devices that you want to connect to determine the specific commands, register sizes, clock modes, and so on that are required to operate the device.

You can see there is no overhead in SPI as there was in UART and I2C. There are no start bits, addresses, stop bits, acknowledge bits, or any other overhead. It is pure, sweet, high-speed data. On the other hand, there is a lot more programming and prearranged setup needed to communicate between two devices. SPI also can drive high and low on the data lines, allowing to slew faster from a 0 to a 1, which leads to the faster transmission rate discussed.

So, let's summarize the pros and cons.

These are the pros:

- Fast data rates of 6-12.5 MHz
- Full-duplex communication
- Simple shift-register hardware can be used
- Multiple slaves
- Bus architecture

These are the cons:

- Single master only
- Four wires needed, plus a slave select wire for each slave.
- Short transmission length dependent on speed, impedance, and capacitance with a max estimated at 3 m

In the next section, we will discuss a very common protocol that is used in nearly every vehicle on the road! Start your engines!

Framed-based serial protocols

Up until now, we have been discussing protocols that have fairly small message sizes in the region of 8-10 bits. What if you want to send more? In the next few sections, you will learn about protocols that support larger message sizes and package them into frames or packets.

You will learn about the following protocols:

- CAN
- Ethernet: UDP and TCP

Understanding CAN

Controller Area Network (CAN) is a message-based protocol that was developed, by Bosch, to reduce the number of wires connecting the ever-growing number of microcontrollers and **Electronic Control Units (ECUs)** in vehicles.

It is a bus-based protocol with two wires acting as a differential pair, CAN-HI and CAN-LO. You learned about differential pairs in the *Single-ended versus differential* section.

> **Ghost and goblins**
> Do you recall the trick we used to provide safe passage to the langis and the signal on their journey? There is a real *twist* to that story.

CAN is a feature-packed protocol that is very robust, reliable, and rapid. Here are some of the features of the protocol:

- Decentralized multi-master communication
- Prioritized messages
- Bus arbitration
- Remote terminal request
- Data integrity with cyclic redundancy checks
- Flexible expandable network
- Centralized diagnostics and configuration
- EMI noise rejection through a twisted differential pair

52   Understanding and Working with Signals

The CAN bus architecture is devilishly simple and is illustrated in the following figure:

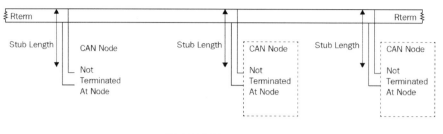

ISO 11898-2 Network

Figure 2.18 – CAN bus architecture

You can see that nodes may be added anywhere on the bus inside of the bus terminations, R_{term}. A consideration when connecting a node is the unterminated stub length, which the standard recommends keeping below 0.3 m.

Now let's see how bits are transmitted on the CAN HI and CAN LO differential twisted pair lines. The figure that follows illustrates the dominant and recessive voltages of the CAN protocol:

> **Zero to hero**
>
> 0 rules the bus with its dominant differential voltage rising up above the minimum threshold.

> **One and done**
>
> 1 sleeps on the bus with its recessive differential voltage, which lies below the minimum threshold.

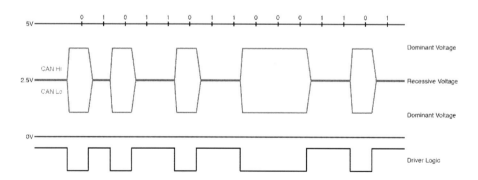

Figure 2.19 – CAN dominant and recessive voltages

By EE JRW – own work, CC BY-SA 4.0, https://commons.wikimedia.org/w/index.php?curid=55237229

Now that you see how bits are placed on the bus, let's look at the CAN frame structure. This will be useful if you find yourself debugging or reading CAN bus traffic. The following figure depicts the segments of a CAN frame:

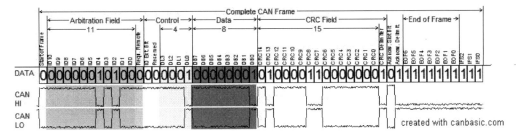

Figure 2.20 – CAN message format

CAN frames begin with a **Start of Frame** (SOF) bit, 0, which is the dominant differential voltage. This may sound a bit similar to what you learned in UART communication, which also started with a logical 0. Much like in UART, the SOF bit in CAN is a transition from an idle state to an active one. Unlike UART, however, the active and dominant state is a high voltage state.

Following the SOF bit is the arbitration field. This can be thought of as the ECU's functional address (for example, the steering module, oxygen sensor, lidar sensor, and so on).

> **Less is best**
> ECUs with a smaller address in the arbitration fields are considered higher priority in the CAN protocol. The smaller address will win the arbitration when two or more devices start transmitting at the same time.

The next bit is the **Remote Transmission Request** (RTR). This is used when one ECU would like to request data directly from another ECU. An RTR is requested by setting the bit to logical 1, the recessive state.

The next six bits are the **Data Length Code** (DLC) section of the frame, which says how long the upcoming data field will be. The data for a CAN message can be 0 to 8 bytes in length.

Immediately following the DLC is the data, which can be 0-64 (0-8 bytes) bits in length.

> **Bit order**
> CAN sends its information with the MSB first.

Next is the **Cyclic Redundancy Check (CRC)** field, which is 15 bits long and is used for error checking the message. The sending ECU performs a checksum calculation on the data field and places this in the CRC field. Once the receiving ECU gets the frame, it runs the same checksum calculation on the data field and verifies that it matches the CRC field in the received frame. The CRC is immediately followed by the CRC delimiter field to give it separation from the ACK bit.

The **Acknowledge (ACK)** bit is next, which is transmitted with a logic 1 recessive so that any receiving ECU can acknowledge receipt of the error-free data during this bit interval. The ACK bit is followed by the ACK delimiter to allow for any timing difference that overruns the ACK bit.

Finally, the **End of Frame (EOF)** field contains seven recessive logic 1 bits, which indicate – you guessed it – the end of the frame.

Okay, one more thing: there is an **Inter Frame Space (IFS)**, which is defined by the CAN controller of the system.

Sweet – that was long. Don't worry, though; CAN is a very well-supported protocol and there are plenty of software and hardware modules that you can find that will do the heavy lifting for you. You will likely only need to dust this knowledge off when things aren't working right and you pull out the old oscilloscope to probe the CAN bus and verify that messages are transmitting properly.

Let's recap the pros and cons of the CAN bus protocol.

These are the pros:

- Decentralized multi-master communication
- Prioritized messages
- Bus arbitration
- RTR
- Data integrity with CRCs
- Flexible, expandable network
- Centralized diagnostics and configuration
- EMI noise rejection through a twisted differential pair
- Maximum cable length of 40 m

This is the only con, really:

- Careful attention to the wiring bus terminations and stub lengths is needed.

In the next section, you will learn about the most ubiquitous networking protocols used in modern times, both in cars and at home.

Ethernet and internet protocols

Ethernet is a framework of protocols and layers that is used in modern networking in nearly every application you interact with today. Ethernet is in your home, the train you ride, the plane you fly in, and definitely in your self-driving car. It consists of both the physical and protocol standards for network-based communication. It all starts with the **Open Systems Interconnection (OSI)** model of the different layers. The following figure illustrates the seven layers of the OSI model and what each layer is tasked with:

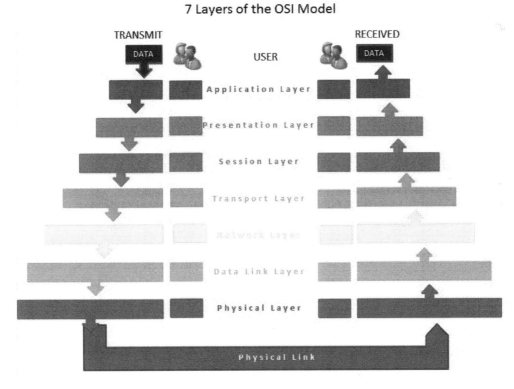

Figure 2.21 – The seven layers of the OSI model

Each of these layers has its own protocol for processing data. It all starts with the raw data, or bits, at the application layer. The data gets processed at each layer to be passed onto the next layer. Each layer wraps the previous layer's frame into a new frame, which is why the model shows the frames getting larger and larger. The following figure illustrates the protocols at each layer:

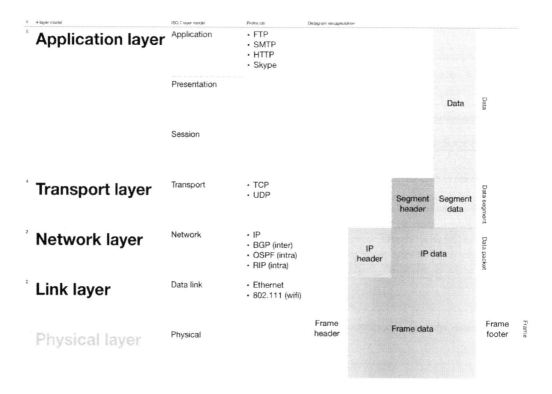

Figure 2.22 – Protocols of the OSI model

We could spend an entire book talking about the details of each layer and protocol. Instead, we will focus on two protocols (UDP and TCP) that you will encounter when working with sensors and actuators in a self-driving car.

Understanding UDP

User Datagram Protocol (UDP) is a very popular protocol for sensors such as lidars, cameras, and radars. It is a connection-less protocol. *Wait – if it's connection-less, how is it sending data?* Connection-less, in this sense, just means that the protocol doesn't verify that it can reach the destination before it sends data. UDP lives on the transport layer of the OSI model. You can see in the following figure that the transport layer is the first layer to add a header:

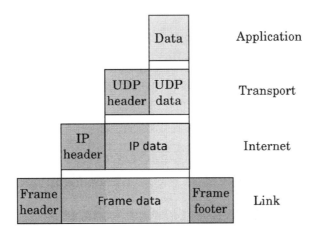

Figure 2.23 – UDP on the transport layer

If you were sending a gift to someone, what would you want them to know about the gift so that they could be confident that it was intended for them and was not swapped for someone else's gift? You might say something like, *Tenretni Olleh, I am sending you this luxurious pair of rainbow pajamas in size large and I hope they fit. Please try them on.* This is exactly what the UDP header's function is. It stores the source port, the destination port, the length of the data including the header, and finally a checksum. The checksum is simply a number that is created with an algorithm before the data is sent to ensure that when it is received, the data is intact and not corrupted. This is done by running the same algorithm on the received data and comparing the number generated to the checksum value. This is akin to sending a picture of the pajamas that were sent to Tenretni so they knew they received the correct gift.

The following figure illustrates the fields within a UDP header and the actual message itself:

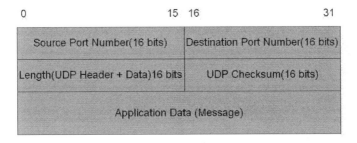

Figure 2.24 – UDP header fields

> **Port, plugs, and sockets**
>
> A port in the Ethernet protocol can be thought of like a power socket in your wall. You plug different devices into the sockets, such as lamps and TVs. Each plug, once connected, serves a specific device power. Similarly, a port is where a digital socket is created for a specific device or protocol to send and/or receive data.

The UDP header is always 8 bytes (64 bits), while the data (message) can be up to 65,507 bytes in length. The following figure is a relevant example, to self-driving cars, of the data (message) field size of a UDP packet from a popular family of high-resolution lidar sensors:

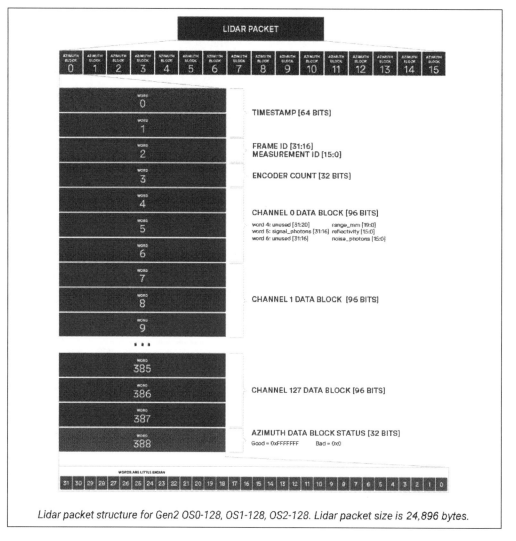

Figure 2.25 – Ouster lidar UDP data structure

You can see from this, if you carefully multiply all the bytes, that you get 389 words * 4 bytes/word * 16 azimuths/packet = 24,896 bytes/packet. This is well within the data limit size of a UDP packet, 65,507 bytes. In order to send this data over UDP, what must the lidar sensor append to this data? You guessed it – there needs to be a UDP header with the 8 bytes of source, destination, data length, and checksum information.

UDP is often used for streaming-type devices such as lidar sensors, cameras, and radars since it does not make sense to resend data if it is not received. Imagine you didn't receive a few azimuths in the lidar sensor example. Would it be useful to you to have that data resent to you? Probably not, since whatever the lasers bounced off is now in the past and likely in a different position. Another reason to use UDP for such devices is that due to the high data rates, it would slow things down tremendously to have to resend lost or corrupted data.

In the next section, we will discuss a protocol that will address cases where you might want to ensure that there is a three-way handshake for each packet of data.

Understanding TCP

If you were going to send a command to turn the steering wheel of your self-driving car, would you be okay if the command never made it, was wrong, or corrupted? Would you be okay if you didn't know whether the steering actuator received the command? Probably not!

This is where **Transmission Control Protocol** (**TCP**) can serve you! TCP operates similarly to UDP...well, actually, it's completely different. Unlike UDP, TCP is a connection-based protocol. This means that each time you want to send data, you need to do a three-way handshake. This is done through a process known as SYN-SYN/ACK-ACK. Let's break that down to understand it better:

- SYN – The client sends a SYN (synchronization) packet with a randomly selected initial sequence number (x), which is used to count the bytes that are being sent. It also sets the SYN bit flag to 1 (more on this later).
- SYN/ACK – The server receives the SYN packet:

1. It increments x by one. This becomes the acknowledgement (ACK) number (x+1), which is the number of the next byte it expects.
2. It then sends a SYN/ACK packet back to the client with the ACK number as well as the server's own randomly selected sequence number (y).

- ACK – The client receives the SYN/ACK packet with the ACK number (x+1) and server sequence number (y):

1. It increments the server's initial sequence number to y+1.
2. It sends an ACK packet with the ACK number (y+1) and ACK bit flag set to 1 back to the server to establish the connection.

The following diagram illustrates the connection sequence:

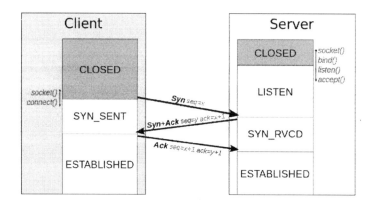

Figure 2.26 – TCP connection sequence diagram

Now the connection is established and data can begin to flow. Each packet that is sent will be followed by an ACK packet with the number of bytes received plus one, indicating that the packet was received intact and what byte number it expects next. The sequence number is incremented by one for SYN and SYN/ACK packets and by the number of bytes of payload received for ACK packets.

You can already see that in order to do all this, the header is going to need more fields than with UDP. The following figure illustrates the fields of a TCP header:

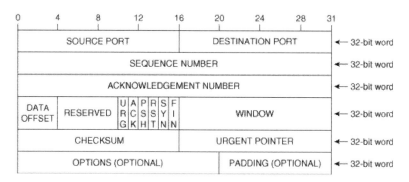

Figure 2.27 – TCP header fields

Let's unpack each field and its purpose:

- **Source port**: This is the port the packet is sent from. This is usually a randomly assigned port number.
- **Destination port**: This is the port the packet is being sent to. This is usually a well-known port number that is dedicated to a specific protocol. An example would be the **Secure Shell (SSH)** port, which is reserved as port number 22. A list of well-known ports can be found at this link: `https://www.iana.org/assignments/service-names-port-numbers/service-names-port-numbers.xhtml`.
- **Sequence number**: This is the number of the first byte being sent in the payload; or, for SYN and SYN/ACK packets, it is the randomly selected initial sequence number.
- **Acknowledgment number**: This is the number of bytes that have been received plus one, indicating the next byte number expected.
- **Data offset**: This is the length of the TCP header, that is, the offset before the payload.
- **Reserved**: These are bits that are unused but reserved for future protocol improvements.
- **URG**: This is the first of six bit flags (set to either `0` or `1`). This is used to mark a packet as urgent.
- **ACK**: This is the `ACK` bit flag, which is set to `1` when a valid acknowledgment number is being sent.
- **PHS**: This is the push bit flag, which is set to `1` when the data should be pushed to the application immediately.
- **RST**: This is the reset bit flag, which is set to `1` when the connection needs to be reset.
- **SYN**: This is the synchronize bit flag, which is set to `1` when the SYN-SYN/ACK connection establishment process is initiated. It indicates that there is a valid sequence number in the sequence number field.
- **FIN**: This is the finish bit flag, which is set to `1` when the connection should be closed after all data is sent.
- **Window**: This is the size of the buffer that the receiving end can accept before losing data.

- **Checksum**: This is the value calculated using an algorithm on `payload+header` that is used to verify that the data received is valid and unchanged.

- **Urgent pointer**: This is the byte number of the first byte of data that is considered urgent. This is valid if the `URG` bit flag is set to `1`.

TCP uses all this header information for the task of ensuring that all data is received, verified, and acknowledged. If data is ever missed, the last valid sequence number can be used to resend the data. Now you can send your steering commands over Ethernet with confidence, knowing that you won't go careening off a cliff!

> Cars use CAN, mostly...
>
> Although we used steering as an example for TCP here, you will typically find that vehicle control commands are sent using CAN bus over Ethernet bus from the factory. Increasingly, though, self-driving car creators are relying on Ethernet for its higher data throughput and security. There is talk of moving to Ethernet bus for factory vehicles in the future. Military aircraft have already started doing so!

Okay – goodness, that was a lot to take in. Do not worry, though: now that you have seen this once and understand it, you can rely on open source tools to parse through this in the future. Where you will find this useful is when things start going wrong and you need to debug the traffic flow of your data.

Speaking of which, Wireshark is a fantastic tool for **sniffing** Ethernet packets on your network and seeing the flow of information for debugging and testing. You can find all the information you need on installation and use at `https://www.wireshark.org/`.

As you can see, TCP is a powerful protocol for connection-based, highly reliable, and secure data transfer. Now get out there and start using the Ethernet protocol with the open source tools listed at the end of this chapter!

Summary

Congratulations, you have completed your quest with your new friends, the langis and the signal! You have had quite an adventure! You battled ghosts and goblins in the form of electromagnetic waves and induced currents. You learned so much along the way about serial versus parallel data transfer; digital versus analog signals; and protocols such as UART, I2C, SPI, CAN, UDP, and TCP and their secret decoder rings! You are now armed with the knowledge you will need when integrating sensors and actuators into your real self-driving car.

In the next chapter, you will learn how to use OpenCV to detect lanes on the road, a vital skill to ensure the safe and legal operation of your self-driving car!

Questions

After reading this chapter, you should be able to answer the following questions:

1. How many wires does each protocol require and what are their names?
2. What are two methods to reduce noise in a signal?
3. What is the difference between serial and parallel data transmission?
4. Which protocols use a bus architecture?
5. Which protocols have a clock signal?
6. What protocol is used widely to send GPS information to other sensors?

Further reading

- Texas Instruments Controller Area Network Physical Layer Requirements (http://www.ti.com/lit/an/slla270/slla270.pdf?HQS=slla270-aaj&ts=1589256007656)
- Texas Instruments Introduction to the Controller Area Network (CAN) (http://www.ti.com/lit/an/sloa101b/sloa101b.pdf)
- Universal Asynchronous Receiver and Transmitter (UART) (https://ieeexplore.ieee.org/document/7586376)
- Understanding the I2C Bus (http://www.ti.com/lit/an/slva704/slva704.pdf?&ts=1589265769229)

Open source protocol tools

You can also refer to the following resources to learn more about the tools for programming with the protocols covered:

- PySerial (https://pypi.org/project/pyserial/) for UART (RS-232, RS-422, RS-485)
- python-periphery (https://python-periphery.readthedocs.io/en/latest/index.html) for UART, I2C, SPI, and more
- smbus2 (https://pypi.org/project/smbus2/) for I2C

- `spidev` (https://pypi.org/project/spidev/) for SPI
- `python-can` (https://pypi.org/project/python-can/) for CAN
- `socket` (https://docs.python.org/3/library/socket.html) for Ethernet TCP, UDP, and more

3
Lane Detection

This chapter will show one of the incredible things possible using computer vision in general and OpenCV in particular: lane detection. You will learn how to analyze an image and build more and more visual knowledge about it, one step after another, applying several filtering techniques, replacing noise and approximation with a better understanding of the image, until you will be able to detect where the lanes are on a straight road or on a turn, and we will apply this pipeline to a video to highlight the road.

You will see that this method relies on several assumptions that might not be true in the real world, though it can be adjusted to correct for that. Hopefully, you will find this chapter quite interesting.

We will cover the following topics:

- Detecting lanes in a road
- Color spaces
- Perspective correction
- Edge detection
- Thresholding
- Histograms
- The sliding window algorithm

- Polynomial fitting
- Video filtering

By the end of this chapter, you will be able to design a pipeline that is able to detect the lanes on a road, using OpenCV.

Technical requirements

Our lane detection pipeline requires quite a lot of code. We will explain the main concepts, and you can find the full code on GitHub at `https://github.com/PacktPublishing/Hands-On-Vision-and-Behavior-for-Self-Driving-Cars/tree/master/Chapter3`.

For the instructions and code in this chapter, you need the following:

- Python 3.7
- The OpenCV-Python module
- The NumPy module
- The Matplotlib module

To identify the lanes, we need some images and a video. While it's easy to find some open source database to use for this, they are usually only available for non-commercial purposes. For this reason, in this book, we will use images and video generated by two open source projects: CARLA, a simulator useful for autonomous driving tasks, and Speed Dreams, an open source video game. All the techniques also work with real-world footage, and you are encouraged to try them on some public datasets, such as CULane or KITTI.

The Code in Action videos for this chapter can be found here:

`https://bit.ly/37pjxnO`

How to perform thresholding

While for a human it is easy to follow a lane, for a computer, this is not something that is so simple. One problem is that an image of the road has too much information. We need to simplify it, selecting only the parts of the image that we are interested in. We will only analyze the part of the image with the lane, but we also need to separate the lane from the rest of the image, for example, using color selection. After all, the road is typically black or dark, and lanes are usually white or yellow.

In the next sections, we will analyze different color spaces, to see which one is most useful for thresholding.

How thresholding works on different color spaces

From a practical point of view, a color space is a way to decompose the colors of an image. You are most likely comfortable with RGB, but there are others.

OpenCV supports several color spaces, and as part of this pipeline, we need to choose the two best channels from a variety of color spaces. Why do we want to use two different channels? For two reasons:

- A color space that is good for white lanes might not be good for yellow ones.
- When there are difficult frames (for example, with shadows on the road or if the lane is discolored), one channel could be less affected than another one.

This might not be strictly necessary for our example, as the lanes are always white, but it is definitely useful in real life.

We will now see how our test image appears in different color spaces, but bear in mind that your case might be different.

RGB/BGR

The starting point will be the following image:

Figure 3.1 – Reference image, from Speed Dreams

The image can, of course, be decomposed into three channels: red, green, and blue. As we know, OpenCV stores the image as BGR (meaning, the first byte is the blue channel, not the red channel), but conceptually, there is no difference.

These are the three channels once separated:

Figure 3.2 – BGR channels: blue, green, and red channels

They all seem fine. We can try to separate the lane by selecting the white pixels. As the white color is (255, 255, 255), we could leave some margin and select the colors above 180 on the scale. To do this operation, we need to create a black image with the same size as the selected channel, then paint all the pixels that are above 180 in the original channel white:

```
img_threshold = np.zeros_like(channel)
img_threshold [(channel >= 180)] = 255
```

This is how the output appears:

Figure 3.3 – BGR channels: blue, green, and red channels, threshold above 180

They all seem good. The red channel also shows part of the car, but since we will not analyze that part of the image, it is not a problem. As the white color has the same value in the red, green, and blue channels, it is kind of expected that the lane should be visible on all three channels. This would not be true for yellow lanes, though.

The value that we choose for the threshold is very important, and unfortunately, it is dependent on the colors used for the lane and on the situation of the road; light conditions and shadows will also affect it.

The following figure shows a totally different threshold, 20-120:

Figure 3.4 – BGR channels: blue, green, and red channels, threshold in the range 20-120

You can select the pixels in the 20-120 range with the following code:

```
img_threshold[(channel >= 20) & (channel <= 120)] = 255
```

The image is probably still usable, as long as you consider that the lane is black, but it would not be recommended.

HLS

The HLS color space divides the color into hue, lightness, and saturation. The result is sometimes surprising:

Figure 3.5 – HLS channels: hue, lightness, and saturation

The hue channel is pretty bad, noisy, and low resolution, while the lightness seems to perform well. The saturation seems to be unable to detect our lane.

Let's try some thresholding:

Figure 3.6 – HLS channels: hue, lightness, and saturation, threshold above 160

The threshold shows that lightness is still a good candidate.

HSV

The HSV color space divides the color into hue, saturation, and value, and it is related to HLS. The result is therefore similar to HLS:

Figure 3.7 – HSV channels: hue, saturation, and value

Hue and saturation are not useful to us, but value looks fine with thresholding applied:

Figure 3.8 – HSV channels: hue, saturation, and value, threshold above 160

As expected, the threshold of value looks good.

LAB

The LAB (CIELAB or CIE L*a*b*) color space divides the color into L* (lightness, from black to white), a* (from green to red), and b* (from blue to yellow):

Figure 3.9 – LAB channels: L*, a*, and b*

L* seems fine, while a* and b* are not useful to us:

Figure 3.10 – LAB channels: L*, a*, and b*, threshold above 160

YCbCr

YCbCr is the last color space that we will analyze. It divides the image into Luma (Y) and two chroma components (Cb and Cr):

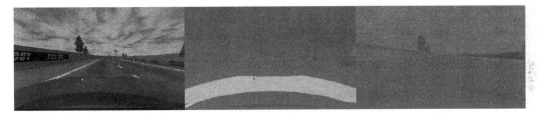

Figure 3.11 – YCbCr channels: Y, Cb, and Cr

This is the result when we apply a threshold:

Figure 3.12 – YCbCr channels: Y, Cb, and Cr, threshold above 160

The threshold confirms the validity of the Luma channel.

Our choice

After some experiments, it seems that the green channel can be used for edge detection, and the L channel from the HLS space could be used as additional thresholding, so we'll stick to these. These settings should be also fine for a yellow line, while different colors might require different thresholds.

Perspective correction

Let's take a step back and start simple. The easiest case that we can have is with a straight lane. Let's see how it looks:

Figure 3.13 – Straight lane, from Speed Dreams

If we were flying over the road, and watching it from a bird's eye view, the lanes would be parallel, but in the picture, they are not, because of the perspective.

The perspective depends on the focal length of the lens (lenses with a shorter focal length show a stronger perspective) and the position of the camera. Once the camera is mounted on a car, the perspective is fixed, so we can take it into consideration and correct the image.

OpenCV has a method to compute the perspective transformation: `getPerspectiveTransform()`.

It takes two parameters, both arrays of four points, identifying the trapezoid of the perspective. One array is the source and one array is the destination. This means that the same method can be used to compute the inverse transformation, by just swapping the parameters:

```
perspective_correction = cv2.getPerspectiveTransform(src, dst)
perspective_correction_inv = cv2.getPerspectiveTransform(dst, src)
```

We need to select the area around the lanes, plus a small margin:

Figure 3.14 – Trapezoid with the region of interest around the lanes

In our case, the destination is a rectangle (as we want to make it straight). *Figure 3.14* shows the green trapezoid (the `src` variable in the previous code) with the original perspective and the white rectangle (the `dst` variable in the previous code), which is the desired perspective. Please notice that for clarity, they have been drawn as overlapping, but the coordinates of the rectangle passed as a parameter are shifted, as if it was starting at *X* coordinate 0.

We can now apply the perspective correction and get our bird's eye view:

```
cv2.warpPerspective(img, perspective_correction, warp_size,
flags=cv2.INTER_LANCZOS4)
```

The `warpPerspective()` method accepts four parameters:

- The source image.
- The transformation matrix, obtained from `getPerspectiveTransform()`.
- The size of the output image. In our case, the width is the same as the original image, but the height is only the height of the trapezoid/rectangle.
- Some flags, to specify the interpolation. `INTER_LINEAR` is a common choice, but I recommend experimenting, and to give `INTER_LANCZOS4` a try.

This is the result of warp using `INTER_LINEAR`:

Figure 3.15 – Warped with INTER_LINEAR

This is the result using `INTER_LANCZOS4`:

Figure 3.16 – Warped with INTER_LANCZOS4

They are very similar, but a closer look shows that the interpolation performed with the `LANCZOS4` resampling is sharper. We will see later that at the end of the pipeline, the difference is significant.

What is clear in both images is that our lines are now vertical, which intuitively could help us.

We'll see in the next section how to leverage this image.

Edge detection

The next step is detecting the edges, and we will use the green channel for that, as during our experiments, it gave good results. Please be aware that you need to experiment with the images and videos taken from the country where you plan to run the software, and with many different light conditions. Most likely, based on the color of the lines and the colors in the image, you might want to choose a different channel, possibly from another color space; you can convert the image into different color spaces using `cvtColor()`, for example:

```
img_hls = cv2.cvtColor(img_bgr, cv2.COLOR_BGR2HLS).astype(np.float)
```

We will stick to green.

OpenCV has several ways to compute edge detection, and we are going to use Scharr, as it performs quite well. Scharr computes a derivative, so it detects the difference in colors in the image. We are interested in the *X* axis, and we want the result to be a 64-bit float, so our call would be like this:

```
edge_x = cv2.Scharr(channel, cv2.CV_64F, 1, 0)
```

As Scharr computes a derivative, the values can be both positive and negative. We are not interested in the sign, but only in the fact that there is an edge. So, we will take the absolute value:

```
edge_x = np.absolute(edge_x)
```

Another issue is that the values are not bounded on the 0-255 value range that we expect on a single channel image, and the values are floating points, while we need an 8-bit integer. We can fix both the issues with the following line:

```
edge_x = np.uint8(255 * edge_x / np.max(edge_x))
```

This is the result:

Figure 3.17 – Edge detection with Scharr, scaled and with absolute values

At this point, we can apply thresholding to convert the image into black and white, to better isolate the pixels of the lanes. We need to choose the intensity of the pixels to select, and in this case, we can go for 20-120; we will select only pixels that have at least an intensity value of 20, and not more than 120:

```
binary = np.zeros_like(img_edge)
binary[img_edge >= 20] = 255
```

The `zeros_like()` method creates an array full of zeros, with the same shape of the image, and the second line sets all the pixels with an intensity between 20 and 120 to 255.

This is the result:

Figure 3.18 – Result after applying a threshold of 20

The lanes are now very visible, but there is some noise. We can reduce that by increasing the threshold:

```
binary[img_edge >= 50] = 255
```

This is how the output appears:

Figure 3.19 – Result after applying a threshold of 50

Now, there is less noise, but we lost the lines on the top.

We will now describe a technique that can help us to retain the full line without having an excessive amount of noise.

Interpolated threshold

In practice, we don't have to choose between selecting the whole line with a lot of noise and reducing the noise while detecting only part of the line. We could apply a higher threshold to the bottom (where we have more resolution, a sharper image, and more noise) and a lower threshold on the top (there, we get less contrast, a weaker detection, and less noise, as the pixels are stretched by the perspective correction, naturally blurring them). We can just interpolate between the thresholds:

```
threshold_up = 15
threshold_down = 60
threshold_delta = threshold_down-threshold_up

for y in range(height):
  binary_line = binary[y,:]
  edge_line = channel_edge[y,:]
  threshold_line = threshold_up + threshold_delta * y/height
  binary_line[edge_line >= threshold_line] = 255
```

Let's see the result:

Figure 3.20 – Result after applying an interpolated threshold, from 15 to 60

Now, we can have less noise at the bottom and detect weaker signals at the top. However, while a human can visually identify the lanes, for the computer, they are still just pixels in an image, so there is still work to do. But we simplified the image very much, and we are making good progress.

Combined threshold

As we mentioned earlier, we also wanted to use the threshold on another channel, without edge detection. We chose the L channel of HLS.

This is the result of thresholding above 140:

Figure 3.21 – L channel with the threshold above 140

Not bad. Now, we can combine it with the edge:

Figure 3.22 – Combination of the two thresholds

The result is noisier, but also more robust.

Before moving forward, let's introduce a picture with a turn:

Figure 3.23 – Lane with a turn, from Speed Dreams

This is the threshold:

Figure 3.24 – Lane with a turn, after the threshold

It still looks good, but we can see that, because of the turn, we no longer have a vertical line. In fact, at the top of the image, the lines are basically horizontal.

Finding the lanes using histograms

How could we understand, more or less, where the lanes are? Visually, for a human, the answer is simple: the lane is a long line. But what about a computer?

If we talk about vertical lines, one way could be to count the pixels that are white, on a certain column. But if we check the image with a turn, that might not work. However, if we reduce our attention to the bottom part of the image, the lines are a bit more vertical:

Figure 3.25 – Lane with a turn, after the threshold, the bottom part

We can now count the pixels by column:

```
partial_img = img[img.shape[0] // 2:, :]   # Select the bottom
part
hist = np.sum(partial_img, axis=0)   # axis 0: columns direction
```

To save the histogram as a graph, in a file, we can use Matplotlib:

```
import matplotlib.pyplot as plt

plt.plot(hist)
plt.savefig(filename)
plt.clf()
```

We obtain the following result:

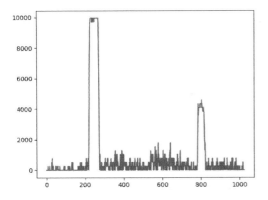 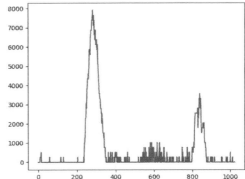

Figure 3.26 – Left: histogram of a straight lane, right: histogram of a lane with a turn

The X coordinates on the histogram represent the pixels; as our image has a resolution of 1024x600, the histogram shows 1,024 data points, with the peaks centered around the pixels where the lanes are.

As we can see, in the case of a straight lane, the histogram identifies the two lines quite clearly; with a turn, the histogram is less clear (because the line makes a turn and, therefore, the white pixels are spread a bit around), but it's still usable. We can also see that in the case of a dotted line, the peek in the histogram is less pronounced, but it is still there.

This looks promising!

Now, we need a way to detect the two peaks. We can use `argmax()` from NumPy, which returns the index of the maximum element of an array, which is one of our peaks. However, we need two. For this, we can split the array into two halves, and select one peak on each one:

```
size = len(histogram)
max_index_left = np.argmax(histogram[0:size//2])
max_index_right = np.argmax(histogram[size//2:]) + size//2
```

Now we have the indexes, which represent the X coordinate of the peaks. The value itself (for example, `histogram[index]`) can be considered the confidence of having identified the lane, as more pixels mean more confidence.

The sliding window algorithm

While we are making progress, the image still has some noise, meaning there are pixels that can reduce the precision. In addition, we only know where the line starts.

The solution is to focus on the area around the line – after all, there is no reason to work on the whole warped image; we could start at the bottom of the line and proceed to "follow it." This is probably one case where an image is worth a thousand words, so this is what we want to achieve:

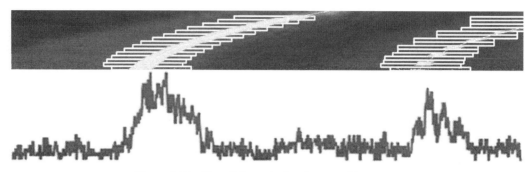

Figure 3.27 – Top: sliding window, bottom: histogram

On the upper part of *Figure 3.27*, each rectangle represents a window of interest. The first window on the bottom of each lane is centered on the respective peak of the histogram. Then, we need a way to "follow the line." The width of each window is dependent on the margin that we want to have, while the height depends on the number of windows that we want to have. These two numbers can be changed to reach a balance between a better detection (reducing the unwanted points and therefore the noise) and the possibility to detect more difficult turns, with a smaller radius (which will require the windows to be repositioned faster).

As this algorithm requires quite some code, we will focus on the left lane for clarity, but the same computations need to also be performed for the right lane.

Initialization

We are only interested in the pixels that have been selected by the thresholding. We can use nonzero() from NumPy:

```
non_zero = binary_warped.nonzero()
non_zero_y = np.array(non_zero[0])
non_zero_x = np.array(non_zero[1])
```

The non_zero variable will contain the coordinates of the pixels that are white, then non_zero_x will contain the *X* coordinates, and non_zero_y the *Y* coordinates.

We also need to set `margin`, the movement that we are allowing to the lane (for example, half of the window width of the sliding window), and `min_pixels`, the minimum number of pixels that we want to detect to accept a new position for the sliding window. Below this threshold, we will not update it:

```
margin = 80
min_pixels = 50
```

Coordinates of the sliding windows

The `left_x` variable will contain the position of the left lane, and we need to initialize it with the value obtained from the histogram.

After setting the stage, we can now cycle through all the windows, and the variable that we will use as the index is `idx_window`. The *X* range is computed from the last position, adding the margin:

```
win_x_left_min = left_x - margin
win_x_left_max = left_x + margin
```

The *Y* range is determined by the index of the window that we are analyzing:

```
win_y_top = img_height - idx_window * window_height
win_y_bottom = win_y_top + window_height
```

Now, we need to select the pixels that are white (from `non_zero_x` and `non_zero_y`) and constrained in the window that we are analyzing.

The NumPy array can be filtered using overloaded operators. To count all the *Y* coordinates that are above `win_y_bottom`, we can, therefore, simply use the following expression:

```
non_zero_y >= win_y_bottom
```

The result is an array with `True` in the pixels selected and `False` on the other ones.

But what we need is pixels between `win_y_top` and `win_y_bottom`:

```
(non_zero_y >= win_y_bottom) & (non_zero_y < win_y_top)
```

We also need the X coordinates, which must be between `win_x_left_min` and `win_x_left_max`. As we need to just count the points, we can add a `nonzero()` call:

```
non_zero_left = ((non_zero_y >= win_y_bottom) &
                 (non_zero_y < win_y_top) &
                 (non_zero_x >= win_x_left_min) &
                 (non_zero_x < win_x_left_max)).nonzero()[0]
```

We need to select the first element because our array is inside another array of one single element.

We will also keep all these values in a variable, to draw the line above the lane later:

```
left_lane_indexes.append(non_zero_left)
```

Now, we just need to update the left lane position with the average of the positions, but only if there are enough points:

```
if len(non_zero_left) > min_pixels:
    left_x = np.int(np.mean(non_zero_x[non_zero_left]))
```

Polynomial fitting

Now, we have potentially selected thousands of points, but we need to make sense of them and obtain a line. For this, we can use `polyfit()`, a method that can approximate a series of points with a polynomial of the specified degree; a second-degree polynomial will be enough for us:

```
x_coords = non_zero_x[left_lane_indexes]
y_coords = non_zero_y[left_lane_indexes]
left_fit = np.polynomial.polynomial.polyfit(y_coords, x_coords,
2)
```

> **Note**
>
> Please notice that `polyfit()` accepts the parameters in the order `(X, Y)`, while we provide them in the order `(Y, X)`. We do so because by mathematical convention, in a polynomial, X is known and Y is computed based on X (for example, Y = X^2 + 3*X+5). However, we know Y and we need to compute X, so we need to provide them in the opposite order.

We are almost done.

The Y coordinates are simply a range:

```
ploty = np.array([float(x) for x in range(binary_warped.shape[0])])
```

Then, we need to compute X from Y, using the generic formula for a polynomial of the second degree (reversed on X and Y):

$x = Ay^2 + By + C;$

This is the code:

```
Left_fitx = left_fit[2] * ploty ** 2 + left_fit[1] * ploty + left_fit[0]
```

This is where we are now:

Figure 3.28 – Lanes drawn on the warped image

We can now call perspectiveTransform() with the inverse perspective transformation to move the pixels to their position in the image. This is the final result:

Figure 3.29 – Lane detected on the image

Congratulations! It has not been particularly easy, but you can now detect a lane on a frame, under the correct conditions. Unfortunately, not all the frames will be good enough for this. Let's see in the next section how we can use the temporal evolution of the video stream to filter the data and improve the precision.

Enhancing a video

Analyzing a video stream in real time can be a challenge from a computational point of view, but usually, it offers the possibility to improve precision, as we can build on knowledge from the previous frames and filter the result.

We will now see two techniques that can be used to detect lanes with better precision when working with video streams.

Partial histogram

If we assume that we correctly detected a lane in the previous few frames, then the lane on the current frame should be in a similar position. This assumption is affected by the speed of the car and the frame rate of the camera: the faster the car, the more the lane could change. Conversely, the faster the camera, the less the lane could have moved between two frames. In a real self-driving car, both these values are known, so they can be taken into consideration if required.

From a practical point of view, this means we can limit the part of the histogram that we analyze, to avoid false detections, analyzing only some histogram pixels (for example, 30) around the average of some of the previous frames.

Rolling average

The main result of our detection is the three values of the polynomial fit, for each lane. Following the same principle of the previous section, we can deduce that they cannot change much between frames, so we could consider the average of some of the previous frames, to reduce noise.

There is a technique called the **exponentially weighted moving average** (or rolling average), which can be used to easily compute an approximate average on some of the last values of a stream of values.

Given `beta`, a parameter greater than zero and typically close to one, the moving average can be computed like this:

```
moving_average = beta * prev_average + (1-beta)*new_value
```

As an indication, the number of frames that most affect the average is given by the following:

```
1 / (1 - beta)
```

So, `beta = 0.9` would average 10 frames, and `beta = 0.95` would average 20 frames.

This concludes the chapter. I invite you to check the full code on GitHub and to play around with it. You can find some real-life footage and try to identify the lanes there.

And don't forget to apply the **camera calibration**, if you can.

Summary

In this chapter, we built a nice pipeline to detect lanes. First, we analyzed different color spaces, such as RGB, HLS, and HSV, to see which channels would be more useful to detect lanes. Then, we used perspective correction, with `getPerspectiveTransform()`, to obtain a *bird's eye view* and make parallel lines on the road also look parallel on the image we analyzed.

We used edge detection with `Scharr()` to detect edges and make our analysis more robust than using only a color threshold, and we combined the two. We then computed a histogram to detect where the lanes start, and we used the "sliding window" technique to "follow" the lane in the image.

Then, we used `polyfit()` to fit a second-order polynomial on the pixels detected, making sense of them, and we used the coefficients returned by the function to generate our curve, after having applied reverse perspective correction on them. Finally, we discussed two techniques that can be applied to a video stream to improve the precision: partial histogram and rolling average.

Using all these techniques together, you can now build a pipeline that can detect the lanes on a road.

In the next chapter, we will introduce deep learning and neural networks, powerful tools that we can use to accomplish even more complex computer vision tasks.

Questions

1. Can you name some color spaces, other than RGB?
2. Why do we apply perspective correction?
3. How can we detect where the lane starts?
4. Which technique can you use to *follow the lane* in the image?
5. If you have many points forming more or less a lane, how can you convert them into a line?
6. Which function can you use for edge detection?
7. What can you use to compute the average of the last N positions of the lane?

Section 2: Improving How the Self-Driving Car Works with Deep Learning and Neural Networks

This section will lead you toward the world of deep learning, hopefully surprising you with what can be achieved with relatively simple and short code.

This section comprises the following chapters:

- *Chapter 4, Deep Learning with Neural Networks*
- *Chapter 5, Deep Learning Workflow*
- *Chapter 6, Improving Your Neural Network*
- *Chapter 7, Detecting Pedestrians and Traffic Lights*
- *Chapter 8, Behavioral Cloning*
- *Chapter 9, Semantic Segmentation*

4
Deep Learning with Neural Networks

This chapter is an introduction to neural networks with Keras. If you have already worked with MNIST or CIFAR-10 image classification datasets, feel free to skip it. But if you have never trained a neural network, this chapter might have some surprises in store for you.

This chapter is quite practical, to give you very quickly something to play with, and we will skip as much theory as reasonably possible and learn how to recognize handwritten numbers (composed of one single digit) with high precision. The theory behind what we do here, and more, will be covered in the next chapter.

We will cover the following topics:

- Machine learning
- Neural networks and their parameters
- Convolutional neural networks
- Keras, a deep learning framework
- The MNIST dataset
- How to build and train a neural network
- The CIFAR-10 dataset

Technical requirements

For the instructions and code in this chapter, you need the following:

- Python 3.7
- NumPy
- Matplotlib
- TensorFlow
- Keras
- The OpenCV-Python module
- A GPU (recommended)

The code for the book can be found here:

https://github.com/PacktPublishing/Hands-On-Vision-and-Behavior-for-Self-Driving-Cars/tree/master/Chapter4

The Code in Action videos for this chapter can be found here:

https://bit.ly/3jfOoWi

Understanding machine learning and neural networks

According to Wikipedia, **machine learning** is *"the study of computer algorithms that improve automatically through experience."*

What that means in practice, at least for what concerns us, is that the algorithm itself is only moderately important, and what is critical is the data that we feed to this algorithm so that it can learn: we need to **train** our algorithm. Putting it in another way, we can use the same algorithm in many different situations as long as we provide the proper data for the task at hand.

For example, during this chapter, we will develop a neural network that is able to recognize handwritten numbers between 0 and 9; most likely, the exact same neural network could be used to recognize 10 letters, and with trivial modifications, it could recognize all letters or even different objects. In fact, we will reuse it basically as it is to recognize 10 objects.

This is totally different from *normal programming*, where different tasks usually require different code; to improve a result, we need to improve the code, and we might not need data at all for an algorithm to be usable (with real data).

That said, this does not mean that the result of a neural network is always good so long as good data is fed to it: difficult tasks require more advanced neural networks to perform well.

To be clear, while the algorithm (meaning the neural network model) is less important than the code in traditional programming, it is still important if you want to get very good results. In fact, with the wrong architecture, your neural network might not be able to learn at all.

Neural networks are only one of the tools that you can use to develop machine learning models, but this is what we will focus on. The accuracy of deep learning is usually quite high, and you might find that applications where less-accurate machine learning techniques are used are heavily constrained by the amount of data and the cost of processing it.

Deep learning can be considered a subset of machine learning, where the computation is performed by several computation layers, which is the *deep* part of the name. From a practical point of view, deep learning is achieved using neural networks.

That brings us to the question: what exactly is a neural network?

Neural networks

Neural networks are somewhat inspired by our brains: a neuron in our brain is a "computational node" that is connected to other neurons. When performing a computation, each of our brain's neurons "senses" the excited state of the neurons that it is connected to and uses these external states to compute its own state. A neuron in a neural network (a perceptron) basically does the same, but here is more or less where the similarities end. To be clear, a perceptron is not a simulation of a neuron, but it is just inspired by it.

The following is a mini neural network, with its neurons:

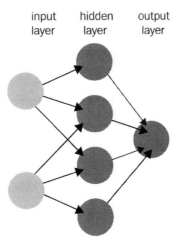

Figure 4.1 – A neural network

The first layer is the input (for example, the pixels of your image) and the output layer is the result (for example, your classification). The hidden layer is where the computation happens. Normally, you have more hidden layers, not just one. Every input can also be called a feature, and in the case of an RGB image, a feature is usually a single channel of a pixel.

In feedforward neural networks, the neurons of a layer are connected only to neurons of the layer before and of the following layers:

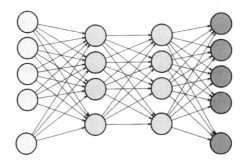

Figure 4.2 – A neural network

But what exactly is a neuron?

Neurons

A neuron is a computation node that produces an output given some input. As for what these inputs and outputs are – well, it depends. We will come back to this point later.

The following is a representation of the typical neuron of a neural network:

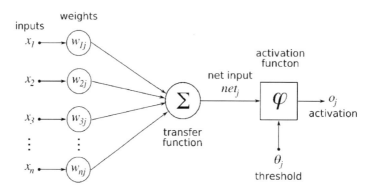

Figure 4.3 – Schematic of a single neuron of a neural network. ©2016 Wikimedia Commons

This needs some explanation. The computation performed by a neuron can be divided into two parts:

- The transfer function computes the sum of every input multiplied by its weight (just a number); what this means is that the state of the neuron depends on the state of its input neurons, but different neurons provide a different contribution. This is just a linear operation:

$$u = \sum_{1=1}^{n} w_i x_i$$

- The activation function is applied to the result of the transfer function, and it should be a **non-linear** operation, typically with a threshold. A function that we will use often, because of its performance, is called **Rectified Linear Unit (ReLU)**.

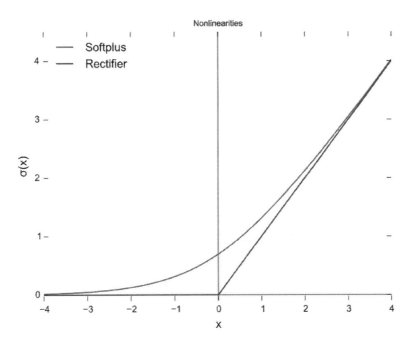

Figure 4.4 – Two activation functions: Softplus and ReLU

There is usually also a **bias**, a value used to shift the activation function.

The combination of a linear function with a non-linear function is non-linear, while the combination of two linear functions is still linear. This is very important because it means that if the activation was linear, then the output of the neurons will be linear, and the combination of different layers would be linear as well. So, the whole neural network would be linear and therefore equivalent to a single layer.

Introducing a non-linear operation in the activation allows a network to compute non-linear functions that become more and more complex as the number of layers grows. This is one of the reasons why the most sophisticated neural networks can literally have hundreds of layers.

Parameters

The bias and the weights are called **parameters**, because they are not fixed but need to change based on the task at hand. We do this during the **training** phase. To be clear, the whole purpose of the training phase is to find the best possible value for these parameters for our task.

This has profound implications, as it means that the same neural network, with different parameters, can solve different problems – very different problems. The trick, of course, is to find the best values (or one approximation) for these parameters. If you are wondering how many parameters a typical neural network can have, the answer is millions. Luckily, this process, called training, can be automated.

An alternative way to imagine a neural network is to consider it as a gigantic system of equations, and the training phase is an attempt to find an approximate solution to it.

The success of deep learning

You've probably noticed that deep learning has seen explosive growth in the past few years, but neural networks are really nothing new. I remember trying to write a neural network (and failing miserably!) more than 20 years ago, after reading a book about it. In fact, they date back to 1965, with some theories being even 20 years older than that.

Many years ago, they were dismissed basically as a curiosity, as they were too computationally demanding to be practical.

However, fast forward some decades, and deep learning is the new black, thanks to some critical advances:

- Computers are much faster and have much more RAM available.
- GPUs can be used to make computations even faster.
- There are many datasets easily available on the internet to train neural networks.
- There are now plenty of tutorials and online courses dedicated to deep learning.
- There are several good open source libraries for neural networks.
- Architectures have become better and more efficient.

It's the perfect storm to make neural networks much more appealing, and there are many applications that seem to be waiting for deep learning, such as voice assistants and, of course, self-driving cars.

There is a special type of neural network that is particularly good at understanding the content of images, and we will pay great attention to them: convolutional neural networks.

Learning about convolutional neural networks

If you look at a classical neural network, you can see that the first layer is composed of inputs, standing on a line. This is not only a graphical representation: for a classical neural network, an input is an input, and it should be independent of the other ones. This is probably fine if you are trying to predict the price of an apartment based on size, ZIP code, and floor number, but it does not seem optimal for an image, where pixels have neighbors and it seems intuitive that keeping this proximity information is important.

Convolutional Neural Networks (**CNNs**) solve exactly this problem, and it turns out that not only can they process images efficiently, but they can also be used with success for natural language processing.

A CNN is a neural network that has at least one convolutional layer, which is inspired by the visual cortex of animals, where individual neurons respond only to stimuli in a small area of the field of vision. Let's see what convolutions really are.

Convolutions

Convolutions are based on the concept of the **kernel**, a matrix that you apply to some pixels to get a single new pixel. Kernels can be used for edge detection or to apply filters to an image, and you normally have the option to define your kernel in image processing programs, if you wish to do so. The following is a 3x3 identity kernel that replicates an image as it is, and we are applying it to a small image:

$$\begin{matrix} 31 & 32 & 33 \\ 41 & 42 & 43 \\ 51 & 52 & 53 \end{matrix} \quad + \quad \begin{bmatrix} 0 & 0 & 0 \\ 0 & 1 & 0 \\ 0 & 0 & 0 \end{bmatrix} \quad ==> \quad 42$$

Figure 4.5 – Part of an image, a 3x3 identity kernel, and the result

Just imagine putting a pixel behind each element of the kernel and multiplying them together, then adding the results to get the value of the new pixel; clearly, you would get a zero for each pixel except the central one, which would be unchanged. This kernel preserves the value of the pixel in the middle and discards all the others. If you slide this convolution kernel over the whole picture, you will get the original image back:

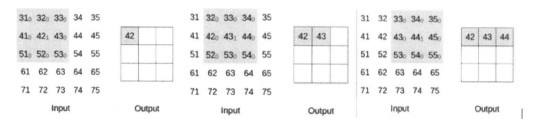

Figure 4.6 – Identity convolution – just copying an image

You can see that as the convolution kernel slides over the image, the pixels are replicated unchanged. You can also see that the resolution is reduced, as we use *valid* padding.

This is another example:

$$\begin{matrix} 2 & 2 & 2 \\ 2 & 3 & 2 \\ 2 & 2 & 2 \end{matrix} + \begin{bmatrix} 0 & -1 & 0 \\ -1 & 5 & -1 \\ 0 & -1 & 0 \end{bmatrix} \implies 7$$

Figure 4.7 – Part of an image, a 3x3 kernel, and the result

Other kernels can be more interesting than the identity kernel. The following kernel (on the left) can detect edges, as seen on the right:

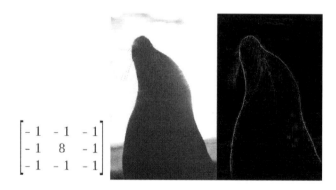

Figure 4.8 – Kernel detecting edges

If you are curious about kernels, please go ahead with OpenCV and have some fun:

```
img = cv2.imread("test.jpg")
kernel = np.array(([-1, -1, -1], [-1, 8, -1], [-1, -1, -1]))
dst = cv2.filter2D(img,-1,kernel)
cv2.imshow("Kernel", cv2.hconcat([img, dst]))
cv2.waitKey(0)
```

Kernels don't need to be 3x3; they can be bigger.

If you imagine starting with the first pixel of the image, you might ask what happens then, as there are no pixels above it or to its left. If you position the top-left corner of a kernel on the top-left pixel of an image, you will lose one pixel on each side of the image, because you can think of it as the kernel *emitting a pixel* from the center. This is not always a problem, because when designing a neural network, you might want the image to get smaller and smaller after each layer.

An alternative is to use padding – for example, pretending that there are black pixels around the image.

The good news is that you don't need to find the values of the kernels; the CNN will find them for you during the training phase.

Why are convolutions so great?

Convolutions have some great advantages. As we have already said, they preserve the proximity of pixels:

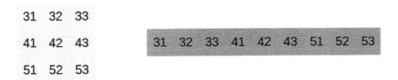

Figure 4.9 – A convolution layer, in yellow, versus a dense layer, in green

As you can see from the previous figure, the convolution knows the topology of the image and can know, for example, that the pixel with the number 43 is right next to the pixel with the number 42, is below the pixel with the number 33, and is above the pixel with the number 53. The dense layer in the same figure does not have this information and might think that the pixel with 43 and the pixel with 51 are close to each other. Not only that, but it does not even know whether the resolution is 3x3, 9x1, or 1x9. Intuitively knowing the topology of pixels is an advantage.

An additional important advantage is that they are computationally efficient.

Another great characteristic of convolutions is that they are very good at recognizing patterns, such as diagonal lines or circles. You might say that they can only do so at a small scale, which is true, but you can combine multiple convolutions to detect patterns at different scales, and they can be surprisingly good at that.

They are also able to detect patterns in different parts of an image.

All these characteristics make them great to work with images, and it is not surprising that they are used so much for object detection.

Enough theory for now. Let's get our hands dirty and write our first neural network.

Getting started with Keras and TensorFlow

There are many libraries dedicated to deep learning, and we will be using Keras, a Python library that uses multiple backends; we will be using TensorFlow as a backend. While the code is specific to Keras, the principles can apply to any other libraries.

Requirements

Before starting, you need to install at least TensorFlow and Keras, using `pip`:

```
pip install tensorflow
pip install keras
```

We are using TensorFlow 2.2, which has integrated GPU support, but if you are using TensorFlow version 1.15 or older, you need to install a separate package to take advantage of a GPU:

```
pip install tensorflow-gpu
```

I would recommend using the most recent versions of both TensorFlow and Keras.

Before starting, let's make sure that everything is in order. You probably want to use a GPU, to speed up training. Unfortunately, getting TensorFlow to use your GPU is not necessarily straightforward; for example, it is very picky with the version of CUDA: if it says CUDA 10.1, it really means it – it is not going to work with 10.0 or with 10.2. Hopefully, this will not affect your games much.

To print the version of TensorFlow, you can use this code:

```
import tensorflow as tf
print("TensorFlow:", tf.__version__)
print("TensorFlow Git:", tf.version.GIT_VERSION)
```

On my computer, that prints this:

```
TensorFlow: 2.1.0
TensorFlow Git: v2.1.0-rc2-17-ge5bf8de410
```

To check the GPU support, you can use this code:

```
print("CUDA ON" if tf.test.is_built_with_cuda() else "CUDA OFF")
print("GPU ON" if tf.test.is_gpu_available() else "GPU OFF")
```

If everything is fine, you should see CUDA ON, meaning that your version of TensorFlow has been built with CUDA support, and GPU ON, meaning that TensorFlow is able to use your GPU.

If your GPU is not NVIDIA, it might require some more work, but it should be possible to configure TensorFlow to run on AMD graphics cards, using ROCm.

Now that you have correctly installed all the software, it is time to use it on our first neural network. Our first task will be to recognize handwritten digits, using a dataset called MNIST.

Detecting MNIST handwritten digits

When you design a neural network, you usually start with a problem that you want to solve, and you might start with a design that you know performs well on a similar task. You need a dataset, basically as big a dataset as you can get. There is not really a rule on that, but we can say that the minimum to train your own neural network might be something around 3,000 images, but nowadays world-class CNNs are trained using literally millions of pictures.

Our first task is to detect handwritten digits, a classical task for CNNs. There is a dataset for that, the MNIST dataset (copyright of Yann LeCun and Corinna Cortes), and it is conveniently present in Keras. MNIST detection is an easy task, so we will achieve good results.

Loading the dataset is easy:

```
from keras.datasets import mnist
(x_train, y_train), (x_test, y_test) = mnist.load_data()
x_train = np.reshape(x_train, np.append(x_train.shape, (1)))
x_test = np.reshape(x_test, np.append(x_test.shape, (1)))
```

reshape just reinterprets the shape from (60000, 28, 28) to (60000, 28, 28, 1), because Keras needs four dimensions.

What did we just load?

The load_data() method returns four things:

- x_train: The images used for training
- y_train: The labels used for training (that is, the correct numbers for each of the handwritten digits)
- x_test: The images used for testing
- y_test: The labels used for testing (that is, the correct numbers for each of the handwritten digits)

Training samples and labels

Let's print the dimensions of the training samples (x) and of the labels (y):

```
print('X Train', x_train.shape, ' - X Test', x_test.shape)
print('Y Train', y_train.shape, ' - Y Test', y_test.shape)
```

It should print something like this:

```
X Train (60000, 28, 28, 1)  - X Test (10000, 28, 28, 1)
Y Train (60000,)  - Y Test (10000,)
```

The x variable represents the input for the CNN, which means that x contains all our images divided into two sets, one for training and one for testing:

- x_train contains 60,000 images intended for training, each with 28x28 pixels and in grayscale (one channel).
- x_test contains 10,000 images intended for testing, each with 28x28 pixels and in grayscale (one channel).

As you can see, the training and testing images have the same resolution and the same number of channels.

The y variable represents the expected output of the CNN, also called the label. For many datasets, somebody manually labels all the images to say what they are. If the dataset is artificial, labeling might be automated:

- y_train is composed of 60,000 numbers belonging to 10 classes, from 0 to 9.
- y_test is composed of 10,000 numbers belonging to 10 classes, from 0 to 9.

For each image, we have one label.

Generally speaking, a neural network can have more than one output, and every output is a number. In the case of a classification task, such as MNIST, the output is a single integer number. In this case, we are particularly lucky, because the output value is actually the number we are interested in (for example, 0 means the number 0, and 1 means the number 1). Usually, you need to convert the number to a label (for example, 0 -> cat, 1 -> dog, and 2 -> duck).

To be precise, our CNN will not output one integer result from 0 to 9, but 10 floating-point numbers, and the position of the highest one will be the label (for example, if the output in position 3 is the highest value, then the output will be 3). We will discuss this more in the next chapter.

To better understand MNIST, let's see five samples from the training dataset and five samples from the testing dataset:

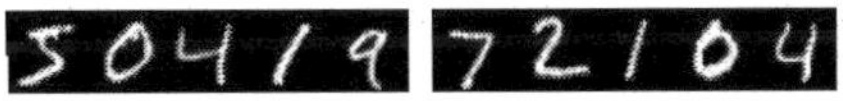

Figure 4.10 – MNIST training and testing dataset samples.
Copyright of Yann LeCun and Corinna Cortes

As you might suspect, the corresponding labels of those images are as follows:

- 5, 0, 4, 1, and 9 for the training samples (y_train)
- 7, 2, 1, 0, and 4 for the testing samples (y_test)

We should also resize the samples so that instead of being in the 0-255 range, they are in the 0-1 range, as that helps the neural network to achieve better results:

```
x_train = x_train.astype('float32')
x_test = x_test.astype('float32')
x_train /= 255
x_test /= 255
```

One-hot encoding

The labels cannot be used directly but need to be converted to a vector using *one-hot encoding*. As the name implies, you get a vector where only one element is hot (for example, its value is 1) while all the other elements are cold (for example, their value is 0). The hot element represents the position of the label, in a vector including all the possible positions. An example should make it easier to understand.

In the case of MINST, you have 10 labels: 0, 1, 2, 3, 4, 5, 6, 7, 8, and 9. The one-hot encoding would therefore use 10 items. This is the encoding of the first three items:

- 0 ==> 1 0 0 0 0 0 0 0 0 0
- 1 ==> 0 1 0 0 0 0 0 0 0 0
- 2 ==> 0 0 1 0 0 0 0 0 0 0

If you have three labels, dog, cat, and fish, your one-hot encoding would be as follows:

- Dog   ==> 1 0 0
- Cat   ==> 0 1 0
- Fish ==> 0 0 1

Keras provides a handy function for that, `to_categorical()`, which accepts the list of labels to transform and the total number of labels:

```
print("One hot encoding: ", keras.utils.to_categorical([0, 1, 2], 10))
```

If your labels are not numeric, you can use `index()` to get access to the index of the specified label and use it to call `to_categorical()`:

```
labels = ['Dog', 'Cat', 'Fish']
print("One hot encoding 'Cat': ", keras.utils.to_categorical(labels.index('Cat'), 10))
```

Training and testing datasets

The x variable contains the images, but why do we have both `x_train` and `x_test`?

We will explain everything in detail in the next chapter, but for now let's just say that Keras needs two datasets: one to train the neural network and one that is used to tune the hyperparameters and to evaluate the performance of the neural network.

It is a bit like having a teacher first explaining things to you, then interrogating you, analyzing your answers to explain better what you did not understand.

Defining the model of the neural network

Now we want to write our neural network, which we can call our model, and train it. We know that it should use convolutions, but we don't know much more than that. Let's take inspiration from an old but very influential CNN: **LeNet**.

LeNet

LeNet was one of the first CNNs. Dating back to 1998, it's pretty small and simple for today's standards. But it is enough for this task.

This is its architecture:

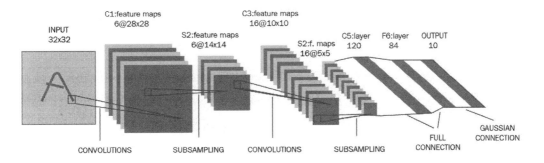

Figure 4.11 – LeNet

LeNet accepts 32x32 images and has the following layers:

- The first layer is composed of six 5x5 convolutions, emitting images of 28x28 pixels.
- The second layer subsamples the image (for example, computing the average of four pixels), emitting images of 14x14 pixels.
- The third layer is composed of 16 5x5 convolutions, emitting images of 10x10 pixels.
- The fourth layer subsamples the image (for example, computing the average of four pixels), emitting images of 5x5 pixels.
- The fifth layer is a fully connected dense layer (that is, all the neurons of the previous layer are connected to all the neurons of this layer) of 120 neurons.

- The sixth layer is a fully connected dense layer of 84 neurons.
- The seventh and last layer is the output, a fully connected dense layer of 10 neurons, because we need to classify the images into 10 classes, for the 10 digits.

We are not trying to recreate LeNet precisely, and our input images are a bit smaller, but we will keep it as a reference.

The code

The first step is defining which type of neural network we are creating, which in Keras usually is `Sequential`:

```
model = Sequential()
```

Now we can add the first convolutional layer:

```
model.add(Conv2D(filters=6, kernel_size=(5, 5),
    activation='relu', padding='same',
    input_shape=x_train.shape[1:]))
```

It accepts the following parameters:

- Six filters, so that we will get six kernels, which means six convolutions.
- Kernel size 5x5.
- ReLU activation.
- `same` padding (for example, using black pixels around the image), to not reduce too much the size of the image too early, and to be closer to LeNet.
- `input_shape` contains the shape of the images.

Then, we add subsampling using `Max Pooling (default size=2x2)`, which emits the value of the pixel with the maximum **activation** (for example, with the maximum value):

```
model.add(MaxPooling2D())
```

Then, we can add the next convolutional layer and the next max pooling layer:

```
model.add(Conv2D(filters=16, kernel_size=(5,5),
    activation='relu'))
model.add(MaxPooling2D())
```

And then we can add the dense layers:

```
model.add(Flatten())
model.add(Dense(units=120, activation='relu'))
model.add(Dense(units=84, activation='relu'))
model.add(Dense(units=num_classes, activation='softmax'))
```

`Flatten()` is used to flatten the 2D outputs of the convolutional layer into a single row of outputs (1D), which is required by the dense layer. Just to be clear, for our use case, the input of a convolutional filter is a grayscale image, and the output is another grayscale image.

The last activation, `softmax`, converts the prediction into a probability, for convenience, and the output with the highest probability will represent the label that the neural network associates to the image.

That's it: just a few lines of code to build a CNN that can recognize handwritten digits. I challenge you to do the same without machine learning!

The architecture

Even if our model definition is pretty straightforward, it can be useful to visualize it and see whether, for example, the dimensions are as expected.

Keras has a very useful function for that – `summary()`:

```
model.summary()
```

And this is the result:

Layer (type)	Output Shape	Param #
conv2d_1 (Conv2D)	(None, 28, 28, 6)	156
max_pooling2d_1 (MaxPooling2	(None, 14, 14, 6)	0
conv2d_2 (Conv2D)	(None, 10, 10, 16)	2416
max_pooling2d_2 (MaxPooling2	(None, 5, 5, 16)	0

```
flatten_1 (Flatten)           (None, 400)                0

dense_1 (Dense)               (None, 120)                48120

dense_2 (Dense)               (None, 84)                 10164

dense_3 (Dense)               (None, 10)                 850
=================================================================
Total params: 61,706
Trainable params: 61,706
Non-trainable params: 0
```

This is very interesting. Firstly, we can see that the dimensions of the output of the convolutional layers are the same as for LeNet: 28x28 and 10x10. This is not necessarily important; it just means that the network is dimensioned as we were expecting.

We can also see that the order of the layers is correct. What is interesting is the third value on each row: the number of parameters. The parameters are the variables that the neural network needs to figure out to actually learn something. They are the variables of our huge system of equations.

In the case of a fully connected dense layer, the number of parameters is obtained by multiplying the number of neurons of the previous layer, plus one, by the number of neurons of the current layer. If you remember the image of a neuron, there was one weight for each neuron it was connected to, so it is kind of intuitive that each of them is a trainable parameter. In addition, there is a parameter for the threshold (bias) of the activation. In the last layer, we therefore have the following:

- 84 inputs ==> 84 weights + 1 bias ==> 85 parameters
- 10 outputs
- 85 x 10 ==> 850 parameters

In the case of a convolutional layer, the number of parameters is given by the area of the kernel plus one, the bias of the activation. In the first layer, we have the following:

- 5x5 kernel ==> 25 + 1 bias ==> 26 parameters
- 6 filters
- 26 x 6 ==> 156 parameters

As you can see, our network has 61,706 parameters. While this might seem like a lot, it's not uncommon for a neural network to have millions of them. How do they impact the training? As a first approximation, we can say that having more parameters enables our network to learn more things, but at the same time, it slows it down and increases the size of the model and the amount of memory it uses. Don't become obsessed with the number of parameters, because not all of them are created equal, but keep an eye on them, in case there is some layer that's using too many. You can see that dense layers tend to use many parameters, and in our case, they hold more than 95% of the parameters.

Training a neural network

Now that we have our neural network, we need to train it. We will talk more about training in the next chapter, but as the name suggests, training is the phase where the neural network *studies* the training dataset and actually learns it. As for how well it learns – that depends.

For the sake of quickly explaining the concepts, we will do an improper comparison with a student trying to learn a book for an exam:

- The book is the training dataset that the student needs to learn.
- Every time that the student reads the whole book is called an epoch. A student might want to read the book more than once, and it is very common for neural networks to do the same and train for more than one epoch.
- The optimizer is like somebody who asks the student questions from an exercise book (the validation dataset; though, in our example, we are going to use the test dataset for validation) to see how well the student is learning. One key difference is that the neural network does not learn from the validation dataset. We will see in the next chapter why this is very good.
- To track their progress and learn in less time, the student can ask the optimizer to ask questions after a certain number of pages; that number of pages would be the batch size.

The first thing to do is to configure the model, using `compile()`:

```
model.compile(loss=categorical_crossentropy, optimizer=Adam(),
    metrics=['accuracy'])
```

Keras has a variety of loss functions that you can use. `loss` is basically a measure of how distant the result of your model is from the ideal output. For classification tasks, we can use `categorical_crossentropy` as a loss function. `optimizer` is the algorithm used to train the neural network. If you imagine the neural network as a giant system of equations, the optimizer is the one that figures out how to change the parameters to improve the result. We will use **Adam**, as this is often a good choice. `metrics` is just some values computed during the training, but they are not used by the optimizer; they are just provided to you as a reference.

We can now run the training, which might take a couple of minutes, and it will print the progress that is being made:

```
history = model.fit(x_train, y_train, batch_size=16,
    epochs=5, validation_data=(x_test, y_test), shuffle=True)
```

We need to provide several parameters:

- `x_train`: The training images.
- `y_train`: The training labels.
- `batch_size`: The default is 32, and usually it's worth trying powers of 2, from 16 to 256; the batch size affects both speed and accuracy.
- `epochs`: The number of times that the CNN will go through the dataset.
- `validation_data`: As we've already said, we are using the test dataset for validation.
- `shuffle`: If we want to shuffle the training data before each epoch, which usually we want to.

The result of the training is `history`, which contains a lot of useful information:

```
print("Min Loss:", min(history.history['loss']))
print("Min Val. Loss:", min(history.history['val_loss']))
print("Max Accuracy:", max(history.history['accuracy']))
print("Max Val. Accuracy:", max(history.history['val_accuracy']))
```

We are talking about minimum and maximum because these values are measured during each epoch, and do not necessarily progress always toward an improvement.

Let's go through what we have here:

- The minimum loss is a measure of how close we come to the ideal output in the training dataset, or how well the neural network learned the training dataset. In general, we want this value to be as small as possible.
- The minimum validation loss is how close we come to the ideal output in the validation dataset, or how well the neural network can do with the validation dataset after training. This is probably the most important value, as it is what we are trying to minimize, so we want this value to be as small as possible.
- The maximum accuracy is the maximum percentage of correct answers (predictions) that our CNN can give using the training dataset. For the student example from earlier, it would tell them how well they had memorized the book. Knowing the book by heart is not bad by itself – it is actually desirable – but the goal is not to memorize the book, but to learn from it. While we expect this value to be as high as possible, it can be misleading.
- The maximum validation accuracy is the maximum percentage of correct answers (predictions) that our CNN can give using the validation dataset. For the student example from earlier, it would tell them how well they had really learned the content of the book, so that they can answer questions that might not be present in the book. This will be an indication of how well our neural network can perform in real life.

This is the result of our CNN:

```
Min Loss: 0.054635716760404344
Min Validation Loss: 0.05480437679834067
Max Accuracy: 0.9842833
Max Validation Accuracy: 0.9835000038146973
```

On your computer, it will probably be slightly different, and in fact it should change a bit every time that you run it.

We can see that the losses are close to zero, which is good. Both the accuracy and the validation accuracy are almost 98.5%, which in general is very good.

We can also plot the evolution over time of these parameters:

```
plt.plot(history_object.history['loss'])
plt.plot(history_object.history['val_loss'])
plt.plot(history_object.history['accuracy'])
plt.plot(history_object.history['val_accuracy'])
plt.title('model mean squared error loss')
plt.ylabel('mean squared error loss')
plt.xlabel('epoch')
plt.legend(['T loss', 'V loss', 'T acc', 'V acc'], loc='upper left')
plt.show()
```

This is the result:

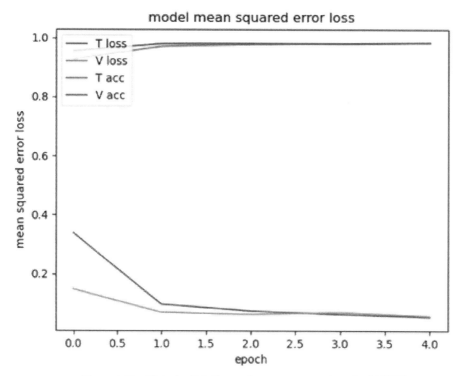

Figure 4.12 – Plot of validation and accuracy over time for MNIST

Both the accuracy and the loss are very good after the first epoch and keep improving.

So far so good. Maybe you think that this was easy. But MNIST is a simple dataset. Let's try CIFAR-10.

CIFAR-10

To use CIFAR-10, we can just ask Keras to use a different dataset:

```
(x_train, y_train), (x_test, y_test) = cifar10.load_data()
```

CIFAR-10 is a more difficult dataset. It contains 32x32 RGB images, containing 10 types of objects:

```
X Train (50000, 32, 32, 3)   - X Test (10000, 32, 32, 3)
Y Train (50000, 1)   - Y Test (10000, 1)
```

It looks similar to MNIST.

In the code on GitHub, to use CIFAR 10, you can simply change the `use_mnist` variable to `False`:

```
use_mnist = False
```

You don't need to change anything else in the code, apart from removing the `reshape()` call because CIFAR-10 uses RGB images and, as a result, it already has three dimensions: width, height, and channels. Keras will adapt the model to the different dimensions and channels, and the neural network will just learn a new dataset!

Let's see the new model:

```
Layer (type)                 Output Shape              Param #
=================================================================
conv2d_1 (Conv2D)            (None, 32, 32, 6)         456

max_pooling2d_1 (MaxPooling2 (None, 16, 16, 6)         0

conv2d_2 (Conv2D)            (None, 12, 12, 16)        2416
```

```
max_pooling2d_2 (MaxPooling2   (None, 6, 6, 16)          0

flatten_1 (Flatten)            (None, 576)               0

dense_1 (Dense)                (None, 120)               69240

dense_2 (Dense)                (None, 84)                10164

dense_3 (Dense)                (None, 10)                850
=================================================================
Total params: 83,126
Trainable params: 83,126
Non-trainable params: 0
```

The model is a bit bigger, because the images are slightly bigger and in RGB format. Let's see how it performs:

```
Min Loss: 1.2048443819999695
Min Validation Loss: 1.2831668125152589
Max Accuracy: 0.57608
Max Validation Accuracy: 0.5572999715805054
```

This is not very good: the loss is high and the validation accuracy is only around 55%.

The next graph is quite important, and you will see it many times, so please take some time to familiarize yourself with it. The following graph shows the evolution of the loss (we use mean squared error) and of the accuracy for each epoch, over time, for our model. On the X axis, you see the number of epochs, and then there are four lines:

- T loss: The training loss
- V loss: The validation loss
- T acc: The training accuracy
- V acc: The validation accuracy:

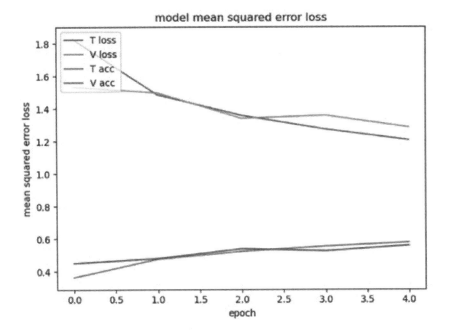

Figure 4.13 – Plot of validation and accuracy over time for CIFAR-10

We can see that the loss is going down, but it has not reached a minimum yet, so it probably means more epochs can be beneficial. The accuracy is low and stays low, probably because the model does not have enough parameters.

Let's see the result with 12 epochs:

```
Min Loss: 1.011266466407776
Min Validation Loss: 1.3062725918769837
Max Accuracy: 0.6473
Max Validation Accuracy: 0.5583999752998352
```

The good news: the loss went down and the accuracy improved. The bad news: the validation loss and validation accuracy did not improve. In practice, our network is learning the training dataset by heart, but it cannot generalize, and therefore it does not perform well on the validation dataset.

Let's try to also significantly increase the size of the network:

```
model.add(Conv2D(filters=64, kernel_size=(3, 3),
    activation='relu', input_shape=x_train.shape[1:]))
model.add(AveragePooling2D())
```

```
model.add(Conv2D(filters=256, kernel_size=(3, 3),
activation='relu'))
model.add(AveragePooling2D())

model.add(Flatten())
model.add(Dense(units=512, activation='relu'))
model.add(Dense(units=256, activation='relu'))
model.add(Dense(units=num_classes, activation = 'softmax'))
```

That gives us this new model:

```
Layer (type)                    Output Shape              Param #
=================================================================
conv2d_1 (Conv2D)               (None, 30, 30, 64)        1792

average_pooling2d_1 (Average    (None, 15, 15, 64)        0

conv2d_2 (Conv2D)               (None, 13, 13, 256)       147712

average_pooling2d_2 (Average    (None, 6, 6, 256)         0

flatten_1 (Flatten)             (None, 9216)              0

dense_1 (Dense)                 (None, 512)               4719104

dense_2 (Dense)                 (None, 256)               131328

dense_3 (Dense)                 (None, 10)                2570
=================================================================
Total params: 5,002,506
Trainable params: 5,002,506
Non-trainable params: 0
```

Wow: we jumped from 83,000 to 5,000,000 parameters! That first dense layer is getting big...

Let's see whether we can see some improvements:

```
Min Loss: 0.23179266978245228
Min Validation Loss: 1.0802633233070373
Max Accuracy: 0.92804
Max Validation Accuracy: 0.65829998254776
```

Now all the values have improved; however, while the training accuracy is now above 90%, the validation accuracy is just 65%:

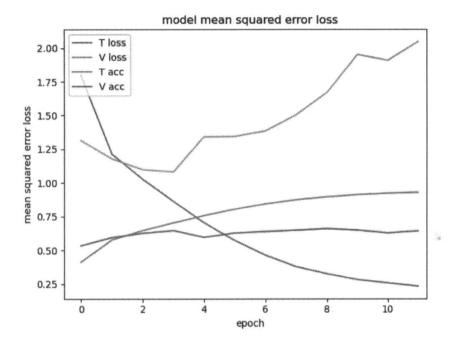

Figure 4.14 – Plot of validation and accuracy over time for CIFAR-10

We see something a bit worrying: while the training loss goes down over time, the validation loss goes up. This situation is called overfitting, and it means that the network is not good at generalizing. It also means that we used way too many epochs for nothing.

Not only that, but if we saved the model at the end, we would not be saving the best one. If you are wondering whether there is a way to save the best model (for example, with the lowest validation loss), then the answer is yes – Keras can do it:

```
checkpoint = ModelCheckpoint('cifar-10.h5', monitor='val_loss', mode='min', verbose=1, save_best_only=True)
```

Here we are telling Keras to do the following:

- Save the model with the name `'cifar-10.h5'`.
- Monitor the validation loss.
- Select the model based on the minimum loss (for example, save only if the validation loss decreases).
- Save only the best model.

You can pass the `checkpoint` object to `model.fit()`:

```
history_object = model.fit(x_train, y_train, batch_size=batch_size, epochs=epochs, validation_data=(x_test, y_test), shuffle=True, callbacks=[checkpoint])
```

This helps, but the model is not good enough. We need something radically better.

In the next chapter, we will learn many things that will hopefully help us to get some better results. Plus, in *Chapter 6, Improving Your Neural Network*, we will apply this knowledge, and more, to improve the results. Now, if you want, you can spend some time trying to tune and improve the network: you can change its size, add filters and layers, and see how it performs.

Summary

This has been a dense chapter! We discussed machine learning in general and deep learning in particular. We talked about neural networks and how convolutions can be used to make faster and more accurate neural networks, leveraging the knowledge of pixel proximity. We learned about weights, bias, and parameters, and how the goal of the training phase is to optimize all these parameters to learn the task at hand.

After verifying the installation of Keras and TensorFlow, we described MNIST, and we instructed Keras to build a network similar to LeNet, to achieve more than 98% accuracy on this dataset, meaning that we can now easily recognize handwritten digits. Then, we saw that the same model does not perform well in CIFAR-10, despite increasing the number of epochs and the size of the network.

In the next chapter, we will study in depth many of the concepts that we introduced here, with the final goal, to be completed by *Chapter 6, Improving Your Neural Network*, of learning how to train a neural network.

Questions

After reading this chapter, you should be able to answer the following questions:

1. What is a perceptron?
2. Can you name an optimizer that tends to perform well in many tasks?
3. What is a convolution?
4. What is a CNN?
5. What is a dense layer?
6. What does the `Flatten()` layer do?
7. Which backend have we been using for Keras?
8. What is the name of one of the first CNNs?

Further reading

- The original LeNet paper: http://yann.lecun.com/exdb/publis/pdf/lecun-01a.pdf
- MNIST: http://yann.lecun.com/exdb/mnist/
- CNNs: https://towardsdatascience.com/a-comprehensive-guide-to-convolutional-neural-networks-the-eli5-way-3bd2b1164a53

5
Deep Learning Workflow

In this chapter, we will go through the steps that you might perform while training your neural network, and when putting it into production. We will discuss more about the theory behind deep learning, to explain better what we actually did in *Chapter 4, Deep Learning with Neural Networks*, but we will stay mostly focused on arguments related to self-driving cars. We will also introduce some concepts that will help us to achieve better precision on CIFAR-10, a famous dataset of small images. We are sure that the theory exposed in this chapter, plus the more practical knowledge associated with *Chapter 4, Deep Learning with Neural Networks*, and *Chapter 6, Improving Your Neural Network*, will give you enough tools to be able to perform tasks that are common in the field of self-driving cars.

In this chapter, we will cover the following topics:

- Obtaining or creating the dataset
- Training, validation, and test datasets
- Classifiers
- Data augmentation
- Defining the model
- How to tune convolutional layers, `MaxPooling` layers, and dense layers
- Training and the role of randomness

- Underfitting and overfitting
- Visualization of activations
- Running inference
- Retraining

Technical requirements

To be able to use the code explained in this chapter, you need to have the following tools and modules installed:

- Python 3.7
- The NumPy module
- The Matplotlib module
- The TensorFlow module
- The Keras module
- The OpenCV-Python module

The code for the chapter can be found at `https://github.com/PacktPublishing/Hands-On-Vision-and-Behavior-for-Self-Driving-Cars/tree/master/Chapter5`.

The Code in Action videos for this chapter can be found here:

`https://bit.ly/3dJrcys`

Obtaining the dataset

Once you have a task that you want to perform with a neural network, the first step is usually to obtain the dataset, which is the data that you need to feed to the neural network. In the tasks that we perform in this book, the dataset is usually composed of images or videos, but it could be anything, or a mix of images and other data.

The dataset represents the input that you feed to your neural network, but as you may have noticed, your dataset also contains the desired output, the labels. We will call x the input to the neural network, and y the output. The dataset is composed of the inputs/features (for example, the images in the MNIST dataset), and the output/labels (for example, the number associated with each image).

We have different dataset types. Let's start with the easiest – the datasets included in Keras – before proceeding to the next ones.

Datasets in the Keras module

Usually a dataset is a lot of data. It's normal to train a neural network on tens of thousands of images, but the best neural networks are trained with many millions of images. So how do we use them?

The easiest way, which is usually mostly helpful for experiments, is to use the datasets included in Keras, as we did in *Chapter 4, Deep Learning with Neural Networks*, using `load_data()`, shown as follows:

```
from keras.datasets import mnist
(x_train, y_train), (x_test, y_test) = mnist.load_data()
```

Keras provides a variety of datasets:

- MNIST – the classification of digits
- CIFAR10 – the classification of small images
- CIFAR100 – the classification of small images
- IMDB movie review sentiment classification
- Reuters newswire classification
- Fashion MNIST dataset
- Boston Housing prices

These datasets are useful in learning how to build neural networks in general. In the next section, we will look at some datasets that are more useful for self-driving cars.

Existing datasets

Luckily, there are several interesting public datasets available, but you have to always carefully check the license to see what you are allowed to do with it, and eventually get or acquire a more permissive license.

The following are some datasets related to self-driving cars that you might want to check:

- BDD100K, a large-scale diverse driving video database; refer to https://bdd-data.berkeley.edu/.
- Bosch small traffic lights database; refer to https://hci.iwr.uni-heidelberg.de/content/bosch-small-traffic-lights-dataset.

- CULane, a large-scale dataset for academic research on traffic lane detection; refer to `https://xingangpan.github.io/projects/CULane.html`.
- KITTI Vision Benchmark Suite; refer to `http://www.cvlibs.net/datasets/kitti/`.
- Mapillary Traffic Sign Dataset; refer to `https://www.mapillary.com/dataset/trafficsign`.

In addition, there are other more generic datasets that you might find interesting, in particular, ImageNet, `http://www.image-net.org/`, an image dataset organized according to the WordNet hierarchy.

This dataset contains millions of URLs pointing to images on the internet, and has been very influential in developing neural networks. We will talk more about this later.

Public datasets are great, but you might consider their content, as it is not uncommon to have some images incorrectly classified. This is not necessarily a big deal for your neural network, but you might still want to get a dataset as good as possible.

If you cannot find a satisfactory dataset, you can always generate one. Let's see how you can quickly build good datasets for self-driving car tasks.

Synthetic datasets

When possible, you might want to generate a dataset from a program that can create *good enough* images. We used this technique in *Chapter 3, Lane Detection*, where we detected pedestrians from Carla, and images from the open source video game Speed Dreams, and you could write your own generator using a 3D engine or 3D modeling software.

These are a relatively easy, quick, and very cheap way to generate massive datasets, and, in fact, are sometimes invaluable, as in many cases you can automatically annotate the images and save a lot of time. However synthetic images tend to be less complex than real images, with the result that your network will probably not perform as well as you think in a real-world scenario. We will use this technique in *Chapter 8, Behavioral Cloning*.

One of the best simulators available, if not the best, is Carla.

Carla, the open source simulator for autonomous driving research, uses the following websites:

- `https://carla.org/`
- `https://github.com/carla-simulator/carla`

You can use it to generate the images that you need for your tasks.

When this is not enough, you have to follow a manual process.

Your custom dataset

Sometimes, you may have no satisfactory alternative and you need to collect the images by yourself. This might require the collection of footage and the classification of thousands of images. If the images are extracted from a video, you might be able to just classify a video, and then extract hundreds or thousands of images from it.

Sometimes this is not the case, and you need to go through tens of thousands of images by yourself. Alternatively, you can use the services of specialized companies to label the images for you.

Sometimes you might have the images, but the classification might be difficult. Imagine having access to video footage of cars, and then having to annotate the images, adding the boxes where the cars are. If you are lucky, you might get access to a neural network that can do the job for you. You might still need to manually go through the result, and reclassify some images, but this can still save a lot of work.

Next, we will learn in depth about these datasets.

Understanding the three datasets

In reality, you don't need one dataset, but ideally three. These are required for training, validation, and testing. Before defining them, please consider that unfortunately sometimes, there is some confusion regarding the meaning of validation and test, typically where only two datasets are available, as in this case, validation and test datasets coincide. We did the same in *Chapter 4, Deep Learning with Neural Networks*, where we used the test dataset as validation.

Let's now define these three datasets, and then we can explain how ideally we should have tested the MNIST dataset:

- **Training dataset**: This is the dataset used to train the neural network, and it is typically the biggest of the three datasets.
- **Validation dataset**: This is usually a hold-out part of the training dataset that is not used for training, but only to evaluate the performance of a model and tune its hyperparameters (for example, the topology of the network or the learning rate of the optimizer).
- **Test dataset**: Ideally this is a throw-away dataset used to evaluate the performance of the model once all the tuning is complete.

You cannot use the training dataset to evaluate the performance of a model because the training dataset is used by the optimizer to train the network, so this is the best case scenario. However, we usually don't need the neural network to perform well in the training dataset but in whatever the user will throw at it. So, we need the network to be able to *generalize*. Going back to the student metaphor from *Chapter 4, Deep Learning with Neural Networks*, a high score in the training dataset means that the student learned the book (the training dataset) by heart, but what we want is the student to have understood the content of the book and be able to apply this knowledge to real-world situations (the validation dataset).

So, if validation represents the real world, why do we need the test dataset? The problem is that while tuning your network, you will make choices that will be biased toward the validation dataset (such as choosing one model instead of another one based on its performance in the validation dataset). As a result, the performance in the validation dataset might still be higher than in the real world.

The test dataset solves this problem as we only apply it after all the tuning. That also explains why ideally, we want to throw away the test dataset after using it only once.

This can be impractical, but not always, as sometimes you can easily generate some samples on demand.

So, how could we use three datasets in the MNIST task? Maybe you remember from *Chapter 4, Deep Learning with Neural Networks*, that the MNIST dataset has 60,000 (60 K) samples for training and 10,000 (10 K) for testing.

Ideally, you could use the following approach:

- The training dataset could use the full 60,000 samples intended for training.
- The validation dataset could use the 10,000 samples intended for testing (as we did).
- The test dataset could be generated on demand, writing digits on the spot.

After discussing the three datasets, we can now see how to split your full dataset into three parts. While this seems an easy operation, you need to be careful in terms of how you go about it.

Splitting the dataset

Given your full dataset, you might need to split it into training, validation, and testing parts. As stated previously, ideally you want the test to be generated on the spot, but if this is not possible, you might choose to use 15-20% of the total dataset for testing.

Of the remaining dataset, you might use 15-20% as validation.

If you have many samples, you might use a smaller percentage for validation and testing. If you have a small dataset, after you are satisfied with your model performance (such as if you chose it because it performs well both on the validation and on the test dataset), you might add the test dataset to the training dataset to get more samples. If you do this, there is no point in evaluating the performance in the test dataset, as effectively, it will become part of the training. In this case, you trust the results in the validation dataset.

But even with the same size, not all splits are created equal. Let's take a practical example.

You want to detect cats and dogs. You have a dataset of 10,000 pictures. You decide to use 8 K for training, 2 K for validation, and testing is done via the real-time recording of a video of 1 dog and 1 cat that you have at home; every time you test, you make a new video. Looks perfect. What can possibly go wrong?

First, you need more or less an equal number of cats and dogs in each dataset. If that's not the case, the network will be biased toward one of them. Intuitively, if during training, the network sees that 90% of the images are of dogs, just predicting always a dog will give you 90% accuracy!

You read that it is a best practice to randomize the order of the samples and you do it. Then you split. Your model performs well in the training, validation, and test datasets. Everything looks good. Then you try with pets of a few friends, and nothing works. What happened?

One possibility is that your split is not good in terms of measuring generalization. Even if you have 10 K images, they might have been taken from 100 pets (including yours), and every dog and cat is present 100 times, in slightly different positions (for example, from a video). If you shuffle the samples, all the dogs and cats will be present in all the datasets, so validation and testing will be relatively easy, as the network *already knows* those pets.

If, instead, you keep 20 pets for validation, and take care to not include pictures of your pets in the training or validation dataset, then your estimation would be much more realistic, and you have a chance to build a neural network that is much better at generalizing.

Now that we have three datasets, it's time to define the task that we need to perform, which typically will be image classification.

Understanding classifiers

Deep learning can be used for many different tasks. For what concerns images and CNN, a very common task is classification. Given an image, the neural network needs to classify it, using one of the labels provided during training. Not surprisingly, a network of this type is called a *classifier*.

To do so, the neural network will have one output for each label (for example, on the 10 digits MNIST dataset, we have 10 labels and so 10 outputs) and only one output should be 1, while all the other outputs should be 0.

How will a neural network achieve this state? Well, it doesn't. The neural network produces floating point outputs as a result of the internal multiplications and sums, and very seldom you get a similar output. However, we can consider the highest value as the hot one (1), and all the others can be considered cold (0).

We usually apply a softmax layer at the end of the neural network, which converts the outputs in to probability, meaning that the sum of the output after softmax will be 1.0. This is quite convenient, as we can easily know how confident the neural network is regarding the prediction. Keras offers a method in the model to get the probability, `predict()`, and one to get the label, `predict_classes()`. The label can easily be converted to the one-hot encoding format, if you need it, using `to_categorical()`.

If you need to go from one-hot encoding to a label, you can use the `argmax()` NumPy function.

Now we know what our task is, classifying images, but we need to be sure that our dataset is similar to what our network will need to detect when deployed in production.

Creating a real-world dataset

When you collect your dataset, either by using your images or an other suitable dataset, you need to take care that the images reflect conditions that you might find in real life. For example, you should try to get *problematic images*, listed as follows, as you will most likely encounter these problems in production:

- Bad light (over-exposed and under-exposed)
- Strong shadows
- Obstacles obstructing the object
- Object partially out of the picture
- Object rotated

If you cannot easily obtain these types of images, you can use data augmentation, which is what our next section is about.

Data augmentation

Data augmentation is the process of increasing the samples in your dataset, and deriving new pictures from the one that you already have; for example, reducing the brightness or rotating them.

Keras includes a convenient way to augment your dataset, `ImageDataGenerator()`, which randomly applies the specified transformations, but unfortunately is not particularly well documented and it lacks some coherence in terms of the parameters. Therefore, we will now analyze some of the most useful transformations. For clarity, we will build a generator with only one parameter, to see the effect, but you will most likely want to use more than one at the same time, which we will do later.

The `ImageDataGenerator()` constructor accepts many parameters, such as the following:

- `brightness_range`: This will change the brightness of the image and it accepts a list of two arguments, the minimum and the maximum brightness, for example, [0.1, 1.5].
- `rotation_range`: This will rotate the image and accept a single parameter that represents the range of rotation in degrees, for example, 60.
- `width_shift_range`: This will shift the image horizontally; it accepts the parameter in different forms. I would recommend using the list of acceptable values, such as [-50, -25, 25, 50].
- `height_shift_range`: This will shift the image vertically; it accepts the parameter in different forms. I would recommend using the list of acceptable values, such as [-50, -25, 25, 50].
- `shear_range`: This is the shear intensity, accepting a number in degrees, such as 60.
- `zoom_range`: This zooms in or zooms out of the image and it accepts a list of two arguments, the minimum and the maximum zoom, such as [0.5, 2].
- `horizontal_flip`: This flips the image horizontally, and the parameter is a Boolean.
- `vertical_flip`: This flips the image vertically, and the parameter is a Boolean.

Of these, the horizontal flip is usually quite effective.

The following figure shows the result of augmenting the images with brightness, rotation, width shift, and height shift:

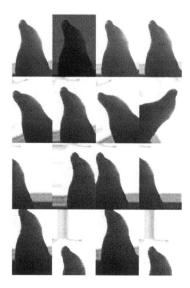

Figure 5.1 – ImageDataGenerator() results. From the top: brightness_range=[0.1, 1.5], rotation_range=60, width_shift_range=[-50, -25, 25, 50], and height_shift_range=[-75, -35, 35, 75]

The following images are generated using shearing, zoom, horizontal flip, and vertical flip:

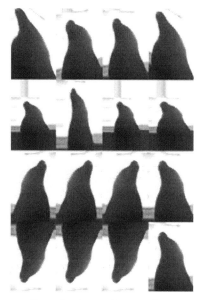

Figure 5.2 – ImageDataGenerator() results. From the top: shear_range=60, zoom_range=[0.5, 2], horizontal_flip=True, and vertical_flip=True

The effects are usually combined, as follows:

```
datagen = ImageDataGenerator(brightness_range=[0.1, 1.5],
rotation_range=60, width_shift_range=[-50, -25, 25, 50],
horizontal_flip=True)
```

And this is the final result:

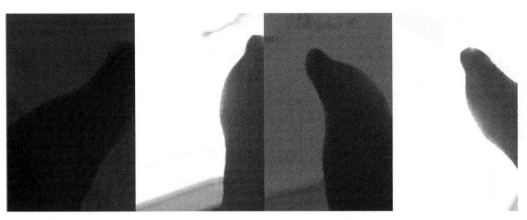

Figure 5.3 – ImageDataGenerator() results. Parameters applied: brightness_range=[0.1, 1.5], rotation_range=60, width_shift_range=[-50, -25, 25, 50], and horizontal_flip=True

Intuitively, the network should become much more tolerant to variations in the image, and it should learn to generalize better.

Please keep in mind that the data augmentation of Keras is more like a data substitution, as it replaces the original images, meaning that the original, unchanged images are not sent to the neural network, unless the random combination is as such that they are presented unchanged.

The great effect of data augmentation is that the samples will change at every epoch. So, to be clear, data augmentation in Keras does not increase the number of samples per epoch, but the samples will change every epoch, according to the specified transformation. You might want to train more epochs.

Next, we will see how to build the model.

The model

Now that you have a dataset of images and you know what you want to do (for instance, a classification), it's time to build your model!

We assume that you are working on a *convolutional neural network*, so you might even just use convolutional blocks, *MaxPooling*, and *dense layers*. But how to size them? How many layers should be used?

Let's do some tests with CIFAR-10, as MINST is too easy, and see what happens. We will not change the other parameters, but just play with these layers a bit.

We will also train for 5 epochs, so as to speed up training. This is not about getting the best neural network; it is about measuring the impact of some parameters.

Our starting point is a network with one convolutional layer, one MaxPooling layer, and one dense layer, shown as follows:

```
model = Sequential()
model.add(Conv2D(8, (3, 3), input_shape=x_train.shape[1:],
activation='relu'))
model.add(MaxPooling2D())
model.add(Flatten())
model.add(Dense(units = 256, activation = "relu"))
model.add(Dense(num_classes))
model.add(Activation('softmax'))
```

The following is a summary of this:

Layer (type)	Output Shape	Param #
conv2d_1 (Conv2D)	(None, 30, 30, 8)	224
max_pooling2d_1 (MaxPooling2	(None, 15, 15, 8)	0
flatten_1 (Flatten)	(None, 1800)	0
dense_1 (Dense)	(None, 256)	461056
dense_2 (Dense)	(None, 10)	2570

```
activation_1 (Activation)    (None, 10)                 0
=================================================================
Total params: 463,850
Trainable params: 463,850
Non-trainable params: 0
```

You can see that this is such a simple network, and it already has 463 K parameters. The number of layers is misleading. You don't necessarily need many layers to get a slow network.

This is the performance:

```
Training time: 90.96391367912292
Min Loss: 0.8851623952198029
Min Validation Loss: 1.142119802236557
Max Accuracy: 0.68706
Max Validation Accuracy: 0.6068999767303467
```

Now, the next step is to tune it. So, let's try that.

Tuning convolutional layers

Let's use 32 channels in the convolutional layer:

```
Total params: 1,846,922

Training time: 124.37444043159485
Min Loss: 0.6110964662361145
Min Validation Loss: 1.0291267457723619
Max Accuracy: 0.78486
Max Validation Accuracy: 0.6568999886512756
```

Not bad! The accuracy increased, and despite being 4 times bigger than before, it is less than 50% slower.

Let's now try to stack 4 layers instead:

```
model.add(Conv2D(8, (3, 3), input_shape=x_train.shape[1:],
activation='relu'))
model.add(Conv2D(8, (3, 3), input_shape=x_train.shape[1:],
activation='relu', padding = "same"))
model.add(Conv2D(8, (3, 3), input_shape=x_train.shape[1:],
activation='relu', padding = "same"))
model.add(Conv2D(8, (3, 3), input_shape=x_train.shape[1:],
activation='relu', padding = "same"))
```

Let's check the size of the network, using `model.summary()` as usual:

```
Total params: 465,602
```

It's just slightly bigger than the initial model! The reason is that most of the parameters are present due to the dense layer, and stacking convolutional layers of the same size does not change the parameters required by the dense layer. And this is the result:

```
Training time: 117.05060386657715
Min Loss: 0.6014562886440754
Min Validation Loss: 1.0268916247844697
Max Accuracy: 0.7864
Max Validation Accuracy: 0.6520000100135803
```

It is very similar – a bit faster and the accuracy is basically the same. The network can now learn more complex functions because it has multiple layers. However, it has a much smaller dense layer, so it loses some accuracy because of that.

Instead of using the *same* padding, let's try to use `valid`, which will reduce the size of the output of the convolutional layer every time:

```
model.add(Conv2D(8, (3, 3), input_shape=x_train.shape[1:],
activation='relu'))
model.add(Conv2D(8, (3, 3), input_shape=x_train.shape[1:],
activation='relu', padding="valid"))
model.add(Conv2D(8, (3, 3), input_shape=x_train.shape[1:],
activation='relu', padding="valid"))
model.add(Conv2D(8, (3, 3), input_shape=x_train.shape[1:],
activation='relu', padding="valid"))
```

The number of parameters decreased significantly, from 465,602:

```
Total params: 299,714
```

We are now using fewer than 300 K parameters, shown as follows:

```
Training time: 109.74382138252258
Min Loss: 0.8018992121839523
Min Validation Loss: 1.0897881112098693
Max Accuracy: 0.71658
Max Validation Accuracy: 0.6320000290870667
```

Very interestingly, the training accuracy dropped 7%, as the network is too small for this task. However, the validation accuracy only went down 2%.

Let's now use the initial model, but with the same padding, as that would give us a slightly bigger image to work with after the convolution:

```
model.add(Conv2D(8, (3, 3), input_shape=x_train.shape[1:],
padding="same", activation='relu'))
```

```
Total params: 527,338
```

We now have more parameters, and this is the performance:

```
Training time: 91.4407947063446
Min Loss: 0.7653912879371643
Min Validation Loss: 1.0724352446556091
Max Accuracy: 0.73126
Max Validation Accuracy: 0.6324999928474426
```

Compared to the reference model, both accuracies improved, and the time is almost unchanged, so this was a positive experiment.

Let's now increase the size of the kernel to 7x7:

```
model.add(Conv2D(8, (7, 7), input_shape=x_train.shape[1:],
padding="same", activation='relu'))
```
```
Total params: 528,298
```

There is a negligible increase in the number of parameters, as the kernels are now bigger. But how does it perform? Let's check:

```
Training time: 94.85121083259583
Min Loss: 0.7786661441159248
Min Validation Loss: 1.156547416305542
Max Accuracy: 0.72674
Max Validation Accuracy: 0.6090999841690063
```

Not well. It is slightly slower and slightly less accurate. It is difficult to know why; maybe it's because the input image is too small.

We know that it is a typical pattern to add a MaxPooling layer after a convolutional layer, so let's see how we can tune it.

Tuning MaxPooling

Let's go back to the previous model and let's just drop `MaxPooling`:

```
Total params: 1,846,250
```

Removing `MaxPooling` means that the dense layer is now 4 times as big, since the resolution of the convolutional layer is no longer reduced:

```
Training time: 121.01851439476013
Min Loss: 0.8000291277170182
Min Validation Loss: 1.2463579467773438
Max Accuracy: 0.71736
Max Validation Accuracy: 0.5710999965667725
```

This does not seem very efficient. Compared to the original network, it is slower, the accuracy improved, but the validation accuracy decreased. Compared to the networks with four convolutional layers, it has the same speed, but a far inferior validation accuracy.

It seems that `MaxPooling` improves generalization while reducing computations. Not surprisingly, it is widely used.

Let's now increase the number of MaxPooling layers:

```
model.add(Conv2D(8, (3, 3), input_shape=x_train.shape[1:],
    activation='relu'))
model.add(Conv2D(8, (3, 3), input_shape=x_train.shape[1:],
    activation='relu', padding = "same"))
```

```
model.add(MaxPooling2D())
model.add(Conv2D(8, (3, 3), input_shape=x_train.shape[1:],
activation='relu', padding = "same"))
model.add(Conv2D(8, (3, 3), input_shape=x_train.shape[1:],
activation='relu', padding = "same"))
model.add(MaxPooling2D())
```

The size is now much smaller because the second convolutional layers are now one fourth of the size:

```
Total params: 105,154
```

Let's check the performance:

```
Training time: 105.30972981452942
Min Loss: 0.8419396163749695
Min Validation Loss: 0.9395202528476715
Max Accuracy: 0.7032
Max Validation Accuracy: 0.6686999797821045
```

While the training accuracy is not great, the validation accuracy is the best that we achieved, and all while using only 100 K parameters!

After tuning the convolutional part of the network, is time to see how we can tune the part composed by dense layers.

Tuning the dense layer

Let's go back to the initial model, and increase the dense layer 4 times, which is to 1,024 neurons:

```
Total params: 1,854,698
```

As expected, the number of parameters increased almost four fold. But what about performance?

```
Training time: 122.05767631530762
Min Loss: 0.6533840216350555
Min Validation Loss: 1.093649614238739
Max Accuracy: 0.7722
Max Validation Accuracy: 0.630299985408783
```

The training accuracy is not bad, but the validation accuracy is lower compared with the best models.

Let's try to use three dense layers:

```
model.add(Dense(units = 512, activation = "relu"))
model.add(Dense(units = 256, activation = "relu"))
model.add(Dense(units = 128, activation = "relu"))
```

Now we get the following parameters:

```
Total params: 1,087,850
```

The number of parameters is now lower:

```
Training time: 111.73353481292725
Min Loss: 0.7527586654126645
Min Validation Loss: 1.1094331634044647
Max Accuracy: 0.7332
Max Validation Accuracy: 0.6115000247955322
```

The result is maybe somehow disappointing. We should probably not count too much on increasing the number of dense layers.

The next step now is to train the network. Let's begin.

Training the network

We are now ready to discuss the training phase in greater depth, which is where the *magic happens*. We will not even attempt to describe the mathematical concepts behind it. We will just discuss in very generic and simplified terms the algorithm that is used to train neural networks.

We need some definitions:

- **Loss function** or **cost function**: A function that computes how far the prediction of the neural network is from the expected label; it could be the **MSE** (which is the **mean squared error**) or something more elaborate.

- **Derivative**: The derivative of a function is a new function that can measure how much a function is changing (and in which direction) in a specific point. For example, if you imagine being in a car, the speed can be your initial function, and its derivative is the acceleration. If the speed is constant, the derivative (for example, the acceleration) is zero; if the speed is increasing, the derivative will be positive and if the speed is decreasing, the derivative will be negative.
- **Local minimum**: The job of a neural network is to minimize the loss function. Given the incredible number of parameters, the function of the neural network can be very complex and therefore reaching a global minimum can be impossible, but the network could still reach a good local minimum.
- **Convergence**: If the network keeps approaching a good local minimum, then it is converging.

Using these definitions, we will now see how the training actually works.

How to train the network

The algorithm is composed of two parts, and, to simplify, let's say that it is performed for every sample and, of course, the whole thing is repeated for every epoch. So, let's see how it works:

- **Forward pass**: At the end of the day, your neural network is just a function with many parameters (weights and possibly biases) and many operations that, when provided with an input, can compute some outputs. In the forward pass, we compute the prediction and the loss.
- **Backward pass**: The optimizer (for example, Adam or stochastic gradient descent) goes *backward* (from the last layer to the first layer) updating all the weights (for instance, all the parameters) trying to minimize the loss function; the *learning rate* (a number between 0 and 1.0, typically worth 0.01 or less) determines how much the weights will be adjusted.

A bigger learning rate makes them train faster, but it might skip local minimums, while a smaller learning rate might converge, but taking too much time. Optimizers are actively researched to improve training speed as much as possible, and they are dynamically changing the learning rate to improve speed and precision.

Adam is an example of an optimizer that can dynamically change the learning rate for each parameter:

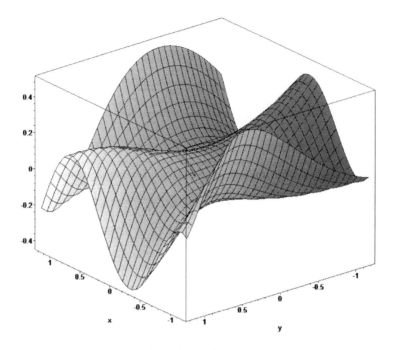

Figure 5.4 – Gradient descent looking for a minimum

While writing an algorithm to train a neural network is very complex, the concept is, in a way, similar to somebody trying to learn to play pool, while repeating the same complex shoot until it works. You choose the point that you want to hit (label), you make your move (forward pass), you evaluate how far you ended up from the target, and then you retry adjusting the power, direction, and all the other variables at play (weights). We also have a way to do this with random initialization. Let's try this next.

Random initialization

You might wonder what the values of the parameters are the first time that you run the neural network. Initializing the weights to zero does not work well, while having small random numbers is quite effective. Keras has a variety of algorithms that you can choose from, and you can also change the standard deviation.

An interesting consequence of this is that the neural network starts with a considerable amount of random data, and you might notice that training the same model on the same dataset actually produces different results. Let's try with our previous basic CIFAR-10 CNN.

The first attempt produces the following results:

```
Min Loss: 0.8791077242803573
Min Validation Loss: 1.1203862301826477
Max Accuracy: 0.69174
Max Validation Accuracy: 0.5996000170707703
```

The second attempt produces the following results:

```
Min Loss: 0.8642362675189972
Min Validation Loss: 1.1310886552810668
Max Accuracy: 0.69624
Max Validation Accuracy: 0.6100000143051147
```

You can try to reduce the randomness using the following code:

```
from numpy.random import seed
seed(1)
import tensorflow as tf
tf.random.set_seed(1)
```

However, if you train on a GPU, there could still be a number of variations. You should take this into consideration while you tune your network model, or you risk disqualifying small improvements due to randomness.

The next stage is to see what overfitting and underfitting are.

Overfitting and underfitting

While training a neural network, you will fight between **underfitting** and **overfitting**. Let's see how:

- Underfitting is where the model is too simple, and it is not able to learn the dataset properly. You need to add parameters, filters, and neurons to increase the capacity of the model.
- Overfitting is where your model is big enough to learn the training dataset, but it is not able to generalize (for example, it *memorizes* the dataset but it is not good when you provide other data).

You can also see it from the plot over time of accuracy and loss:

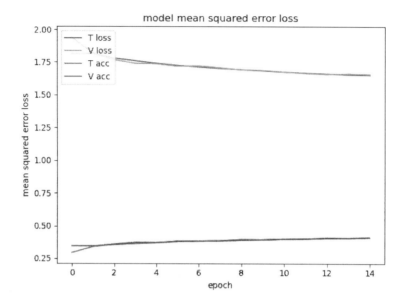

Figure 5.5 – Underfitting: the model is too small (7,590 parameters) and is not learning much

The preceding graph shows an extreme underfitting, and the accuracies stay very low. Now refer to the following graph:

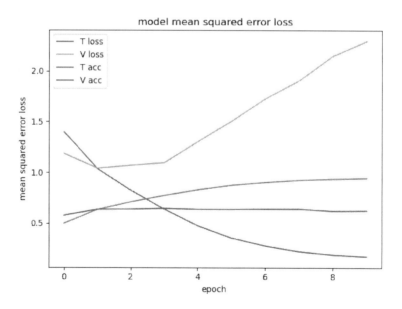

Figure 5.6 – Overfitting: the model is very big (29,766,666 parameters) and is not generalizing well

Figure 5.6 shows a somewhat extreme example of a neural network in overfitting. You may notice that while the training loss keeps decreasing with the epochs, the validation loss reaches a minimum at epoch one, and then keeps increasing. The minimum of the validation loss is where you want to stop your training. In *Chapter 6, Improving Your Neural Network*, we will see a technique that allows us to do more or less that—*early stopping*.

While you might hear that overfitting is a big problem, actually it could be a good strategy first trying to get a model that can overfit the training dataset, and then apply techniques that can reduce the overfitting and improve generalization. However, this is good only if you can overfit the training dataset with a very high degree of accuracy.

We will see very effective ways to reduce overfitting in *Chapter 6, Improving Your Neural Network*, but one thing to consider is that a smaller model is less prone to overfit, and it is usually also faster. So, while you are trying to overfit the training dataset, try not to use a model that is extremely big.

In this section, we have seen how to use the graph of the losses to understand where we are in the training of our network. In the next section, we will see how to visualize the activations in order to get an idea of what our network is learning.

Visualizing the activations

Now we can train a neural network. Great. But what exactly is the neural network able to see and understand? That's a difficult question to answer, but as convolutions output an image, we could try to show this. Let's now try to show the activation for the first 10 images of the MINST test dataset:

1. First, we need to build a model, derived from our previous model, that reads from the input and gets as output the convolutional layer that we want. The name can be taken from the summary. We will visualize the first convolutional layer, `conv2d_1`:

```
conv_layer = next(x.output for x in model.layers if
    x.output.name.startswith(conv_name))
act_model = models.Model(inputs=model.input,
outputs=[conv_layer])
activations = act_model.predict(x_test[0:num_predictions,
    :, :, :])
```

2. Now, for each test image, we can take all the activations and chain them together to get an image:

```
col_act = []
for pred_idx, act in enumerate(activations):
    row_act = []
    for idx in range(act.shape[2]):
        row_act.append(act[:, :, idx])
    col_act.append(cv2.hconcat(row_act))
```

3. And then we can show it:

```
plt.matshow(cv2.vconcat(col_act), cmap='viridis')
plt.show()
```

This is the result for the first convolutional layer, conv2d_1, which has 6 channels, 28x28:

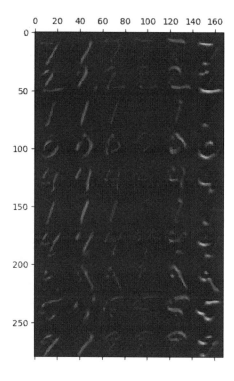

Figure 5.7 – MNIST, activations of the first convolutional layer

This looks interesting, but trying to understand the activations, and what the channels learned to recognize, always involves some guesswork. The last channel seems to focus on horizontal lines, and the third and fourth channels are not very strong, which might mean that the network is not properly trained or it is already bigger than required. But it looks good.

Let's now check the second layer, `conv2d_2`, which has 16 channels, 10x10:

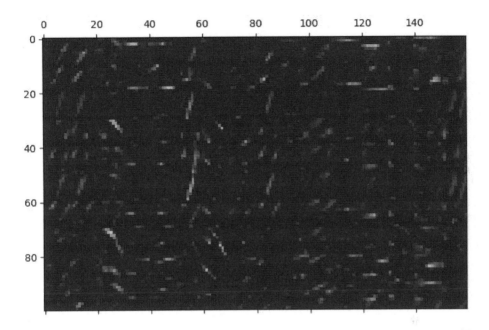

Figure 5.8 – MNIST, activations of the second convolutional layer

Now it's more complex – the outputs are much smaller, and we have more channels. It seems that some channels are detecting horizontal lines, and some of them are focusing on diagonal or vertical lines. And what about the first MaxPooling layer, `max_pooling2d_1`? It's a lower resolution than the original channel, at 10x10, but as it selects the maximum activation, it should be understandable. Refer to the following screenshot:

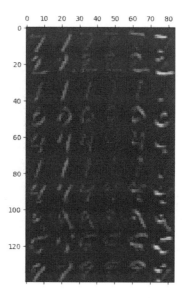

Figure 5.9 – MNIST, activations of the first MaxPooling layer

Indeed, the activation looks good. Just for fun, let's check the second MaxPooling layer, `max_pooling2d_2`, which is only 5x5:

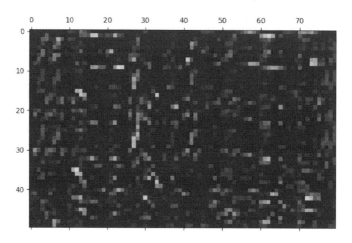

Figure 5.10 – MNIST, activations of the second MaxPooling layer

Now it looks chaotic, but it still looks like some channels are recognizing horizontal lines and some are focusing on vertical ones. Here is when the dense layers will come into play, as they try to make sense of these activations that are difficult to understand but not at all random.

Visualizing the activation is useful to get an idea of what the neural network is learning, and how the channels are used, and it is another tool that you can use while training your neural network, above all when you feel that it is not learning well and you are looking for problems.

Now we will talk about inference, which is actually the whole point of training a neural network.

Inference

Inference is the process of giving an input to your network and getting a classification or prediction. When the neural network has been trained and deployed in production, we use it, for example, to classify images or to decide how to drive in a road, and this process is called inference.

The first step is to load the model:

```
model = load_model(os.path.join(dir_save, model_name))
```

Then you simply call `predict()`, which is the method for inference in Keras. Let's try with the first test sample of MNIST:

```
x_pred = model.predict(x_test[0:1, :, :, :])
print("Expected:", np.argmax(y_test))
print("First prediction probabilities:", x_pred)
print("First prediction:", np.argmax(x_pred))
```

This is the result for my MNIST network:

```
Expected: 7
First prediction probabilities: [[6.3424804e-14 6.1755254e-06 2.5011676e-08 2.2640785e-07 9.0170204e-08 7.4626680e-11 5.6195684e-13 9.9999273e-01 1.9735349e-09 7.3219508e-07]]
First prediction: 7
```

The result of `predict()` is an array of probabilities, which is very handy for evaluating the confidence of the network. In this case, all the numbers are very close to zero, except for the number 7, which is therefore the prediction of the network, with a confidence above 99.999%! In real life, unfortunately, you seldom see a network working so well!

After inference, sometimes you want to periodically retrain on new samples, to improve the network. Let's see what this entails next.

Retraining

Sometimes, once you get a neural network that performs well, you job is done. Sometimes, however, you might want to retrain it on new samples, to get better precision (as your dataset is now bigger) or to get fresher results if your training dataset becomes obsolete relatively quickly.

In some cases, you might even want to retrain continuously, for example, every week, and have the new model automatically deployed in production.

In this case, it's critical that you have a strong procedure in place to verify the performance of your new model in the validation dataset and, hopefully, in a new, throwaway test dataset. It may also be advisable to keep a backup of all the models and try to find a way to monitor the performance in production, to quickly identify anomalies. In the case of a self-driving car, I expect a model to undergo rigorous automated and manual testing before being deployed in production, but other industries that don't have safety concerns might be much less strict.

With this, we conclude our topic on retraining.

Summary

This has been a dense chapter, but hopefully you got a better overview of what neural networks are and how to train them.

We talked a lot about the dataset, including how to get correct datasets for training, validation, and testing. We described what a classifier is and we implemented data augmentation. Then we discussed the model and how to tune the convolutional layers, the MaxPooling layers, and the dense layers. We saw how training is done, what backpropagation is, discussed the role of randomness on the initialization of the weights, and we saw graphs of underfitting and overfitting networks. To understand how well our CNN is doing, we went as far as visualizing the activations. Then we discussed inference and retraining.

This means that you now have sufficient knowledge to choose or create a dataset and train a neural network from scratch, and you will be able to understand if a change in the model or in the dataset improves precision.

In *Chapter 6, Improving Your Neural Network*, we will see how to apply all this knowledge in practice, so as to improve the precision of a neural network significantly.

Questions

After reading this chapter, you should be able to answer the following questions:

1. Can you reuse the test dataset?
2. What is data augmentation?
3. Does data augmentation in Keras add images to your dataset?
4. Which layer tends to have the highest number of parameters?
5. Watching the plot of the losses, how can you tell that a network is overfitting?
6. Is it always bad to have a network that overfits?

6
Improving Your Neural Network

In *Chapter 4, Deep Learning with Neural Networks*, we designed a network that is able to achieve almost 93% accuracy in the training dataset, but that translated to less than 66% accuracy in the validation dataset.

In this chapter, we will continue working on that neural network, with the aim to improve the validation accuracy significantly. Our goal is to reach at least 80% validation accuracy. We will apply some of the knowledge acquired in *Chapter 5, Deep Learning Workflow*, and we will also learn new techniques that will help us very much, such as batch normalization.

We will cover the following topics:

- Reducing the number of parameters
- Increasing the size of the network and the number of layers
- Understanding batch normalization
- Improving validation with early stopping
- Virtually increasing the dataset size with data augmentation
- Improving validation accuracy with dropout
- Improving validation accuracy with spatial dropout

Technical requirements

The full source code for the chapter can be found here: `https://github.com/PacktPublishing/Hands-On-Vision-and-Behavior-for-Self-Driving-Cars/tree/master/Chapter6`

This chapter requires the following software prerequisites, and a basic knowledge of the following would help to understand the chapter better:

- Python 3.7
- The NumPy module
- The Matplotlib module
- The TensorFlow module
- The Keras module
- The OpenCV-Python module
- A recommended GPU

The Code in Action videos for this chapter can be found here: `https://bit.ly/3dGIdJA`

A bigger model

Training your own neural network is an art; you need intuition, some luck, a lot of patience, and all the knowledge and help that you can find. You will also need money and time to either buy a faster GPU, use clusters to test more configurations, or pay to get a better dataset.

But there are no real recipes. That said, we will divide our journey into two phases, as explained in *Chapter 5*, *Deep Learning Workflow*:

- Overfitting the training dataset
- Improving generalization

We will start from where we left off in *Chapter 4*, *Deep Learning with Neural Networks*, with our basic model reaching 66% validation accuracy on CIFAR-10, and then we will improve it significantly, first to make it faster, and then to make it more precise.

The starting point

The following is the model that we developed in *Chapter 4, Deep Learning with Neural Networks*, a model that overfits the dataset because it achieves a high training accuracy value at relatively low validation accuracy:

```
model.add(Conv2D(filters=64, kernel_size=(3, 3), activation='relu',
    input_shape=x_train.shape[1:]))
model.add(AveragePooling2D())
model.add(Conv2D(filters=256, kernel_size=(3, 3),
    activation='relu'))
model.add(AveragePooling2D())

model.add(Flatten())
model.add(Dense(units=512, activation='relu'))
model.add(Dense(units=256, activation='relu'))
model.add(Dense(units=num_classes, activation = 'softmax'))
```

It is a shallow but relatively big model as it has the following number of parameters:

```
Total params: 5,002,506
```

We previously trained it for 12 epochs, with these results:

```
Training time: 645.9990749359131
Min Loss: 0.12497963292273692
Min Validation Loss: 0.9336215916395187
Max Accuracy: 0.95826
Max Validation Accuracy: 0.6966000199317932
```

The training accuracy is actually good enough for us (here, in this run, it is higher than in *Chapter 5, Deep Learning Workflow*, mostly because of randomness), but the validation accuracy is low too. It is overfitting. So, we could even keep it as a starting point, but it would be nice to tune it a bit and see whether we can do better or make it faster.

We should also keep an eye on five epochs, as we might do some tests on fewer epochs, to speed up the whole process:

```
52s 1ms/step - loss: 0.5393 - accuracy: 0.8093 - val_loss: 0.9496 - val_accuracy: 0.6949
```

When you use fewer epochs, you are betting on being able to understand the evolution of the curves, so you are trading speed of development for accuracy of your choices. Sometimes, this is fine, but sometimes it is not.

Our model is too big, so we will start reducing its size and speeding up the training a bit.

Improving the speed

Our model is not just very big – in fact, it is too big. The second convolutional layer has 256 filters and, combined with the 512 neurons of the dense layer, they use a high number of parameters. We can do better. We know that we could split them into layers of 128 filters, and this would save almost half of the parameters, as the dense layer now needs half of the connections.

We can try that. We learned in *Chapter 4, Deep Learning with Neural Networks*, that to not lose resolution after a convolution, we can use padding in the *same* way on both the layers (dense layers omitted), as follows:

```
model.add(Conv2D(filters=64, kernel_size=(3, 3),
activation='relu',
    input_shape=x_train.shape[1:]))
model.add(AveragePooling2D())

model.add(Conv2D(filters=128, kernel_size=(3, 3),
    activation='relu', padding="same"))
model.add(Conv2D(filters=128, kernel_size=(3, 3),
    activation='relu', padding="same"))
model.add(AveragePooling2D())
```

Here, we can see that the number of parameters now is lower:

```
Total params: 3,568,906
```

Let's check the full results:

```
Training time: 567.7167596817017
Min Loss: 0.1018450417491654
Min Validation Loss: 0.8735350118398666
Max Accuracy: 0.96568
Max Validation Accuracy: 0.7249000072479248
```

Nice! It is faster, the accuracy went up slightly, and also, the validation improved!

Let's do the same on the first layer, but this time without increasing the resolution so as not to increase the parameters, since, between two convolutional layers, the gain is lower:

```
model.add(Conv2D(filters=32, kernel_size=(3, 3),
    activation='relu', input_shape=x_train.shape[1:]))
model.add(Conv2D(filters=32, kernel_size=(3, 3),
activation='relu',
    input_shape=x_train.shape[1:], padding="same"))
model.add(AveragePooling2D())

model.add(Conv2D(filters=128, kernel_size=(3, 3),
    activation='relu', padding="same"))
model.add(Conv2D(filters=128, kernel_size=(3, 3),
    activation='relu', padding="same"))
model.add(AveragePooling2D())
```

When we try this, we get these results:

```
Training time: 584.955037355423
Min Loss: 0.10728564778155182
Min Validation Loss: 0.7890052844524383
Max Accuracy: 0.965
Max Validation Accuracy: 0.739300012588501
```

This is similar to before, though the validation accuracy improved slightly.

Next, we will add more layers.

Increasing the depth

The previous model is actually an excellent starting point.

But we will add more layers, to increase the number of non-linear activations and to be able to learn more complex functions. This is the model (dense layers omitted):

```
model.add(Conv2D(filters=32, kernel_size=(3, 3),
activation='relu', input_shape=x_train.shape[1:],
padding="same"))
model.add(Conv2D(filters=32, kernel_size=(3, 3),
activation='relu', input_shape=x_train.shape[1:],
padding="same"))
model.add(AveragePooling2D())

model.add(Conv2D(filters=128, kernel_size=(3, 3),
```

```
activation='relu', padding="same"))
model.add(Conv2D(filters=128, kernel_size=(3, 3),
activation='relu', padding="same"))
model.add(AveragePooling2D())

model.add(Conv2D(filters=256, kernel_size=(3, 3),
activation='relu', padding="same"))
model.add(Conv2D(filters=256, kernel_size=(3, 3),
activation='relu', padding="same"))
model.add(AveragePooling2D())
```

This is the result:

```
Training time: 741.1498856544495
Min Loss: 0.22022022939510644
Min Validation Loss: 0.7586277635633946
Max Accuracy: 0.92434
Max Validation Accuracy: 0.7630000114440918
```

The network is now significantly slower and the accuracy went down (maybe because more epochs are required), but the validation accuracy improved.

Let's try now to reduce the dense layers, as follows (convolutional layers omitted):

```
model.add(Flatten())
model.add(Dense(units=256, activation='relu'))
model.add(Dense(units=128, activation='relu'))
model.add(Dense(units=num_classes, activation = 'softmax'))
```

Now, we have fewer parameters:

```
Total params: 2,162,986
```

But something very bad happened:

```
Training time: 670.0584089756012
Min Loss: 2.3028031995391847
Min Validation Loss: 2.302628245162964
Max Accuracy: 0.09902
Max Validation Accuracy: 0.10000000149011612
```

Both the validations dropped! In fact, they are now 10%, or if you prefer, the network is now producing a random result—it did not learn!

You might conclude that we broke it. In fact, that is not the case. It's enough to run it again, using the randomness to our advantage, and our network learns as expected:

```
Training time: 686.5172057151794
Min Loss: 0.24410496438018978
Min Validation Loss: 0.7960220139861107
Max Accuracy: 0.91434
Max Validation Accuracy: 0.7454000115394592
```

However, this is not a very good sign. This might be due to the increase in layers, as networks with more layers are more difficult to train, due to the fact that the original input can have problems in terms of being propagated to the upper layers.

Let's check the graph:

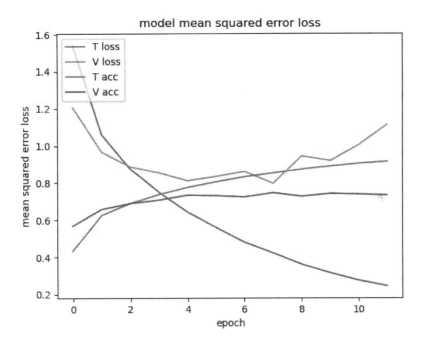

Figure 6.1 – Losses and accuracies graph

You can see that while the training loss (blue line) keeps decreasing, the validation loss (orange line) after some epochs starts to increase. As explained in *Chapter 5, Deep Learning Workflow*, this means that the model is overfitting. This is not necessarily the best model, but we will continue developing it.

In the next section, we will simplify this model.

A more efficient network

Training the previous model requires 686 seconds on my laptop, and achieves a validation accuracy of 74.5%, and a training accuracy of 91.4%. Ideally, to improve the efficiency, we want to keep accuracy at the same level while reducing the training time.

Let's check some of the convolutional layers:

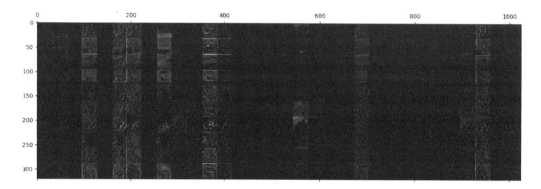

Figure 6.2 – First convolutional layer, 32 channels

We have already seen these activation graphs in *Chapter 5*, *Deep Learning Workflow*, and we know that channels that are black do not achieve a big activation, so they don't contribute much to the result. In practice, it looks like half of the channels are not in use. Let's try to halve the number of channels in every convolutional layer:

```
model.add(Conv2D(filters=16, kernel_size=(3, 3),
    activation='relu', input_shape=x_train.shape[1:],
    padding="same"))
```
```
model.add(Conv2D(filters=16, kernel_size=(3, 3),
    activation='relu',
        input_shape=x_train.shape[1:], padding="same"))
```
```
model.add(AveragePooling2D())
```
```
model.add(Conv2D(filters=32, kernel_size=(3, 3),
    activation='relu',
        padding="same"))
```
```
model.add(Conv2D(filters=32, kernel_size=(3, 3),
    activation='relu',
        padding="same"))
```
```
model.add(AveragePooling2D())
```

```
model.add(Conv2D(filters=64, kernel_size=(3, 3),
activation='relu',
    padding="same"))
```
```
model.add(Conv2D(filters=64, kernel_size=(3, 3),
activation='relu',
    padding="same"))
```

This is what we get as the result:

```
Total params: 829,146
```

As expected, the number of parameters is now much less, and training is much faster:

```
Training time: 422.8525400161743
```
```
Min Loss: 0.27083665314182637
```
```
Min Validation Loss: 0.8076118688702584
```
```
Max Accuracy: 0.90398
```
```
Max Validation Accuracy: 0.7415000200271606
```

Here we see that we lost some accuracy also, but not too much:

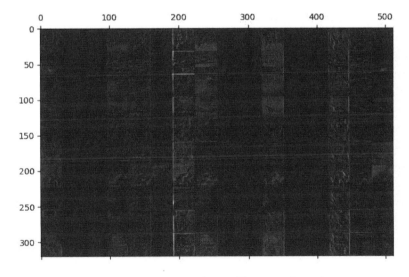

Figure 6.3 – First convolutional layer, 16 channels

Now it's a bit better. Let's check the second layer:

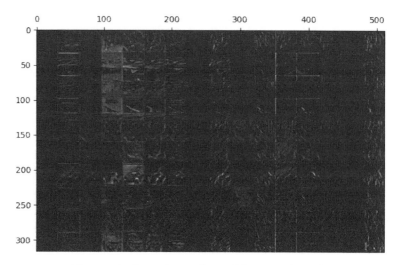

Figure 6.4 – Second convolutional layer, 16 channels

This is also better. Let's check the fourth convolutional layer:

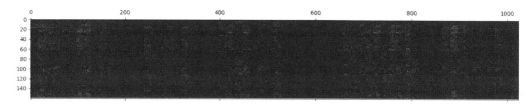

Figure 6.5 – Fourth convolutional layer, 64 channels

It seems a bit empty. Let's halve the third and fourth layers:

```
Total params: 759,962
```

We then get these results:

```
Training time: 376.09818053245544
Min Loss: 0.30105597005218265
Min Validation Loss: 0.8148738072395325
Max Accuracy: 0.89274
Max Validation Accuracy: 0.7391999959945679
```

The training accuracy went down, but the validation accuracy is still fine:

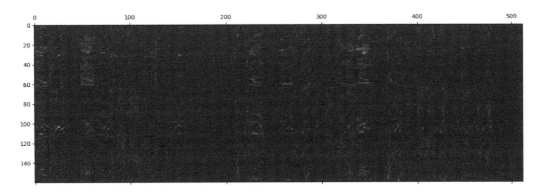

Figure 6.6 – Fourth convolutional layer, 32 channels

Let's check the sixth convolutional layer:

Figure 6.7 – Sixth convolutional layer, 128 channels

It's a bit empty. Let's also halve the last two convolutional layers:

```
Total params: 368,666
```

It is much smaller, with these results:

```
Training time: 326.9148383140564
Min Loss: 0.296858479853943
Min Validation Loss: 0.7925313812971115
Max Accuracy: 0.89276
Max Validation Accuracy: 0.7425000071525574
```

It still looks good. Let's check the activations:

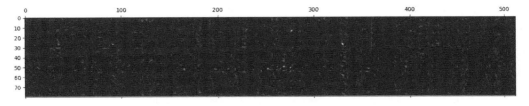

Figure 6.8 – Sixth convolutional layer, 64 channels

You can see that now, many channels are activated, which hopefully is an indication that the neural network is better at taking advantage of its resources.

Comparing this model with the one built in the previous section, you can see that this model can be trained in a bit less than half the time, the validation accuracy is almost unchanged, and the training accuracy decreased a bit, but not much. So, it is indeed more efficient.

In the next section, we will discuss batch normalization, a layer very common on modern neural networks.

Building a smarter network with batch normalization

We normalize the input that we provide to the network, constraining the range from 0 to 1, so it could be beneficial to do that also in the middle of the network. This is called **batch normalization**, and it does wonders!

In general, you should add the batch normalization after the output that you want to normalize, and before the activation, but adding it after the activation might provide faster performance, and this is what we will do.

This is the new code (dense layers omitted):

```
model.add(Conv2D(filters=16, kernel_size=(3, 3), activation='relu',
    input_shape=x_train.shape[1:], padding="same"))
model.add(Conv2D(filters=16, kernel_size=(3, 3), activation='relu',
    input_shape=x_train.shape[1:], padding="same"))
model.add(BatchNormalization())
model.add(AveragePooling2D())

model.add(Conv2D(filters=32, kernel_size=(3, 3), activation='relu',
    padding="same"))
model.add(Conv2D(filters=32, kernel_size=(3, 3), activation='relu',
    padding="same"))
model.add(BatchNormalization())
model.add(AveragePooling2D())

model.add(Conv2D(filters=64, kernel_size=(3, 3), activation='relu',
```

```
        padding="same"))
model.add(Conv2D(filters=64, kernel_size=(3, 3),
activation='relu',
        padding="same"))
model.add(BatchNormalization())
model.add(AveragePooling2D())
```

The number of parameters increased just a bit:

```
Total params: 369,114
```

This is the result:

```
Training time: 518.0608556270599
Min Loss: 0.1616916553277429
Min Validation Loss: 0.7272815862298012
Max Accuracy: 0.94308
Max Validation Accuracy: 0.7675999999046326
```

Not bad, even if unfortunately, now it is much slower. But we can add even more batch normalization, to see whether this improves the situation:

```
Training time: 698.9837136268616
Min Loss: 0.13732857785719446
Min Validation Loss: 0.6836542286396027
Max Accuracy: 0.95206
Max Validation Accuracy: 0.7918999791145325
```

Yes, both the accuracies improved. We are actually very close to our initial goal of having 80% accuracy. But let's go further and see what we can do.

Until now, we only used ReLU activation, but even if it is used very much, it's not the only one. Keras supports a variety of activations, and sometimes it is worth experimenting with. We will stick to ReLU.

Let's check some activations:

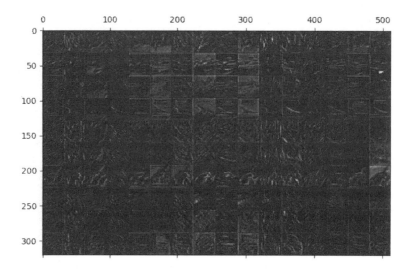

Figure 6.9 – Second convolutional layer, 16 channels, batch normalization

Now, all the channels of the second layer are learning. Very good!

Here is the result of the fourth layer:

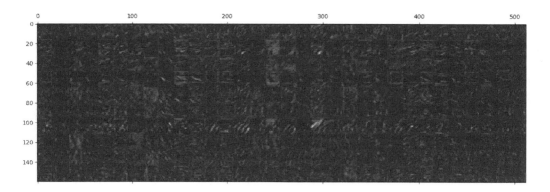

Figure 6.10 – Fourth convolutional layer, 32 channels, batch normalization

Here is the result of the sixth layer:

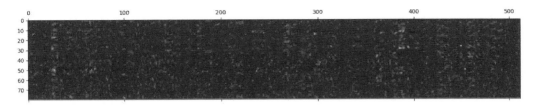

Figure 6.11 – Sixth convolutional layer, 64 channels, batch normalization

It is starting to look good!

Let's try to visualize the effect of batch normalization on the activations of the first layer before and after batch normalization:

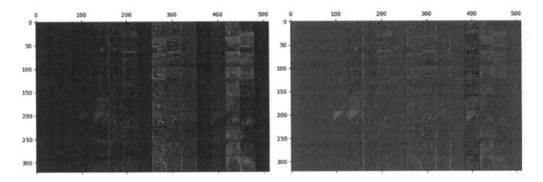

Figure 6.12 – First convolutional layer, 16 channels, before and after batch normalization

You can see that the intensity of the channels is now more uniform; there are no longer channels without activity and channels with very strong activations. However, the channels that are inactive are still without real information.

Let's also check the second layer:

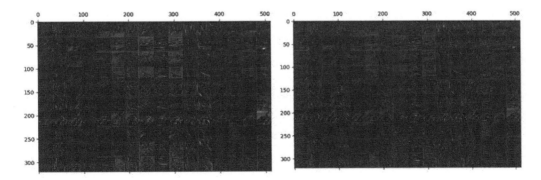

Figure 6.13 – Second convolutional layer, 16 channels, before and after batch normalization

Here, it is maybe less evident, but you can still see that the difference between the channels is reduced, as clearly, they have been normalized. Intuitively, this helps propagate weaker signals through layers, and it has some regularization effect, which results in better validation accuracy.

Now that we have talked about batch normalization, it is time to discuss further what a batch is and what implications the size of a batch has.

Choosing the right batch size

During training, we have a high number of samples, typically from thousands to millions. If you remember, the optimizer will compute the loss function and update the hyperparameters to try to reduce the loss. It could do this after every sample, but the result could be noisy, with continuous changes that can slow down the training. At the opposite end, the optimizer could update the hyperparameters only once per epoch – for example, using the average of the gradients – but this typically leads to bad generalization. Usually, there is a range on the batch size that performs better than these two extremes, but unfortunately, it depends on the specific neural network.

A larger batch size can marginally improve the training time on a GPU, but if your model is big, you might find that the memory of your GPU is a limit to how big your batch size can be.

Batch normalization is also affected by the size of the batch, as small batches reduce its effectiveness (as there is not enough data do to a proper normalization).

Given these considerations, the best thing to do is to just try. Normally, you can try using 16, 32, 64, and 128, and eventually extend the range if you see that the best value is at the limit of the range.

As we have seen, the best batch size can improve accuracy and possibly increase the speed, but there is another technique that can help us to improve the validation accuracy while speeding up, or at least simplifying, the training: early stopping.

Early stopping

When should we stop training? That's a good question! Ideally, you want to stop at the minimum validation error. While you cannot know this in advance, you can check the losses and get an idea of how many epochs you need. However, when you train your network, sometimes you need more epochs depending on how you tune your model, and it is not simple to know in advance when to stop.

We already know that we can use `ModelCheckpoint`, a callback of Keras, to save the model with the best validation error seen during training.

But there is also another very useful callback, `EarlyStopping`, which stops the training when a predefined set of conditions happen:

```
stop = EarlyStopping(min_delta=0.0005, patience=7, verbose=1)
```

The most important parameters to configure early stopping are the following:

- `monitor`: This decides which parameter to monitor, by default: validation loss.
- `min_delta`: If the difference in validation loss between epochs is below this value, the loss is considered to not have changed.
- `patience`: This is the number of epochs with no validation improvement to allow before stopping the training.
- `verbose`: This is instructing Keras to provide more information.

The reason why we need early stopping is that with data augmentation and dropout, we will need many more epochs, and instead of guessing when it is time to stop, we will use early stopping to do that for us.

Let's talk now about data augmentation.

Improving the dataset with data augmentation

It's time to use data augmentation, and basically, increase the size of our dataset.

From this moment, we will no longer care about the accuracy of the training dataset, as this technique will reduce it, but we will focus on the validation accuracy, which is expected to improve.

We also expect to need more epochs, as our dataset is now more difficult, so we will now set the epochs to `500` (though we don't plan to reach it) and use `EarlyStopping` with a patience of 7.

Let's try with this augmentation:

```
ImageDataGenerator(rotation_range=15, width_shift_range=[-5, 0, 5],
    horizontal_flip=True)
```

You should take care not to overdo things because the network might learn a dataset too different from validation, and in this case, you will see the validation accuracy stuck at 10%.

This is the result:

```
Epoch 00031: val_loss did not improve from 0.48613
Epoch 00031: early stopping
Training time: 1951.4751739501953
Min Loss: 0.3638068118467927
Min Validation Loss: 0.48612626193910835
Max Accuracy: 0.87454
Max Validation Accuracy: 0.8460999727249146
```

Early stopping interrupted the training after 31 epochs, and we reached a validation accuracy of above 84% –not bad. As expected, we need many more epochs now. This is a graph of the losses:

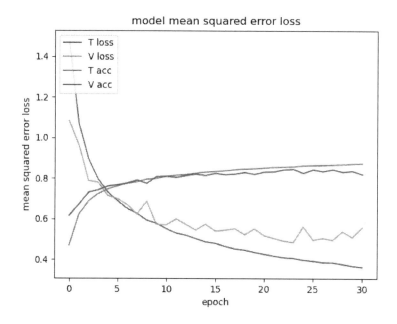

Figure 6.14 – Losses with data augmentation and early stopping

You can see how the training accuracy kept increasing, while the validation accuracy at some point decreased. The network is still overfitting a bit.

Let's check the activations of the first convolutional layer:

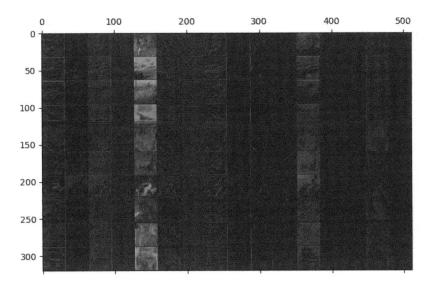

Figure 6.15 – First convolutional layer, 16 channels, with data augmentation and early stopping

It's marginally better, but it can probably improve again.

We can try to augment the data a little more:

```
ImageDataGenerator(rotation_range=15, width_shift_range=[-8,
-4, 0,
    4, 8], horizontal_flip=True, height_shift_range=[-5, 0, 5],
    zoom_range=[0.9, 1.1])
```

This is the result:

```
Epoch 00040: early stopping
Training time: 2923.3936190605164
Min Loss: 0.5091392234659194
Min Validation Loss: 0.5033097203373909
Max Accuracy: 0.8243
Max Validation Accuracy: 0.8331999778747559
```

This model is slower and less accurate. Let's see the graph:

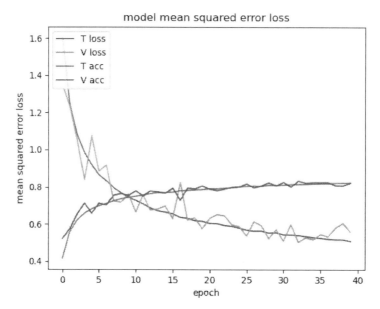

Figure 6.16 – Losses with more data augmentation and early stopping

Maybe it needs more patience. We will stick to the previous data augmentation then.

In the next section, we will analyze a simple but effective way to increase the validation accuracy using the dropout layer.

Improving the validation accuracy with dropout

A source of overfitting is the fact that the neural network relies more on some neurons to draw its conclusions, and if those neurons are wrong, the network is wrong. One way to reduce this problem is simply to randomly shut down some neurons during training while keeping them working normally during inference. In this way, the neural network learns to be more resistant to errors and to generalize better. This mechanism is called **dropout**, and obviously, Keras supports it. Dropout increases the training time, as the network needs more epochs to converge. It might also require a bigger network, as some neurons are randomly deactivated during training. It is also more useful when the dataset is not very big for the network, as it is more likely to overfit. In practice, as dropout is meant to reduce overfitting, it brings little benefit if your network is not overfitting.

A typical value of dropout for dense layers is 0.5, though we might use a bit less, as our model is not overfitting much. We will also increase the *patience* to 20, as the model needs more epochs to be trained now and the validation loss can fluctuate for more time.

Let's try to add some dropout to the dense layers:

```
model.add(Flatten())
model.add(Dense(units=256, activation='relu'))
model.add(Dropout(0.4))
model.add(Dense(units=128, activation='relu'))
model.add(Dropout(0.2))
model.add(Dense(units=num_classes, activation = 'softmax'))
```

This is the result:

```
Epoch 00097: early stopping
Training time: 6541.777503728867
Min Loss: 0.38114651718586684
Min Validation Loss: 0.44884318161308767
Max Accuracy: 0.87218
Max Validation Accuracy: 0.8585000038146973
```

A bit disappointing. It took a lot of time to train, with small gains. We assume that our dense layers are a bit small.

Let's increase the size of the layers by 50%, and we will also increase the dropout of the first dense layer while reducing the dropout of the second one:

```
model.add(Flatten())
model.add(Dense(units=384, activation='relu'))
model.add(Dropout(0.5))
model.add(Dense(units=192, activation='relu'))
model.add(Dropout(0.1))
model.add(Dense(units=num_classes, activation='softmax'))
```

It is, of course, bigger, as we can see here:

```
Total params: 542,426
```

It has a slightly better result:

```
Epoch 00122: early stopping
Training time: 8456.040931940079
```

```
Min Loss: 0.3601766444931924
Min Validation Loss: 0.4270844452492893
Max Accuracy: 0.87942
Max Validation Accuracy: 0.864799976348877
```

As we improve the validation accuracy, even small gains are difficult to achieve.

Let's check the graph:

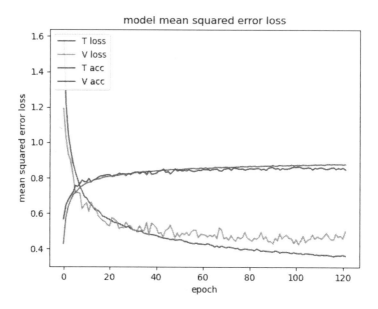

Figure 6.17 – Losses with more data augmentation and dropout on dense layers

There is a bit of overfitting, so let's try to fix it. We can also use `Dropout` in the convolutional layers.

Let's try this:

```
model.add(Conv2D(filters=16, kernel_size=(3, 3),
activation='relu', input_shape=x_train.shape[1:],
    padding="same"))
model.add(BatchNormalization())
model.add(Dropout(0.5))
model.add(Conv2D(filters=16, kernel_size=(3, 3),
activation='relu', input_shape=x_train.shape[1:],
    padding="same"))
model.add(BatchNormalization())
```

```
model.add(AveragePooling2D())
model.add(Dropout(0.5))
```

This is the disappointing result:

```
Epoch 00133: early stopping
Training time: 9261.82032418251
Min Loss: 0.6104169194960594
Min Validation Loss: 0.4887285701841116
Max Accuracy: 0.79362
Max Validation Accuracy: 0.8417999744415283
```

The network did not improve!

Here, we see an interesting case—the validation accuracy is significantly higher than the training accuracy. How is that possible?

Assuming that your split is correct (for example, you don't have a validation set that is too easy or containing images too similar to the training dataset), two factors can create this situation:

- Data augmentation can potentially make the training dataset harder than the validation dataset.
- Dropout is active during the training phase and deactivated during the prediction phase, so this means that the training dataset can be significantly harder than the validation dataset.

In our case, the culprit is the dropout. You don't necessarily need to avoid this situation, if it is justified, but in our case, the validation accuracy went down, so we need to fix our dropout, or maybe increase the size of the network.

I find Dropout more difficult to use with the convolutional layers, and I would personally not use a big dropout in that case. Here, there are some guidelines:

- No batch normalization right after Dropout, as normalization would suffer.
- Dropout is more effective after MaxPooling than before.
- Dropout after a convolutional layer drops single pixels, but SpatialDropout2D drops channels, and it is recommended on the first few layers at the beginning of the neural network.

I ran another few (long!) experiments and I decided to increase the size of the convolutional layers, reduce the dropout, and use `Spatial Dropout` in a couple of layers. I ended up with this neural network, which is what I consider my final version.

This is the code of the convolutional layers:

```
model = Sequential()
model.add(Conv2D(filters=32, kernel_size=(3, 3),
activation='relu', input_shape=x_train.shape[1:],
padding="same"))
model.add(BatchNormalization())
model.add(Conv2D(filters=32, kernel_size=(3, 3),
activation='relu', input_shape=x_train.shape[1:],
padding="same"))
model.add(BatchNormalization())
model.add(AveragePooling2D())
model.add(SpatialDropout2D(0.2))

model.add(Conv2D(filters=48, kernel_size=(3, 3),
activation='relu',
    padding="same"))
model.add(BatchNormalization())
model.add(Conv2D(filters=48, kernel_size=(3, 3),
activation='relu',
    padding="same"))
model.add(BatchNormalization())
model.add(AveragePooling2D())
model.add(SpatialDropout2D(0.2))

model.add(Conv2D(filters=72, kernel_size=(3, 3),
activation='relu',
    padding="same"))
model.add(BatchNormalization())
model.add(Conv2D(filters=72, kernel_size=(3, 3),
activation='relu',
    padding="same"))
model.add(BatchNormalization())
model.add(AveragePooling2D())
model.add(Dropout(0.1))
```

And this is the part with the dense layers:
```
model.add(Flatten())
model.add(Dense(units=384, activation='relu'))
model.add(Dropout(0.5))
model.add(Dense(units=192, activation='relu'))
model.add(Dropout(0.1))
model.add(Dense(units=num_classes, activation='softmax'))
```

These are the results:

```
Epoch 00168: early stopping
Training time: 13122.931826591492
Min Loss: 0.4703261657243967
Min Validation Loss: 0.3803714614287019
Max Accuracy: 0.84324
Max Validation Accuracy: 0.8779000043869019
```

There is an improvement in the validation accuracy:

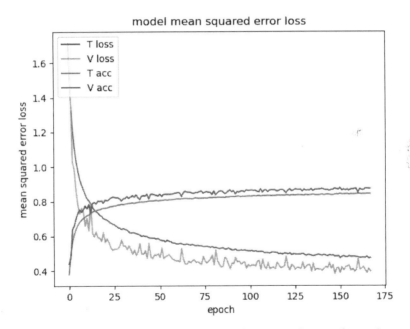

Figure 6.18 – Losses with more data augmentation and dropout on dense and convolutional layers

Congratulations! Now you have an idea of how to train a neural network, and feel free to experiment and go crazy! Every task is different, and the possibilities are really endless.

For fun, let's train it again and to see how the same logical model performs on MNIST.

Applying the model to MNIST

Our previous MNIST model achieved 98.3% validation accuracy and, as you might have noticed, the closer you get to 100%, the more difficult it is to improve the model.

Our CIFAR-10 is trained on a different task than MNIST, but let's see how it performs:

```
Epoch 00077: early stopping
Training time: 7110.028198957443
Min Loss: 0.04797766085289389
Min Validation Loss: 0.02718053938352254
Max Accuracy: 0.98681664
Max Validation Accuracy: 0.9919000267982483
```

Here is the graph for it:

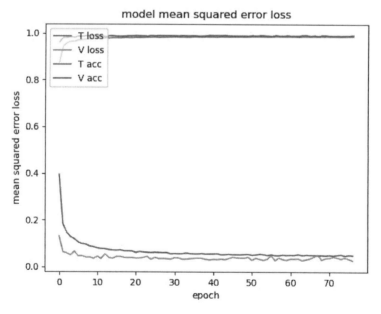

Figure 6.19 – MNIST, losses

I wish every task was as easy as MNIST!

Out of curiosity, these are the activations of the first layer:

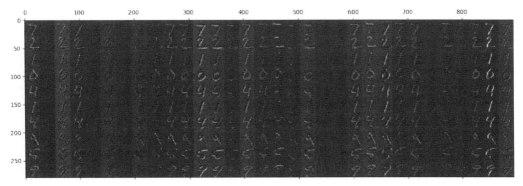

Figure 6.20 – MNIST, activations of the first convolutional level

As you can see, many channels are activated, and they easily detect the most important features of the numbers.

This could be an excellent time for you to try the code in GitHub and experiment with it.

Now it's your turn!

If you have some time, you should really experiment with a public dataset, or even create your own dataset and train a neural network from scratch.

If you are out of ideas, you could use CIFAR-100.

Remember that training a neural network usually is not linear—you might have to guess what can help you, or you might try many different things. And remember to repeat, going back and forth, because while your model evolves, the importance of different techniques and different layers can change.

Summary

This has been a very practical chapter, showing one way to proceed when training a neural network. We started from a big model, achieving 69.7% validation accuracy, and then we reduced its size and added some layers to increase the number of non-linear activations. We used batch normalization to equalize the contribution of all the channels and then we learned about early stopping, which helped us to decide when to stop the training.

After learning how to automatically stop the training, we applied it immediately with data augmentation, which increases not only the size of the dataset but also the number of epochs required to properly train the network. We then introduced `Dropout` and `SpatialDropout2D`, a powerful way to reduce overfitting, though not always easy to use.

We ended up with a network achieving 87.8% accuracy.

In the next chapter, we will train a neural network that will be able to drive a car on an empty track!

Questions

After this chapter, you will be able to answer the following questions:

1. Why do we want to use more layers?
2. Is a network with more layers automatically slower than a shallower one?
3. How do we know how to stop training the model?
4. Which Keras function can we use to stop the training before the model starts to overfit?
5. How can you normalize the channels?
6. How can you effectively make your dataset bigger and more difficult?
7. Does dropout make your model more robust?
8. If you use data augmentation, would you expect the training to become slower or faster?
9. If you use dropout, would you expect the training to become slower or faster?

7
Detecting Pedestrians and Traffic Lights

Congratulations on covering deep learning and progressing to this new section! Now that you know the basics of how to build and tune neural networks, it is time to move toward more advanced topics.

If you remember, in *Chapter 1, OpenCV Basics and Camera Calibration*, we already detected pedestrians using OpenCV. In this chapter, we will learn how to detect objects using a very powerful neural network called **Single Shot MultiBox Detector (SSD)**, and we will use it to detect not only pedestrians but also vehicles and traffic lights. In addition, we will train a neural network to detect the color of the traffic lights using transfer learning, a powerful technique that can help you achieve good results using a relatively small dataset.

In this chapter, we will cover the following topics:

- Detecting pedestrians, vehicles, and traffic lights
- Collecting images with CARLA
- Object detection with **Single Shot MultiBox Detector (SSD)**

- Detecting the color of a traffic lights
- Understanding transfer learning
- The ideas behind Inception
- Recognizing traffic lights and their colors

Technical requirements

To be able to use the code explained in this chapter, you need to have installed the following tools and modules:

- The Carla simulator
- Python 3.7
- The NumPy module
- The TensorFlow module
- The Keras module
- The OpenCV-Python module
- A GPU (recommended)

The code for this chapter can be found at `https://github.com/PacktPublishing/Hands-On-Vision-and-Behavior-for-Self-Driving-Cars/tree/master/Chapter7`.

The Code in Action videos for this chapter can be found here:

`https://bit.ly/3o8C79Q`

Detecting pedestrians, vehicles, and traffic lights with SSD

When a self-driving car is on a road, it surely needs to know where the lanes are and detect obstacles (including people!) that can be present on the road, and it also needs to detect traffic signs and traffic lights.

In this chapter, we will take a big step forward, as we will learn how to detect pedestrians, vehicles, and traffic lights, including the traffic light colors. We will use Carla to generate the images that we need.

Solving our task is a two-step process:

1. Firstly, we will detect vehicles, pedestrians, and traffic lights (no color information), where we will use a pre-trained neural network called SSD.
2. Then, we will detect the color of the traffic lights, where we will need to train a neural network starting from a pre-trained neural network called **Inception v3**, using a technique called transfer learning, and we will also need to collect a small dataset.

So, let's begin by using Carla to collect the images.

Collecting some images with Carla

We need some pictures of a street, with pedestrians, vehicles, and traffic lights. We can use Carla for that, but this time, we will discuss in further detail how to collect the dataset with Carla. You can find Carla at `https://carla.org/`.

You can find the binaries for Linux and Windows on the Carla GitHub page:

`https://github.com/carla-simulator/carla/releases`

The installation instruction can be found on the Carla website:

`https://carla.readthedocs.io/en/latest/start_quickstart/`

If you are using Linux, Carla starts with the `CarlaUE4.sh` command, while on Windows, it is called `CarlaUE4.exe`. We will just call it `CarlaUE4`. You can run it without arguments, or you could manually set the resolution, as follows:

```
CarlaUE4 -windowed -ResX=640 -ResY=480
```

In Carla, you can move around the track using some keys:

- *W*: Forward
- *S*: Backward
- *A*: Left, sideways
- *D*: Right, sideways

In addition, in Carla, you can use the mouse, pressing the left mouse button and moving the cursor to change the angle of the view and to move along other angles.

You should see something like this:

Figure 7.1 – Carla – default track

While the server is sometimes useful, you probably want to run some of the files present in `PythonAPI\util` and `PythonAPI\examples`.

For this task, we are going to change track, using `Town01`. You can do this using the `PythonAPI\util\config.py` file, as follows:

```
python config.py -m=Town01
```

You should now see a different track:

Figure 7.2 – The Town01 track

Your city is empty, so we need to add some vehicles and some pedestrians. We can do this using `PythonAPI\examples\spawn_npc.py`, as follows:

```
python spawn_npc.py  -w=100 -n=100
```

The `-w` parameter specifies the number of walkers, and `-n` the number of vehicles, that you want to create. Now, you should see some action:

Figure 7.3 – The Town01 track with vehicles and pedestrians

Much better.

Carla is intended to run as a server to which you can connect multiple clients, which should allow more interesting simulations.

When you run Carla, it starts a server. You can go around a bit using the server, but most likely, you will want to run a client as it can provide much more functionality. If you run a client, you will have two windows with Carla, which are expected:

1. Let's run a client using `PythonAPI\examples\manual_control.py`, as follows:

   ```
   python manual_control.py
   ```

   You might see something like the following:

Figure 7.4 – The Town01 track using manual_control.py

You can see a lot of statistics on the left, and you can toggle them using the *F1* key. You will notice that now you have a vehicle, and you can change it with the *Backspace* key.

2. You can move with the same keys as before, but this time, the behavior is more useful and realistic, as there is some physical simulation. You can also use the arrow keys to move.

You can use the *Tab* key to change camera, and the *C* key changes the weather, as we can see in the following screenshot:

Figure 7.5 – The Town01 track; hard rain at noon and clear sky at sunset

Carla has many sensors, one of which is the RGB camera, and you can switch between them using `, the backtick key. Now, refer to the following screenshots:

Figure 7.6 – The Town01 track – left: depth (raw), right: semantic segmentation

The preceding screenshots show a couple of very interesting sensors:

- The depth sensor, which provides the distance from the camera for each pixel
- The semantic segmentation sensor, which classifies every object using a different color

At the time of writing, the full list of camera sensors is as follows:

- Camera RGB
- Camera depth (raw)
- Camera depth (grayscale)

- Camera depth (logarithmic grayscale)
- Camera semantic segmentation (CityScapes Palette)
- Lidar (raycast)
- **Dynamic Vision Sensor (DVS)**
- Camera RGB distorted

Lidar is a sensor that detects the distance of an object using a laser; the DVS, also called the neuromorphic camera, is a camera that records local changes of brightness, overcoming some limitations of RGB cameras. Camera RGB distorted is just an RGB camera simulating the effects of a lens, and of course, you can customize the distortion as needed.

The following screenshot shows the Lidar camera view:

Figure 7.7 – The Lidar camera view

The following screenshot shows the output of DVS:

Figure 7.8 – DVS

You can now just go around and collect some images from the RGB camera, or you can use the ones in the GitHub repository.

Now that we have some images, it is time to detect pedestrians, vehicles, and traffic lights, using a pre-trained network called SSD.

Understanding SSD

In previous chapters, we created a classifier, a neural network able to tell what is present in a picture from a predefined set of options. Later in this chapter, we will see a pre-trained neural network that can classify images in a very precise way.

SSD stands out compared to many neural networks, as it is able to detect multiple objects in the same picture. The details of SSD are a bit complicated, and if you are interested, you can check the *Further reading* section for some inspiration.

Not only can SSD detect multiple objects, but it can also output the area where the object is present! Internally, this is done by checking 8,732 positions at different aspect ratios. SSD is also fast enough that with a good GPU, it can be used to analyze videos in real time.

But where can we find SSD? The answer is the TensorFlow detection model zoo. Let's see what this is.

Discovering the TensorFlow detection model zoo

The TensorFlow detection model zoo is a useful collection of pre-trained neural networks, which supports several architectures trained on several datasets. We are interested in SSD, so we will focus on that.

Of the datasets supported by the model zoo, we are interested in COCO. **COCO** is the Microsoft **Common Objects in Context** dataset, a collection of 2,500,000 (2.5 million) images, classified by type. You can find a link with the 90 labels of COCO in the *Further reading* section, but we are interested in the following ones:

- 1: person
- 3: car
- 6: bus
- 8: truck
- 10: traffic light

You might also be interested in the following:

- 2: bicycle
- 4: motorcycle
- 13: stop sign

Notably, SSD trained on COCO is available on several versions, using different neural networks as the backend to reach the desired speed/precision ratio. Refer to the following screenshot:

Model name	Speed (ms)	COCO mAP[^1]	Outputs
ssd_mobilenet_v1_coco	30	21	Boxes
ssd_mobilenet_v1_0.75_depth_coco ☆	26	18	Boxes
ssd_mobilenet_v1_quantized_coco ☆	29	18	Boxes
ssd_mobilenet_v1_0.75_depth_quantized_coco ☆	29	16	Boxes
ssd_mobilenet_v1_ppn_coco ☆	26	20	Boxes
ssd_mobilenet_v1_fpn_coco ☆	56	32	Boxes
ssd_resnet_50_fpn_coco ☆	76	35	Boxes
ssd_mobilenet_v2_coco	31	22	Boxes
ssd_mobilenet_v2_quantized_coco	29	22	Boxes
ssdlite_mobilenet_v2_coco	27	22	Boxes
ssd_inception_v2_coco	42	24	Boxes

Figure 7.9 – The TensorFlow detection model zoo of SSDs trained on COCO

Here, the mAP column is the mean average precision, so the higher the better. MobileNet is a neural network developed to perform particularly well on mobiles and embedded devices, and thanks to its performance, it is a classical choice for SSD when you need to perform inference in real time.

To detect the objects on the road, we will use an SSD built using **ResNet50** as a backbone, a neural network with 50 layers developed by Microsoft Research Asia. A characteristic of ResNet is the presence of **skip connections**, shortcuts that can connect a layer to another one, skipping some layers in the middle. This helps in solving the **vanishing gradient problem**. With deep neural networks, the gradient during training can become so small that the network can basically stop learning.

But how do we use ssd_resnet_50_fpn_coco, our selected model? Let's check it out!

Downloading and loading SSD

On the model zoo page, if you click on **ssd_resnet_50_fpn_coco**, you get a URL that Keras needs to download the model from; at the time of writing, the URL is as follows:

```
http://download.tensorflow.org/models/object_detection/
ssd_resnet50_v1_fpn_shared_box_predictor_640x640_coco14_
sync_2018_07_03.tar.gz
```

The full name of the model is the following:

```
ssd_resnet50_v1_fpn_shared_box_predictor_640x640_coco14_
sync_2018_07_03.
```

To load the model, you can use the following code:

```
url = 'http://download.tensorflow.org/models/object_detection/'
+ model_name + '.tar.gz'
model_dir = tf.keras.utils.get_file(fname=model_name,
untar=True, origin=url)

print("Model path: ", model_dir)
model_dir = pathlib.Path(model_dir) / "saved_model"
model = tf.saved_model.load(str(model_dir))
model = model.signatures['serving_default']
```

If this is the first time that you have run this code, it will take more time because Keras will download the model and save it on your hard drive.

Now that we have loaded the model, is time to use it to detect some objects.

Running SSD

Running SSD requires just a few lines of code. You can load the image (with a resolution of 299x299) with OpenCV, then you need to convert the image into a tensor, a type of multi-dimensional array used by TensorFlow that is similar to NumPy arrays. Refer to the following code:

```
img = cv2.imread(file_name)
img = cv2.cvtColor(img, cv2.COLOR_BGR2RGB)
input_tensor = tf.convert_to_tensor(img)
input_tensor = input_tensor[tf.newaxis, ...]
# Run inference
output = model(input_tensor)
```

Please note that we feed the network with an RGB image, not BGR. You might remember from the previous chapters that OpenCV uses pictures in BGR format, so we need to pay attention to the order of the channels.

As you can see, running SSD is quite easy, but the output is relatively complex, and it needs some code to be converted into a useful and more compact form. The `output` variable is a Python dictionary, but the values that it contains are tensors, so you need to convert them.

For example, printing `output['num_detections']`, which contains the number of predictions (for example, objects found in the image), would give the following as a result:

```
tf.Tensor([1.], shape=(1,), dtype=float32)
```

For the conversion, we can use `int()`.

All the other tensors are arrays, and they can be converted using their `numpy()` function. So then, your code might look like this:

```
num_detections = int(output.pop('num_detections'))
output = {key: value[0, :num_detections].numpy()
          for key, value in output.items()}
output['num_detections'] = num_detections
```

There are still the following two things to fix:

- The detection classes are floating point, while, as they are our labels, they should be integers.
- The coordinates of the boxes are in percentage form.

We can fix these problems with just a few lines of code:

```
output['detection_classes'] = 
    output['detection_classes'].astype(np.int64)
output['boxes'] = [
    {"y": int(box[0] * img.shape[0]),
    "x": int(box[1] * img.shape[1]),
    "y2": int(box[2] * img.shape[0]),
    "x2": int(box[3] * img.shape[1])}
        for box in output['detection_boxes']]
```

Let's apply SSD to this image:

Figure 7.10 – Image from Town01

We get this output:

```
{
'detection_scores': array([0.4976843, 0.44799107, 0.36753723,
    0.3548107 ], dtype=float32),
'detection_classes': array([ 8, 10,  6,  3], dtype=int64),
'detection_boxes': array([
    [0.46678272, 0.2595877, 0.6488052, 0.40986294],
    [0.3679817, 0.76321596, 0.45684734, 0.7875406],
    [0.46517858, 0.26020002, 0.6488801, 0.41080648],
    [0.46678272, 0.2595877, 0.6488052, 0.40986294]],
    dtype=float32),
'num_detections': 4,
'boxes': [{'y': 220, 'x': 164, 'y2': 306, 'x2': 260},
          {'y': 174, 'x': 484, 'y2': 216, 'x2': 500},
          {'y': 220, 'x': 165, 'y2': 306, 'x2': 260},
          {'y': 220, 'x': 164, 'y2': 306, 'x2': 260}]
}
```

This is what the code means:

- `detection_scores`: A higher score means higher confidence in the prediction.
- `detection_classes`: The predicted labels – in this case, truck (`8`), traffic light (`10`), bus (`6`), and car (`3`).
- `detection_boxes`: The original boxes, with coordinates in percentage form.
- `num_detections`: The number of predictions.
- `boxes`: The boxes with coordinates converted to the resolution of the original image.

Please notice that three predictions are basically in the same area, and they are ordered by score. We will need to fix this overlapping.

To be able to better see what has been detected, we will now annotate the image.

Annotating the image

To properly annotate the image, we need to perform the following operations:

1. Consider only the labels that are interesting to us.
2. Remove the overlapping of labels.
3. Draw a rectangle on each prediction.
4. Write the label and its score.

To remove the overlapping labels, it's enough to compare them, and if the center of the boxes is similar, we will keep only the label with a higher score.

This is the result:

Figure 7.11 – Image from Town01, annotated with SSD only

It's a good starting point, even if other images are not recognized so well. The vehicle has been recognized as a truck, which is not completely accurate, but we don't really care about that.

The main problem is that we know that there is a traffic light, but we don't know the color. Unfortunately, SSD cannot help us; we need to do it by ourselves.

In the next section, we will develop a neural network that is able to detect the color of the traffic light, using a technique called transfer learning.

Detecting the color of a traffic light

In principle, we could try to detect the color of a traffic light using some computer vision technique – for example, checking the red and the green channel could be a starting point. In addition, verifying the luminosity of the bottom and upper part of the crossing light should help. This could work, even if some crossing lights can be problematic.

However, we will use deep learning, as this task is well-suited to exploring more advanced techniques. We will also go the extra mile to use a small dataset, even though it would be easy for us to create a big dataset; the reason being that we don't always have the luxury of easily increasing the size of the dataset.

To be able to detect the color of a traffic light, we need to complete three steps:

1. Collect a dataset of crossing lights.
2. Train a neural network to recognize the color.
3. Use the network with SSD to get the final result.

There is a traffic light dataset that you could use, the *Bosch Small Traffic Lights* dataset; however, we will generate our own dataset using Carla. Let's see how.

Creating a traffic light dataset

We are going to create a dataset using Carla. In principle, it could be as big as we want. The bigger the better, but a big dataset would make training slower and, of course, it will require some more time to be created. In our case, as the task is simple, we will create a relatively small dataset of a few hundreds of images. We will explore **transfer learning** later, a technique that can be used when the dataset is not particularly big.

> **Tip**
> On GitHub, you can find the dataset that I created for this task, but if you have some time, collecting the dataset by yourself could be a nice exercise.

Creating this dataset is a three-step task:

1. Collect images of streets.
2. Find and crop all the traffic lights.
3. Classify the traffic lights.

The first task of collecting images is very simple. Just start Carla using `manual_control.py` and press the *R* key. Carla will start recording and it will stop after you press *R* again.

Consider that we want to record four types of images:

- Red lights
- Yellow lights
- Green lights
- The back of traffic lights (negative samples)

The reason why we want to collect the back of the traffic light is that SSD is recognizing it as a traffic light, but we have no use for it, so we don't want to use it. These are **negative samples**, and they could also include pieces of road or buildings or anything that SSD wrongly classifies as a traffic light.

So, while you record your images, please try to get enough samples for each category.

These are some example of images that you might want to collect:

Figure 7.12 – Town01 – left: red light, right: green light

The second step is applying SSD and extracting the image of the crossing light. It's quite simple; refer to the following code:

```
obj_class = out["detection_classes"][idx]
if obj_class == object_detection.LABEL_TRAFFIC_LIGHT:
    box = out["boxes"][idx]
    traffic_light = img[box["y"]:box["y2"],
box["x"]:box["x2"]]
```

In the previous code, assuming that the `out` variable contains the result of running the SSD, calling `model(input_tensor)`, and `idx` contains the current detection among the predictions, you just need to select the detections containing traffic lights and crop them using the coordinates that we computed earlier.

I ended up with 291 detections, with images like these:

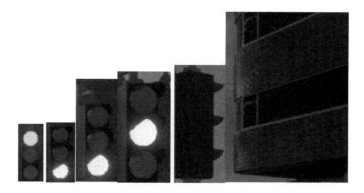

Figure 7.13 – Town01, from the left: small red light, small green light, green light, yellow light, back of a traffic light, piece of a building wrongly classified as a traffic light

As you can see, the images have different resolutions and ratios, and that's perfectly fine.

There are also some images that are completely unrelated, such as a piece of a building, and these are excellent negative samples for things that are not a traffic light because SSD misclassified them, so it is also a way to improve the output of SSD.

The last step is just classifying the images. With a few hundred pictures of this type, it takes only a few minutes. You can create a directory for each label and move the appropriate images there.

Congratulations, now you have a custom dataset to detect the color of traffic lights.

As you know, the dataset is small, so, as we already said, we are going to use transfer learning. The next section will explain what it is.

Understanding transfer learning

Transfer learning is a very appropriate name. From a conceptual point of view, indeed, it is about taking what a neural network learned on one task and transferring this knowledge to a different but related task.

There are several approaches to transfer learning; we will discuss two, and we will choose one of them and use it to detect the colors of the traffic lights. In both cases, the starting point is a neural network that has been pre-trained on a similar task – for example, a classification of images. We will talk more about this in the next section, *Getting to know ImageNet*. We are focusing on a **Convolutional Neural Network** (**CNN**) used as a classifier, as this is what we need to recognize the color of the traffic lights.

The first approach is to load the pre-trained neural network, adapting the number of outputs to the new problem (either replacing some or all the dense layers or sometimes just adding an additional dense layer), and basically keep training it on the new dataset. You might need to use a small learning rate. This approach might work if the number of samples in the new dataset is smaller than the dataset used for the original training, but still significantly big. For example, the size of our custom dataset could be 10% of the site of the original dataset. One drawback is that training might take a long time, as typically you are training a relatively big network.

A second approach, the one that we are going to follow, is similar to the first one, but you are going to freeze all the convolutional layers, meaning that their parameters are fixed and will not change during training. This has the advantage that training is much faster as you don't need to train the convolutional layers. The idea here is that the convolutional layers have been trained on a huge dataset, and they are able to detect so many features that it is going to be fine for the new task also, while the real classifier, composed of the dense layers, can be replaced and trained from scratch.

Intermediate approaches are also possible, where you train some of the convolutional layers, but typically keep at least the first layers frozen.

Before seeing how to do transfer learning with Keras, let's think a bit more about what we just discussed. A key assumption is that this hypothetical network that we want to learn from has been trained on a huge dataset, where the network can learn to recognize many features and patterns. Turns out that there is a very big dataset that fits the bill—ImageNet. Let's talk a bit more about it.

Getting to know ImageNet

ImageNet is a huge dataset, and at the time of writing, it is composed of 14,197,122 (over 14 million) images! In reality, it does not provide the images, but just the URLs to download the images. Those images are classified on 27 categories and a total of 21,841 subcategories! These subcategories, called synsets, are based on a classification hierarchy called **WordNet**.

ImageNet has been a very influential dataset, thanks also to a competition used to measure the advancements in computer vision: the **ImageNet Large-Scale Visual Recognition Challenge (ILSVRC)**.

These are the main categories:

- `amphibian`
- `animal`
- `appliance`

- `bird`
- `covering`
- `device`
- `fabric`
- `fish`
- `flower`
- `food`
- `fruit`
- `fungus`
- `furniture`
- `geological formation`
- `invertebrate`
- `mammal`
- `musical instrument`
- `plant`
- `reptile`
- `sport`
- `structure`
- `tool`
- `tree`
- `utensil`
- `vegetable`
- `vehicle`
- `person`

The number of subcategories is impressively high; as an example, the `tree` category has 993 subcategories, covered by more than half a million of pictures!

Surely, a neural network performing well on this dataset will be very good at recognizing patterns on many types of images, and it might also have a quite big capacity. So, yes, it will overfit your dataset, but as we know how to deal with overfitting, we will keep an eye on this problem, but not get too worried about it.

As so much research has been devoted to performing well on ImageNet, it's not surprising that many of the most influential neural networks have been trained on it.

One, in particular, stood out when it first appeared in 2012—AlexNet. Let's see why.

Discovering AlexNet

When AlexNet was released in 2012, it was over 10% more precise than the best neural network of the time! Clearly, these solutions have been studied extensively, and some are now very common.

AlexNet introduced several ground-breaking innovations:

- Multi-GPU training where AlexNet was trained half on one GPU and half on another one, allowing the model to be twice the size.
- ReLU activation instead of Tanh, which apparently allowed the training to be six times faster.
- Overlapping pooling added, where AlexNet used max-pooling of 3x3, but the pooling area is moved only by 2x2, meaning that there is an overlap between pools. According to the original paper, this gave a 0.3–0.4% improvement in accuracy. In Keras, you can achieve similar overlapping pooling using `MaxPooling2D(pool_size=(3,3), strides=(2,2))`.

With over 60 million parameters, AlexNet was pretty big, so to reduce overfitting, it made extensive use of data augmentation and dropout.

While AlexNet was state-of-the-art and ground-breaking in 2012, by today's standards, it is quite inefficient. In the next section, we will discuss a neural network that can achieve substantially better accuracy than AlexNet using only one-tenth of the parameters: **Inception**.

The ideas behind Inception

Having a huge dataset like ImageNet at our disposal is great, but it would be much easier to have a neural network already trained with it. It turns out that Keras provides several of them. One is ResNet, which we have already encountered. Another one, which is very influential and with great innovations, is Inception. Let's talk a bit about it.

Inception is a family of neural networks, meaning that there are several of them, refining the initial concept. Inception was designed by Google, and the version that participated in the ILSVRC 2014 (ImageNet) competition and won is called **GoogLeNet**, in honor of the LeNet architecture.

If you are wondering whether Inception took its name from the famous movie *Inception*, yes it did, because they wanted to go deeper! And Inception is a deep network, with a version called `InceptionResNetV2` arriving at a staggering 572 layers! This, of course, is if we count every layer, including the activations. We are going to use Inception v3, which has *only* 159 layers.

We will focus on Inception v1, because it is easier, and we will briefly discuss some improvements added later, as they can be a source of inspiration for you.

A key observation made by Google is that given the variety of positions where a subject can be on a picture, it is difficult to know in advance which kernel size of a convolutional layer would be the best, so they added 1x1, 3x3, and 5x5 convolutions in parallel to cover the main cases, plus max pooling, as it is often useful, and concatenated the results. One advantage of doing it in parallel is that the network does not get too deep, which keeps the training easier.

What we just described is the **naïve** Inception block:

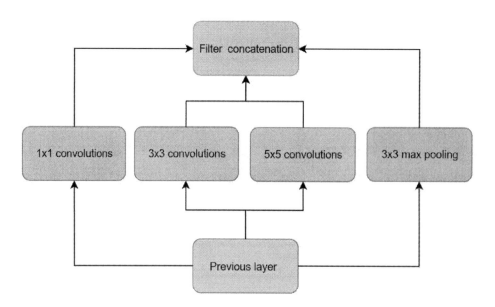

Figure 7.14 – Naïve Inception block

You might have noticed a 1x1 convolution. What's that? Just multiplying a channel by a number? Not exactly. The 1x1 convolution is very cheap to perform, as there is only 1 multiplication instead of 9 (as in 3x3 convolutions) or 25 (as in 5x5 convolutions), and it can be used to change the number of filters. In addition, you can add a ReLU, introducing a non-linear operation that increases the complexity of the functions that the network can learn.

This module is called naïve because it is too computationally expensive. As the number of channels grows, the 3x3 and 5x5 convolutions become slow. The solution is to put 1x1 convolutions in front of them, to reduce the number of channels where the more expensive convolutions need to operate:

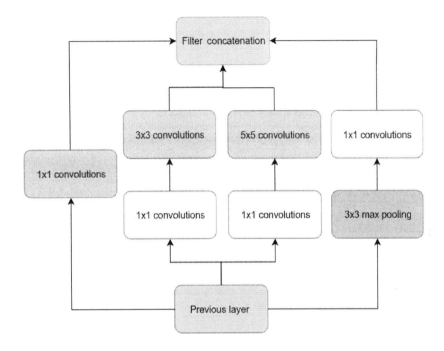

Figure 7.15 – Inception block including dimension reductions

The key to understanding this block is to remember that the 1x1 convolutions are used to reduce the channels and improve performance significantly.

For example, the first Inception block in GoogLeNet has an input of 192 channels, and the 5x5 convolution would create 32 channels, so the number of multiplications would be proportional to 25 x 32 x 192 = 153,600.

They added a 1x1 convolution with an output of 16 filters, so the number of multiplications would be proportional to 16 x 192 + 25 x 32 x 16 = 3,072 + 12,800 = 15,872. Almost a 10x reduction. Not bad!

One more thing. For the concatenation to work, all the convolutions need to have an output of the same size, which means that they need the padding, which keeps the same resolution of the input image. And what about max pooling? It also needs to have an output of the same size as the convolutions, so even if it finds the maximum in a 3x3 grid, it cannot reduce the size.

In Keras, this means it would be something like this:

```
MaxPooling2D(pool_size=(3, 3), padding='same', strides=(1, 1))
```

The `strides` parameter indicates how many pixels to move after calculating the maximum. By default, it's set at the same value of `pool_size`, which in our example would reduce the size 3 times. Setting it to `(1, 1)` with the same padding has the effect of not changing the size. The Conv2D layers also have a `strides` parameter, which can be used to reduce the size of the output; however, usually it is more effective to do so using a max pooling layer.

Inception v2 introduced some optimizations, among them the following:

- A 5x5 convolution is similar to two stacked 3x3 convolutions, but slower, so they refactored it with 3x3 convolutions.
- A 3x3 convolution is equivalent to a 1x3 convolution followed by a 3x1 convolution, but using two convolutions is 33% faster.

Inception v3 introduced the following optimizations:

- Factorized 7x7 convolutions, created using several smaller and faster convolutions
- Some batch normalization layers

Inception-ResNet introduced the residual connections typical of ResNet, to skip some layers.

Now that you have a better understanding of the concepts behind Inception, let's see how to use it in Keras.

Using Inception for image classification

Loading Inception in Keras could not be simpler, as we can see here:

```
model = InceptionV3(weights='imagenet', input_shape=(299,299,3))
```

As Inception can tell us the content of an image, let's try it with the test image that we used at the beginning of the book:

```
img = cv2.resize(preprocess_input(cv2.imread("test.jpg")), (299, 299))
out_inception = model.predict(np.array([img]))
```

```
out_inception = imagenet_utils.decode_predictions(out_
inception)
print(out_inception[0][0][1], out_inception[0][0][2], "%")
```

This is the result:

```
sea_lion 0.99184495 %
```

It is indeed right: our image depicts a sea lion from the Galapagos Islands:

Figure 7.16 – Recognized by Inception as a sea lion with 0.99184495 confidence

But we want to use Inception for transfer learning, not for image classification, so we need to use it in a different way. Let's see how.

Using Inception for transfer learning

The loading for transfer learning is a bit different, because we need to remove the classifier on top of Inception, as follows:

```
base_model = InceptionV3(include_top=False, input_shape=
    (299,299,3))
```

With input_shape, we use the original size of Inception, but you could use a different shape, as long as it has 3 channels and the resolution is at least 75x75.

The important parameter is `include_top`, as setting it to `False` would remove the top part of Inception—the classifier with the dense filters—which means that the network will be ready for transfer learning.

We will now create a neural network that is based on Inception but can be modified by us:

```
top_model = Sequential()
top_model.add(base_model) # Join the networks
```

Now, we can add a classifier on top of it, as follows:

```
top_model.add(GlobalAveragePooling2D())
top_model.add(Dense(1024, activation='relu'))
top_model.add(Dropout(0.5))
top_model.add(Dense(512, activation='relu'))
top_model.add(Dropout(0.5))
top_model.add(Dense(n_classes, activation='softmax'))
```

We added some dropout, as we expect Inception to overfit quite a lot on our dataset. But please pay attention to the `GlobalAveragePooling2D`. What it does is compute the average of the channels.

We could use `Flatten`, but as Inception outputs 2,048 convolutional channels of 8x8, and we are using a dense layer with 1,024 neurons, the number of parameters would be huge—134,217,728! Using `GlobalAveragePooling2D`, we need only 2,097,152 parameters. Even counting the parameters of Inception, the saving is quite significant—24,427,812 parameters instead of 156,548,388.

There is one more thing that we need to do: freeze the layers of Inception that we don't want to train. In this case, we want to freeze all of them, but this might not always be the case. This is how you can freeze them:

```
for layer in base_model.layers:
    layer.trainable = False
```

Let's check how our network looks. Inception is too big, so I will only show the data of the parameters:

```
Total params: 21,802,784
Trainable params: 21,768,352
Non-trainable params: 34,432
```

Please note that `summary()` will actually print two summaries: one for Inception and one for our network; this is the output of the first summary:

```
Model: "sequential_1"
```

Layer (type)	Output Shape	Param #
inception_v3 (Model)	(None, 8, 8, 2048)	21802784
global_average_pooling2d_1 (	(None, 2048)	0
dense_1 (Dense)	(None, 1024)	2098176
dropout_1 (Dropout)	(None, 1024)	0
dense_2 (Dense)	(None, 512)	524800
dropout_2 (Dropout)	(None, 512)	0
dense_3 (Dense)	(None, 4)	2052

```
Total params: 24,427,812
Trainable params: 2,625,028
Non-trainable params: 21,802,784
```

As you can see, the first layer is Inception. In the second summary, you also have a confirmation that Inception has the layers frozen, because we have more than 21 million non-trainable parameters, matching exactly the total number of parameters of Inception.

To reduce the overfitting and to compensate for the small dataset, we will use data augmentation:

```
datagen = ImageDataGenerator(rotation_range=5, width_shift_range=[-5, -2, -1, 0, 1, 2, 5], horizontal_flip=True, height_shift_range=[-30, -20, -10, -5, -2, 0, 2, 5, 10, 20, 30])
```

I only applied a small rotation because traffic lights are usually pretty straight, and I also added only a small width shift because the traffic lights are detected by a neural network (SSD), so the cut tends to be very consistent. I also added a higher height shift because I saw that SSD sometimes wrongly cut the traffic lights, removing one-third of it.

Now that the network is ready, we just need to feed it our dataset.

Feeding our dataset to Inception

Let's assume that you loaded your dataset in two variables: `images` and `labels`.

Inception needs some preprocessing, to map the values of the images to the `[-1, +1]` range. Keras has a function that takes care of this, `preprocess_input()`. Please take care to import it from the `keras.applications.inception_v3` module, because there are other functions with the same name and different behavior in other modules:

```
from keras.applications.inception_v3 import preprocess_input
images = [preprocess_input(img) for img in images]
```

We need to divide the dataset into training and validation, which is easy, but we also need to randomize the order, to be sure that the split is meaningful; for example, my code loads all the images with the same label, so a split without randomization would put only one or two labels in validation, and one of them might even not be present in training.

NumPy has a very handy function to generate new index positions, `permutation()`:

```
indexes = np.random.permutation(len(images))
```

Then, you can use **for comprehension**, a feature of Python, to change the order in your lists:

```
images = [images[idx] for idx in indexes]
labels = [labels[idx] for idx in indexes]
```

If your labels are numeric, you can use `to_categorical()` to convert them into one-hot encoding.

Now, it's just a matter of slicing. We will use 20% of the samples for validation, so the code can be like this:

```
idx_split = int(len(labels_np) * 0.8)
x_train = images[0:idx_split]
x_valid = images[idx_split:]
y_train = labels[0:idx_split]
y_valid = labels[idx_split:]
```

Now, you can train the network as usual. Let's see how it performs!

Performance with transfer learning

The performance of the model is very good:

```
Min Loss: 0.028652783162121116
Min Validation Loss: 0.011525456588399612
Max Accuracy: 1.0
Max Validation Accuracy: 1.0
```

Yes, 100% accuracy and validation accuracy! Not bad, not bad. Actually, it's very rewarding. However, the dataset was very simple, so it was fair to expect a very good result.

This is the graph of the losses:

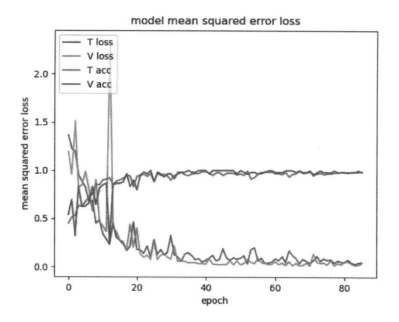

Figure 7.17 – Losses with transfer learning from Inception

The problem is that despite the great results, the network does not work too well on my test images. Probably, it overfits, and I suspect that as the images are normally smaller than the native resolution of Inception, the network might experience patterns that are a result of interpolation instead of true patterns in the images, and maybe get confused by them, but that's just my theory.

To get good results, we need to try harder.

Improving transfer learning

We can assume that the network is overfitting, and the standard response would be to increase the dataset. In this case, it would be easy to do that, but let's pretend that we cannot do it, so we can explore other options that can be useful to you in similar cases.

There are some very easy things that we can do to reduce overfitting:

- Increase the variety of the data augmentation.
- Increase dropout.

Despite the fact that Inception is clearly able to process tasks much more complex than this, it is not optimized for this specific task, and it is also possible that it could benefit from a bigger classifier, so I will add a layer:

- This is the new data augmentation, after a few tests:

  ```
  datagen = ImageDataGenerator(rotation_range=5, width_
  shift_range= [-10, -5, -2, 0, 2, 5, 10],
  zoom_range=[0.7, 1.5],
  height_shift_range=[-10, -5, -2, 0, 2, 5, 10],
  horizontal_flip=True)
  ```

- This is the new model, with more dropout and an additional layer:

  ```
  top_model.add(GlobalAveragePooling2D())
  top_model.add(Dropout(0.5))
  top_model.add(Dense(1024, activation='relu'))
  top_model.add(BatchNormalization())
  top_model.add(Dropout(0.5))
  top_model.add(Dense(512, activation='relu'))
  top_model.add(Dropout(0.5))
  top_model.add(Dense(128, activation='relu'))
  top_model.add(Dense(n_classes, activation='softmax'))
  ```

- I added a dropout after the global average pooling, to reduce overfitting, and I also added a batch normalization layer, which can also help to reduce overfitting.
- Then, I added a dense layer, but I did not put a dropout on it, because I noticed the network had problems training with so much dropout.

  Even if we don't want to increase the dataset, we can still do something about it. Let's look at the distribution of the classes:

  ```
  print('Labels:', collections.Counter(labels))
  ```

  This is the result:

  ```
  Labels: Counter({0: 123, 2: 79, 1: 66, 3: 23})
  ```

As you see, the dataset has much more green than yellow or red and not many negative samples.

In general, it is not good to have imbalanced labels, and the network was indeed predicting more green lights than there were, because statistically, it is more rewarding to predict a green than any other label. To improve this situation, we can instruct Keras to customize the loss in a way that predicting a wrong red would be worse than predicting a wrong green, as this would have an effect similar to making the dataset balanced.

You can do this with these two lines of code:

```
n = len(labels)
class_weight = {0: n/cnt[0], 1: n/cnt[1], 2: n/cnt[2], 3: n/cnt[3]}
```

The following is the result:

```
Class weight: {0: 2.365, 1: 4.409, 2: 3.683, 3: 12.652}
```

As you can see, the loss penalty would be less for green (label 0) than for the other ones.

This is how the network performs:

```
Min Loss: 0.10114006596268155
Min Validation Loss: 0.012583946840742887
Max Accuracy: 0.99568963
Max Validation Accuracy: 1.0
```

Not much different than before, but this time, the network works better and nails all the traffic lights in my test images. This should be a reminder to not trust the validation accuracy completely unless you are sure that your validation dataset is excellent.

This is the graph of the losses:

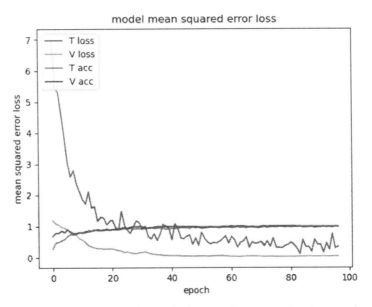

Figure 7.18 – Losses with transfer learning from Inception, improved

Now that we have a good network, it's time to complete our task, using the new network in combination with SSD, as detailed in the next section.

Recognizing traffic lights and their colors

We are almost done. From the code using SSD, we just need to manage the traffic light in a different way. So, when the label is `10` (traffic light), we need to do the following:

- Crop the area with the traffic light.
- Resize it to 299x299.
- Preprocess it.
- Run it through our network.

Then, we will get the prediction:

```
img_traffic_light = img[box["y"]:box["y2"], box["x"]:box["x2"]]
img_inception = cv2.resize(img_traffic_light, (299, 299))
img_inception = np.array([preprocess_input(img_inception)])
prediction = model_traffic_lights.predict(img_inception)
label = np.argmax(prediction)
```

If you run the code of this chapter that is in GitHub, the label 0 is the green light, 1 is yellow, 2 is red, and 3 means that it is not a traffic light.

The whole process involves first detecting objects with SSD, and then using our network to detect the color of traffic lights, if any are present in the image, as explained in the following diagram:

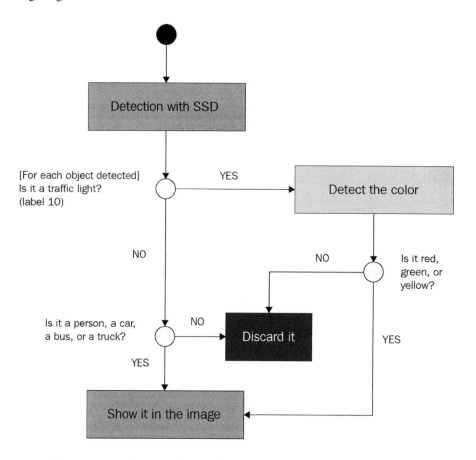

Figure 7.19 – A diagram showing how to use SSD and our network together

These are examples obtained running SSD followed by our network:

Figure 7.20 – Some detections with traffic lights

The colors of the traffic lights are now detected properly. There are some false detections: for example, in the preceding figure, the image on the right marks a person where there is a tree. Unfortunately, this can happen. In a video, we could require detection for a few frames before accepting it, always considering that in a real self-driving car, you cannot introduce high latency, because the car needs to react quickly to what's happening on the street.

Summary

In this chapter, we focused on pre-trained neural networks, and how we can leverage them for our purposes. We combined two neural networks to detect pedestrians, vehicles, and traffic lights, including their color. We first discussed how to use Carla to collect images, and then we discovered SSD, a powerful neural network that stands out for its capacity to detect not only objects, but also their position in an image. We also saw the TensorFlow detection model zoo and how to use Keras to download the desired version of SSD, trained on a dataset called COCO.

In the second part of the chapter, we discussed a powerful technique called transfer learning, and we studied some of the solutions of a neural network called Inception, which we trained on our dataset using transfer learning, to be able to detect the colors of traffic lights. In the process, we also talked about ImageNet, and we saw how achieving 100% validation accuracy was misleading, and as a result, we had to reduce the overfitting to improve the real precision of the network. In the end, we succeeded in using the two networks together—one to detect pedestrians, vehicles, and traffic lights, and one to detect the color of the traffic lights.

Now that we know how to build knowledge about the road, it's time to move forward to the next task—driving! In the next chapter, we will literally sit in the driving seat (of Carla), and teach our neural network how to drive, using a technique called behavioral cloning, where our neural network will try to mimic our behavior.

Questions

You should now be able to answer the following questions:

1. What is SSD?
2. What is Inception?
3. What does it mean to freeze a layer?
4. Can SSD detect the color of a traffic light?
5. What is transfer learning?
6. Can you name some techniques to reduce overfitting?
7. Can you describe the idea behind the Inception block?

Further reading

- SSD: `https://arxiv.org/abs/1512.02325`
- TensorFlow model zoo: `https://github.com/tensorflow/models/blob/master/research/object_detection/g3doc/detection_model_zoo.md`
- COCO labels: `https://github.com/tensorflow/models/blob/master/research/object_detection/data/mscoco_label_map.pbtxt`
- Vanishing gradient problem: `https://en.wikipedia.org/wiki/Vanishing_gradient_problem`
- The Bosch Small Traffic Lights dataset: `https://hci.iwr.uni-heidelberg.de/content/bosch-small-traffic-lights-dataset`
- ImageNet: `http://www.image-net.org/`
- Inception paper: `https://static.googleusercontent.com/media/research.google.com/en//pubs/archive/43022.pdf`
- AlexNet paper: `https://papers.nips.cc/paper/4824-imagenet-classification-with-deep-convolutional-neural-networks.pdf`

8
Behavioral Cloning

In this chapter, we are going to train a neural network to control the steering wheel of a car, effectively teaching it how to drive a car! Hopefully, you will be surprised by how simple the core of this task is, thanks to deep learning.

To achieve our goal, we will have to modify one of the examples of the CARLA simulator, first to save the images required to create the dataset, then to use our neural network to drive. Our neural network will be inspired by the architecture of Nvidia DAVE-2, and we will also see how to better visualize where the neural network focuses its attention.

In this chapter, we will cover the following topics:

- Teaching a neural network how to drive with behavioral cloning
- The Nvidia DAVE-2 neural network
- Recording images and the steering wheel from Carla
- Recording three video streams
- Creating the neural network
- Training a neural network for regression
- Visualizing the saliency maps
- Integrating with Carla for self-driving
- Training bigger datasets using generators

Technical requirements

To be able to use the code explained in this chapter, you need to have installed the following tools and modules:

- The Carla simulator
- Python 3.7
- The NumPy module
- The TensorFlow module
- The Keras module
- The `keras-vis` module
- The OpenCV-Python module
- A GPU (recommended)

The code for this chapter can be found at `https://github.com/PacktPublishing/Hands-On-Vision-and-Behavior-for-Self-Driving-Cars/tree/master/Chapter8`.

The Code in Action videos for this chapter can be found here:

`https://bit.ly/3kjIQLA`

Teaching a neural network how to drive with behavioral cloning

A self-driving car is a complicated ensemble of hardware and software. The hardware of a normal car is already very complex, usually with thousands of mechanical pieces, and a self-driving car adds many sensors to that. The software is not any simpler, and in fact, rumor has it that already 15 years ago, a world-class carmaker had to take a step back, because the complexity of the software was getting out of control. To give you an idea, a sports car can have more than 50 CPUs!

Clearly, making a self-driving car that is safe and reasonably fast is an incredible challenge, but despite this, we will see how powerful a dozen of lines of code can be. For me, it was an enlightening moment to realize that something so complex as driving could be coded in such a simple way. But I should not have been surprised because, with deep learning, data is more important than the code itself, at least to a certain extent.

We don't have the luxury of testing on a real self-driving car, so we will use Carla, and we will train a neural network that can generate the steering angle after having been fed the video of the camera. We are not using other sensors, though, in principle, you could use all the sensors that you can imagine, just modifying the network to accept this additional data.

Our goal is to teach Carla how to make a *lap*, using a part of the **Town04** track, one of the tracks included in Carla. We want our neural network to drive a bit straight, and then make some turns to the right until it reaches the initial point. In principle, to teach the neural network, we just need to drive Carla, recording images of the road and the corresponding steering angle that we applied, a process called **behavioral cloning**.

Our task is divided into three steps:

- Building the dataset
- Designing and training the neural network
- Integrating the neural network in Carla

We are going to take inspiration from the DAVE-2 system, created by Nvidia. So, let's start describing it.

Introducing DAVE-2

DAVE-2 is a system designed by Nvidia to train a neural network to drive a car, intended as a proof of concept to demonstrate that, in principle, a single neural network could be able to steer a car on a road. Putting it another way, our network could be trained to drive a real car on a real road, if enough data is provided. To give you an idea, Nvidia used around 72 hours of video, at 10 frames per second.

The idea is very simple: we feed the neural network a video stream, and the neural network will simply generate the steering angle, or something equivalent. The training is created by a human driver, and the system collects data from the camera (training data) and from the steering wheel moved by the pilot (training labels). This is called *behavioral cloning* because the network is trying to clone the behavior of the human driver.

Unfortunately, this would be a bit too simple, as most of the labels would simply be 0 (the driver going straight), so the network would have problems learning how to move to the middle of the lane. To alleviate this issue, Nvidia uses three cameras:

- One on the center of the car, which is the real human behavior
- One on the left, simulating what to do if the car is too much on the left
- One on the right, simulating what to do if the car is too much on the right

For the left and right cameras to be useful, it is, of course, necessary to change the steering angle associated with their videos, to simulate a correction; so, the *left* camera needs to be associated with a turn *more to the right* and the *right* camera needs to be associated with a turn *more to the left*.

The following diagram shows the system:

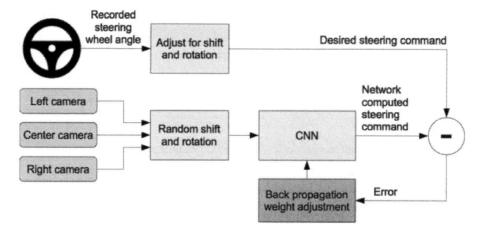

Figure 8.1 – Nvidia DAVE-2 system

To make the system more robust, Nvidia adds random shift and rotation, adjusting the steering for it, but we will not do that. However, we are going to use three video streams, as suggested by them.

How do we get the three video streams and the steering angle? Of course, from Carla, which we will use quite a lot during this chapter. Before starting to write some code, let's get familiar with `manual_control.py`, a file that we will copy and modify.

Getting to know manual_control.py

Instead of writing a full client code to do what we need, we will change the `manual_control.py` file, from `PythonAPI/examples`.

I will usually say where the code to alter is located, but you really need to check GitHub to see it.

Before starting, please consider that the code of this chapter might be stricter than usual on the version requirements, in particular the visualization part, as it uses a library that has not been updated.

My recommendation is to use Python 3.7 and to install TensorFlow version 2.2, Keras 2.3, and `scipy` 1.2, as follows:

```
pip install tensorflow==2.2.0
pip install keras==2.3.1
pip install scipy==1.2.3
```

If you now look at `manual_control.py`, the first thing that you might notice is this block of code:

```
try:
  sys.path.append(glob.glob('../carla/dist/carla-*%d.%d-%s.egg'
% (
    sys.version_info.major,
    sys.version_info.minor,
    'win-amd64' if os.name == 'nt' else 'linux-x86_64'))[0])
except IndexError:
  pass
```

It loads an `egg` file containing the code for Carla, which is located in the `PythonAPI/carla/dist/` folder. As an alternative, you can also install Carla using a command such as the following, of course with the name of your `egg` file:

```
python -m easy_install carla-0.9.9-py3.7-win-amd64.egg
```

After this, you will probably notice that the code is organized into the following classes:

- `World`: The virtual world where our vehicle moves, which includes the map and all the actors (vehicles, pedestrians, and sensors).
- `KeyboardControl`: This reacts to the keys pressed by the user, and it has some logic to convert the binary on/off keys for steering, braking, and accelerating to a wider range of values, based on how long they are pressed for, making the car much easier to control.
- `HUD`: This renders all the information related to the simulation, such as speed, steering, and throttle, and it manages the notifications that can show some information to the user, for a few seconds.
- `FadingText`: This class is used by the HUD class to show notifications that disappear after a few seconds.
- `HelpText`: This class displays some text using `pygame`, a gaming library used by Carla.
- `CollisionSensor`: This is a sensor that is able to detect collisions.
- `LaneInvasionSensor`: This is a sensor that is able to detect that you crossed a lane line.
- `GnssSensor`: This is a GPS/GNSS sensor that provides the GNSS position inside the OpenDRIVE map.

- `IMUSensor`: This is the inertial measurement unit, which uses a gyroscope to detect the accelerations applied to the car.
- `RadarSensor`: A radar, providing a two-dimensional map of the elements detected, including their speed.
- `CameraManager`: This is a class that manages the camera and prints it.

There are also a couple of other notable methods:

- `main()`: This is mostly dedicated to parsing the arguments received by the OS.
- `game_loop()`: This mostly initializes pygame, the Carla client, and all the related objects, and it also implements the game loop, where, 60 times per second, the keys are analyzed and the most updated image is shown on the screen.

The visualization of the frame is triggered by `game_loop()`, with the following line:

```
world.render(display)
```

The `world.render()` method calls `CameraManager.render()`, which displays the last frame available.

If you checked the code, you may have noticed that Carla uses a weak reference to avoid circular references. A **weak reference** is a reference that does not prevent an object from being garbage-collected, which is useful in some scenarios, such as a cache.

When you work with Carla, there is one important thing to consider. Some of your code runs on the server, while some of it runs on the client, and it might not be easy to draw a line between the two. This can have unintended consequences, such as your model running 10 to 30 times slower, probably because it is serialized to the server, though this is just my speculation after seeing this problem. For this reason, I run my inference in the `game_loop()` method, which surely runs on the client.

This also means that the frames are computed on the server and sent to the client.

An unfortunate additional thing to consider is that the API of Carla is not stable, and version 0.9.0 removed many functionalities that should be added back soon.

The documentation is also not particularly updated with these missing APIs, so don't be surprised if things don't work as expected. Hopefully, this will be fixed soon. In the meantime, you can use an older version. We used Carla 0.9.9.2, and there are still some rough edges, but it is good enough for our needs.

Now that we know more about CARLA, let's see how we can record our dataset, starting with only one video stream.

Recording one video stream

In principle, recording one video stream with Carla is very simple, because there is already an option to do so. If you run `manual_control.py`, from the `PythonAPI/examples` directory, when you press *R*, it starts to record.

The problem is that we also want the steering angle. Normally, you could save this data in a database of some type, a CSV file, or a pickle file. To keep things simpler and focused on the core task, we will just add the steering angle and some other data to the filename. This makes it a bit easier for you to build the dataset, as you might want to record multiple runs dedicated to fixing a specific problem, and you can just move the files to a new directory and easily preserve all the information without having to update the path on a database.

But if you don't like it, feel free to use a better system.

We could write a client from scratch that integrates with the Carla server and does what we need, but for simplicity and to better isolate the changes required, we will just copy `manual_control.py` to a file called `manual_control_recording.py`, and we will just add what we need.

Please remember that this file should run in the `PythonAPI/examples` directory.

The first thing that we want to do is change track to `Town04`, because it is more interesting than the default track:

```
client.load_world('Town04')
client.reload_world()
```

The previous code needs to go in the `game_loop()` method.

The variable client is clearly the client connecting to the Carla server.

We also need to change the spawn point (the place where the simulation starts) to be fixed, because normally, this changes every time:

```
spawn_point = spawn_points[0] if spawn_points else carla.Transform()
```

Now, we need to change the name of the file. While we are at it, we will not only save the steering angle, but also the throttle and the brake. We will not use them, but if you want to experiment, they will be there for you. The following method should be defined in the `CameraManager` class:

```
def set_last_controls(self, control):
    self.last_steer = control.steer
```

```
            self.last_throttle = control.throttle
            self.last_brake = control.brake
```

Now, we can save the file as follows:

```
image.save_to_disk('_out/%08d_%s_%f_%f_%f.jpg' % (image.frame,
    camera_name, self.last_steer, self.last_throttle,
    self.last_brake))
```

The `image.frame` variable contains the number of the current frame, and `camera_name` for now is not important, but it will have the `MAIN` value.

The `image` variable also contains the current image that we want to save.

You should get names similar to the following:

```
00078843_MAIN_0.000000_0.500000_0.000000.jpg
```

In the previous file name, you can identify the following components:

- The frame number (`00078843`)
- The camera (`MAIN`)
- The steering angle (`0.000000`)
- The throttle (`0.500000`)
- The brake (`0.000000`)

This is the image, in my case:

Figure 8.2 – One frame from Carla, steering 0 degrees

This frame is fine, but not great. I should have stayed in another lane, or the steering should have been slightly pointed toward the right. In the case of behavioral cloning, the car learns from you, so how you drive is important. Controlling Carla with a keyboard is not great, and when recording, it works worse because of the time spent saving the images.

The real problem is that we need to record three cameras, not just one. Let's see how to do that.

Recording three video streams

To record three video streams, the starting point is to have three cameras.

By default, Carla has the following five cameras:

- A classical *third-person* view, from the back, above the car
- From the front of the car, toward the road (looking forward)
- From the front of the car, toward the car (looking backward)
- From far above
- From the left

Here, you can see the first three cameras:

Figure 8.3 – Cameras from above, toward the road, and toward the car

The second camera looks very interesting to us.

The following are taken from the remaining two cameras:

Figure 8.4 – Carla cameras from far above and from the left

The last camera is also somehow interesting, though we do not want to record the car in our frames. We are missing the camera from the right because, for some reason, the authors of Carla haven't added it to the list.

Luckily, changing the cameras or adding a new one is quite simple. This is the definition of the original cameras, the `CameraManager` constructor:

```
bound_y = 0.5 + self._parent.bounding_box.extent.y
self._camera_transforms = [
    (carla.Transform(carla.Location(x=-5.5, z=2.5),
        carla.Rotation(pitch=8.0)), Attachment.SpringArm),
    (carla.Transform(carla.Location(x=1.6, z=1.7)),
        Attachment.Rigid),
    (carla.Transform(carla.Location(x=5.5, y=1.5, z=1.5)),
        Attachment.SpringArm),
    (carla.Transform(carla.Location(x=-8.0, z=6.0),
        carla.Rotation(pitch=6.0)), Attachment.SpringArm),
    (carla.Transform(carla.Location(x=-1, y=-bound_y, z=0.5)),
        Attachment.Rigid)]
```

As a first attempt, we can keep just the second and the fifth camera, but we want them at comparable positions. Carla has been written using a very famous engine for video-games: *Unreal Engine 4*. In *Unreal Engine*, the *z* axis is the vertical one (up and down), the *x* axis is for forward and backward, and the *y* axis is for lateral movements, left and right. So, we want the cameras to have the same *x* and *z* coordinates. We also want a third camera, from the right. For this, it is enough to change the sign of the *y* coordinates. This is the resulting code, only for the cameras:

```
(carla.Transform(carla.Location(x=1.6, z=1.7)), Attachment.
Rigid),
(carla.Transform(carla.Location(x=1.6, y=-bound_y, z=1.7)),
    Attachment.Rigid),
(carla.Transform(carla.Location(x=1.6, y=bound_y, z=1.7)),
    Attachment.Rigid)
```

You could probably stop here. I ended up moving the lateral cameras more to the side, which can be done by changing bound_y:

```
bound_y = 4
```

These are the images that we get now:

Figure 8.5 – New cameras: from the left, from the front (main camera), and from the right

Now, it should be easier to understand that the left and right cameras can be used to teach the neural network how to correct the trajectory, if it is not in the correct location, compared to the main camera. This, of course, assumes that the stream recorded by the main camera is the intended position.

Even if the correct cameras are now available, they are not in use. We need to add them, in World.restart(), as follows:

```
self.camera_manager.add_camera(1)
self.camera_manager.add_camera(2)
```

The `CameraManager.add_camera()` method is defined as follows:

```
camera_name = self.get_camera_name(camera_index)

if not (camera_index in self.sensors_added_indexes):
    sensor = self._parent.get_world().spawn_actor(
            self.sensors[self.index][-1],
            self._camera_transforms[camera_index][0],
            attach_to=self._parent,
            attachment_type=self._camera_transforms[camera_index][1])
    self.sensors_added_indexes.add(camera_index)
    self.sensors_added.append(sensor)
    # We need to pass the lambda a weak reference to self to avoid
    # circular reference.
    weak_self = weakref.ref(self)
    sensor.listen(lambda image: CameraManager._save_image(weak_self,       image, camera_name))
```

What this code does is the following:

1. Sets up a sensor, using the specified camera
2. Adds the sensor to a list
3. Instructs the sensor to call a lambda function that invokes the `save_image()` method

The following `get_camera_name()` method is used to get a meaningful name to the camera, based on its index, which is dependent on the cameras that we defined earlier:

```
def get_camera_name(self, index):
    return 'MAIN' if index == 0 else ('LEFT' if index == 1 else
        ('RIGHT' if index == 2 else 'UNK'))
```

Before looking at the code of `save_image()`, let's discuss a small issue.

Recording three cameras for every frame is kind of slow, resulting in low **Frames Per Second (FPS)**, which makes it difficult to drive the car. As a consequence, you would over-correct, recording a sub-optimal dataset where you basically teach the car how to zig-zag. To limit this problem, we will record only one camera view for each frame, then we rotate to the next camera view for the next frame, and we will cycle through all three camera views during recording. After all, consecutive frames are similar, so it is not a huge problem.

The camera used by Nvidia was recording at 30 FPS, but they decided to skip most of the frames, recording only at 10 FPS, because the frames were very similar, increasing the training time without adding much information. You would not record at the highest speed, but your dataset would be better, and if you want a bigger dataset, you can always just drive more.

The `save_image()` function needs to first check whether this is a frame that we want to record:

```
if self.recording:
    n = image.frame % 3

    # Save only one camera out of 3, to increase fluidity
    if (n == 0 and camera_name == 'MAIN') or (n == 1 and
        camera_name == 'LEFT') or (n == 2 and camera_name ==
'RIGHT'):
        # Code to convert, resize and save the image
```

The second step is to convert the image into a format suitable for OpenCV, as we are going to use it to save the image. We need to convert the raw buffer to NumPy, and we also need to drop one channel, because Carla produces images with BGRA, with four channels: blue, green, red, and alpha (transparency):

```
img = np.frombuffer(image.raw_data, dtype=np.dtype('uint8'))
img = np.reshape(img, (image.height, image.width, 4))
img = img[:, :, :3]
```

Now, we can resize the image, crop the part that we need, and save it:

```
img = cv2.resize(img, (200, 133))
img = img[67:, :, :]

cv2.imwrite('_out/%08d_%s_%f_%f_%f.jpg' % (image.frame, camera_
name, self.last_steer, self.last_throttle, self.last_brake),
img).
```

You can see in the code repository in GitHub that I recorded a fair amount of frames, enough to drive for one or two turns, but if you want to drive along the whole track, you will need many more frames, and the better you drive, the better it is.

Now that we have the cameras, we need to use them to build the dataset that we need.

Recording the dataset

To build the dataset, clearly, you need to record at least the turns that you expect your network to make. The more the better. But you should also record movements that help your car correct the trajectory. The left and right camera already help quite a lot, but you should also record a few stints where the car is close to the edge of the road, and the steering wheel is turning it toward the center.

For example, consider something like the following:

Figure 8.6 – Car close to the left, steering to the right

If there are turns that don't go the way you want, you can try to record them more than once, as I did.

Now, you might see the advantage of encoding the steering wheel in the name of the image. You can group these correction stints, or whatever you prefer, on dedicated directories, and take them in and out of the dataset as required.

If you want, you can even manually select a part of the pictures, to correct for wrong steering angles, though this might not be necessary if there is a limited number of frames with the wrong angle.

Despite saving only one camera per frame, you might still find it difficult to drive, above all in regard to the speed. I personally prefer to limit the throttle so that the car does not go too fast, but I can still slow down if I want.

The throttle can usually reach the value of 1, so to limit it, it is enough to use a line of code similar to the following, in the `KeyboardControl ._parse_vehicle_keys()` method:

```
self._control.throttle = min(self._control.throttle + 0.01,
0.5)
```

To increase fluidity, you might run the client with a lower resolution:

```
python manual_control_packt.py --res 480x320
```

You can also lower the resolution of the server, as follows:

```
CarlaUE4   -ResX=480-ResY=320
```

Now that you have the raw dataset, it's time to create the real dataset, with the proper steering angles.

Preprocessing the dataset

The dataset that we recorded is raw, meaning that it needs some preprocessing before being ready to be used.

The most important thing to do is to correct the steering angle for the left and right camera.

For convenience, this is done by an additional program so that you can eventually change it without having to record the frames again.

To start, we need a method to extract the data from the name (we assume the file is a JPG or a PNG):

```
def expand_name(file):
    idx = int(max(file.rfind('/'), file.rfind('\\')))
    prefix = file[0:idx]
    file = file[idx:].replace('.png', '').replace('.jpg', '')
    parts = file.split('_')

    (seq, camera, steer, throttle, brake, img_type) = parts

    return (prefix + seq, camera, to_float(steer),
        to_float(throttle), to_float(brake), img_type)
```

The `to_float` method is just a convenience to convert -0 to 0.

Now, changing the steering angle is simple:

```
(seq, camera, steer, throttle, brake, img_type) = expand_name(file_name)

    if camera == 'LEFT':
        steer = steer + 0.25
    if camera == 'RIGHT':
        steer = steer - 0.25
```

I added a correction of 0.25. If your camera is closer to the car, you might want to use a smaller number.

While we are at it, we can also add the frames mirrored, to increase the size of the dataset a bit.

Now that we have converted the dataset, we are ready to train a neural network similar to DAVE-2 to learn how to drive.

Modeling the neural network

To create our neural network, we will take inspiration from DAVE-2, which is a surprisingly simple neural network:

- We start with a lambda layer, to confine the image pixels in the (-1, +1) range:

    ```
    model = Sequential()
    model.add(Lambda(lambda x: x/127.5 - 1., input_shape=(66, 200, 3)))
    ```

- Then, there are three convolutional layers with kernel size 5 and strides (2,2), which halves the output resolution, and three convolutional layers with kernel size 3:

    ```
    model.add(Conv2D(24, (5, 5), strides=(2, 2), activation='elu'))
    model.add(Conv2D(36, (5, 5), strides=(2, 2), activation='relu'))
    model.add(Conv2D(48, (5, 5), strides=(2, 2), activation='relu'))
    ```

```
model.add(Conv2D(64, (3, 3), activation='relu'))
model.add(Conv2D(64, (3, 3), activation='relu'))
```

- Then, we have the dense layers:

```
model.add(Flatten())
model.add(Dense(1164, activation='relu'))
model.add(Dense(100, activation='relu'))
model.add(Dense(50, activation='relu'))
model.add(Dense(10, activation='relu'))
model.add(Dense(1, activation='tanh'))
```

I am always amazed when I think that these few lines of code are enough to somehow allow a car to drive by itself on a real road!

While it looks more or less similar to other neural networks that we saw before, there is a very important difference—the last activation is not a softmax function, because this is not a classifier, but a neural network that needs to perform a *regression* task, predicting the correct steering angle given an image.

We say that a neural network is performing a regression when it is trying to predict a value in a potentially continuous interval—for example, between –1 and +1. By comparison, in a classification task, the neural network is trying to predict which label is more likely correct and probably represents the content of the image. A neural network that can distinguish between cats and dogs is therefore a classifier, while a network that tries to predict the cost of an apartment based on the size and location is performing regression.

Let's see what we need to change to use a neural network for regression.

Training a neural network for regression

As we have already seen, a difference is the lack of a softmax layer. In its place, we used Tanh (hyperbolic tangent), an activation useful to generate values in the range (-1, +1), which is the range that we need for the steering angle. However, in principle, you could not even have an activation and directly use the value of the last neuron.

The following figure shows the Tanh function:

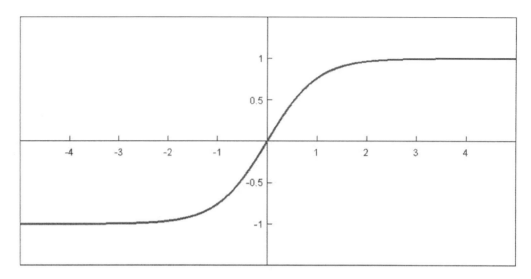

Figure 8.7 – The tanh function

As you can see, Tanh will limit the range of the activation to the (-1, +1) range.

Usually, when we train a classifier, as in the case of MNIST or CIFAR-10, we use `categorical_crossentropy` as a loss and `accuracy` as a metric. However, for regression, we need to use `mse` for the loss and we can optionally use `cosine_proximity` as a metric.

The cosine proximity is an indication of similarity for vectors. So, 1 means that they are identical, 0 that they are perpendicular, and -1 that they are opposite. The loss and metric code snippet looks as follows:

```
model.compile(loss=mse, optimizer=Adam(), metrics=
    ['cosine_proximity'])
```

The rest of the code is as it is for classifiers, except that we don't need to use one-hot encoding.

Let's see the graph for the training:

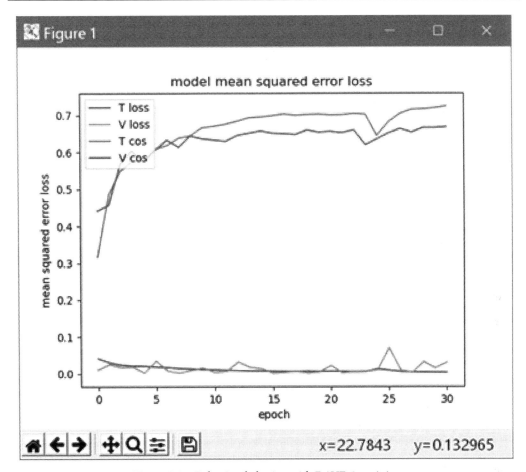

Figure 8.8 – Behavioral cloning with DAVE-2, training

You can see slight overfitting. This is the value of the losses:

```
Min Loss: 0.0026791724107401277
Min Validation Loss: 0.0006011795485392213
Max Cosine Proximity: 0.72493887
Max Validation Cosine Proximity: 0.6687041521072388
```

The loss, in this case, is the mean square error between the steering angle recorded for training and the angle computed by the network. We can see that the validation loss is quite good. If you have time, you can try to experiment with the model, adding dropouts or even changing the whole structure.

Soon, we will integrate our neural network with Carla and see how it drives, but before that, it could be legit to wonder whether the neural network is actually focusing its attention on the right parts of the road. The next section will show us how to do this, using a technique called **saliency maps**.

Visualizing the saliency maps

To understand what the neural network is focusing its attention on, we should use a practical example, so let's choose an image:

Figure 8.9 – Test image

If we had to drive on this road, as humans, we would pay attention to the lanes and the wall, though admittedly, the wall is not as important as the last lane is before that.

We already know how to get an idea of what a **CNN** (short for **convolutional neural network**) such as DAVE-2 is taking into consideration: as the output of a convolution layer is an image, we can visualize it as follows:

Figure 8.10 – Part of the activations of the first convolutional layer

This is a good starting point, but we would like something more. We would like to understand which pixels contribute the most to the prediction. For that, we need to get a **saliency map**.

Keras does not directly support them, but we can use `keras-vis`. You can install it with `pip`, as follows:

```
sudo pip install keras-vis
```

The first step to get a saliency map is to create a model that starts with the input of our model but ends with the layer that we want to analyze. The resulting code is very similar to what we saw for the activations, except that for convenience, we also need the index of the layer:

```
conv_layer, idx_layer = next((layer.output, idx) for idx, layer in
    enumerate(model.layers) if layer.output.name.startswith(name))
act_model = models.Model(inputs=model.input, outputs=[conv_layer])
```

While not necessary in our case, you might want to change the activation to become linear, then reload the model:

```
conv_layer.activation = activations.linear
sal_model = utils.apply_modifications(act_model)
```

Now, it is just a matter of calling `visualize_saliency()`:

```
grads = visualize_saliency(sal_model, idx_layer,
    filter_indices=None, seed_input=img)
plt.imshow(grads, alpha=.6)
```

We are interested in the saliency map of the last layer, the output, but as an exercise, we will go through all the convolutional layers to see what they understand.

Let's see the saliency map for the first convolutional layer:

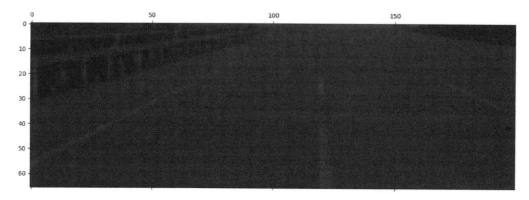

Figure 8.11 – Saliency map of the first convolutional layer

Not very impressive, as there is no saliency and we only see the original image.

Let's see how the map of the second layer looks:

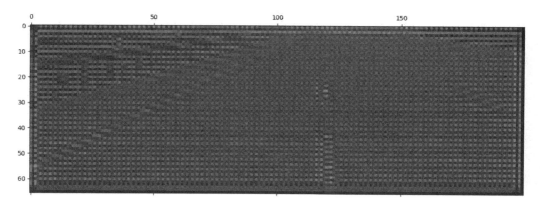

Figure 8.12 – Saliency map of the second convolutional layer

This is an improvement, but even if we see some attention in the middle line, on the wall and the land after the right lane, it is not very clear. Let's see the third layer:

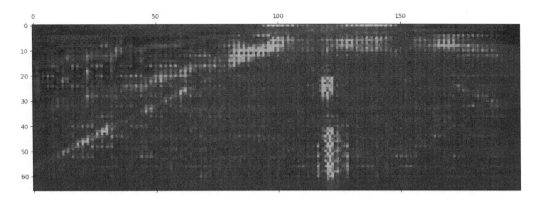

Figure 8.13 – Saliency map of the third convolutional layer

Now we are talking! We can see great attention on the central and left line, and some attention focused on the wall and the right line. The network seems to be trying to understand where the road ends. Let's also see the fourth layer:

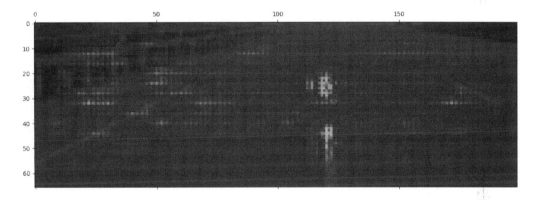

Figure 8.14 – Saliency map of the fourth convolutional layer

Here, we can see that the attention is mostly focused on the central line, but there are also sparks of attention on the left line and on the wall, as well as a bit on the whole road.

We can also check the fifth and last convolutional layer:

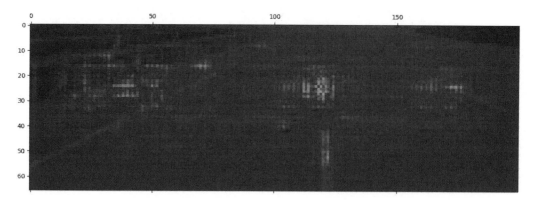

Figure 8.15 – Saliency map of the fifth convolutional layer

The fifth layer is similar to the fourth layer, plus with some more attention on the left line and on the wall.

We can also visualize the saliency map for dense layers. Let's see the result for the last layer, which is what we consider the real saliency map for this image:

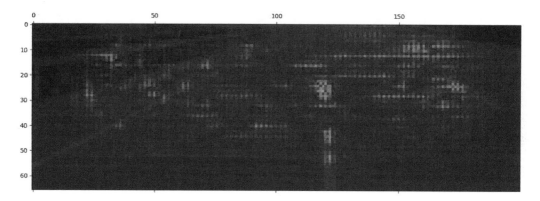

Figure 8.16 – Saliency map of the output layer

The last saliency map, the most important one, shows great attention to the central line and the right line, plus some attention on the upper-right corner, which could be an attempt to estimate the distance from the right lane. We can also see some attention on the wall and the left lane. So, all in all, it seems promising.

Let's try with another image:

Figure 8.17 – Second test image

This is an interesting image, as it is taken from a part of the road where the network has not been trained, but it still behaved very well.

Let's see the saliency map of the third convolutional layer:

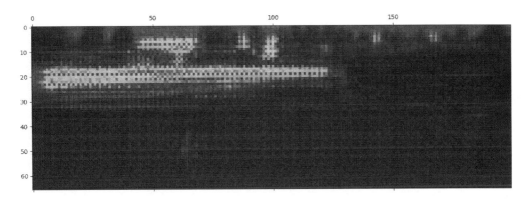

Figure 8.18 – Saliency map of the third convolutional layer

The neural network seems very concerned with the end of the road and it seems to have detected a couple of trees as well. If it was trained for braking, I bet it would do so!

Let's see the final map:

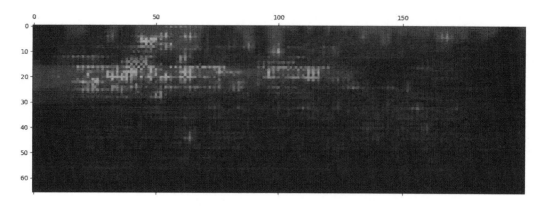

Figure 8.19 – Saliency map of the output layer

This is pretty similar to the previous one, but there is some attention to the central line and the right line, and a tiny amount on the road in general. Looks good to me.

Let's try with the last image, taken from the training to teach when to turn right:

Figure 8.20 – Third test image

This is the final saliency map for it:

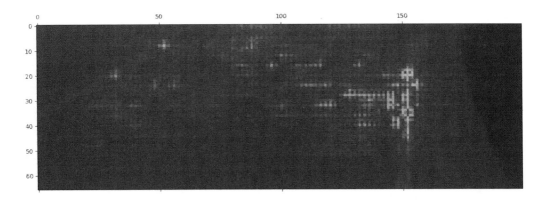

Figure 8.21 – Saliency map of the output layer

You can see that the neural network is giving attention mostly to the right line, also keeping an eye on the whole road and with some spark of attention dedicated to the left line.

As you can see, the saliency map can be a valid tool to understand the behavior of the network a bit more and do a kind of sanity check on its interpretation of the world.

Now it is finally time to integrate with Carla and see how we are performing in the real world. Fasten your seatbelt, because we are going to drive, and our neural network will be in the driver's seat!

Integrating the neural network with Carla

We will now integrate our neural network with Carla, to achieve self-driving.

As before, we start by making a copy of `manual_control.py`, which we could call `manual_control_drive.py`. For simplicity, I will only write the code that you need to change or add, but you can find the full source code on GitHub.

Please remember that this file should run in the `PythonAPI/examples` directory.

In principle, letting our neural network take control of the steering wheel is quite simple, as we just need to analyze the current frame and set the steering. However, we also need to apply some throttle, or the car will not move!

It's also very important that you run the inference phase in the game loop, or that you are really sure that it is running on the client, else the performance will drop substantially and your network will have a hard time driving due to the excess of latency between receiving the frame and sending the instruction to drive.

As the Carla client changes the car every time, the effect of the throttle will change, sometimes making your car too fast or too slow. You therefore need a way to change the throttle with a key, or you could always use the same car, which will be our solution.

You can get a list of the cars available in Carla with the following line of code:

```
vehicles = world.get_blueprint_library().filter('vehicle.*')
```

At the time of writing, this produces the following list:

```
vehicle.citroen.c3
vehicle.chevrolet.impala
vehicle.audi.a2
vehicle.nissan.micra
vehicle.carlamotors.carlacola
vehicle.audi.tt
vehicle.bmw.grandtourer
vehicle.harley-davidson.low_rider
vehicle.bmw.isetta
vehicle.dodge_charger.police
vehicle.jeep.wrangler_rubicon
vehicle.mercedes-benz.coupe
vehicle.mini.cooperst
vehicle.nissan.patrol
vehicle.seat.leon
vehicle.toyota.prius
vehicle.yamaha.yzf
vehicle.kawasaki.ninja
vehicle.bh.crossbike
vehicle.tesla.model3
vehicle.gazelle.omafiets
vehicle.tesla.cybertruck
vehicle.diamondback.century
vehicle.audi.etron
vehicle.volkswagen.t2
vehicle.lincoln.mkz2017
vehicle.mustang.mustang
```

In `World.restart()`, you can select the car of your choice:

```
bp=self.world.get_blueprint_library().filter(self._actor_
filter)
blueprint = next(x for x in bp if x.id == 'vehicle.audi.tt')
```

Carla uses actors, which can represent vehicles, walkers, sensors, traffic lights, traffic signs, and so on; actors are created from templates called **blueprints**. Later, in the same function, the code (which you don't need to modify) creates a vehicle using `try_spawn_actor()`:

```
self.player = self.world.try_spawn_actor(blueprint, spawn_
point)
```

If you run the code now, you will see the car but with the wrong point of view. Pressing the *Tab* key will fix it:

Figure 8.22 – Left: default initial camera, right: camera for self-driving

If you want to start from the point where I was training the car, you should also set the starting point in the same method:

```
spawn_point = spawn_points[0] if spawn_points else carla.
Transform()
```

If you don't do that, the car will be spawned in a random position, and it might have more problems driving.

In `game_loop()`, we also need to select the proper track:

```
client.load_world('Town04')
client.reload_world()
```

If you run it now, after pressing *Tab*, you should see something like the following:

Figure 8.23 – Image from Carla, ready for self-driving

If you press *F1*, you can remove the information on the left.

For convenience, we want to be able to trigger the self-driving mode on and off, so we need a variable for that, such as the following, and one to hold the computed steering angle in the constructor of `KeyboardControl`:

```
self.self_driving = False
```

Then, in `KeyboardControl.parse_events()`, we will intercept the *D* key and switch the self-driving functionality on and off:

```
elif event.key == K_d:
    self.self_driving = not self.self_driving
    if self.self_driving:
        world.hud.notification('Self-driving with Neural Network')
    else:
        world.hud.notification('Self-driving OFF')
```

The next step is resizing and saving the last image received from the server, when it is still in BGR format, in `CameraManager._parse_image()`. This is shown here:

```
array_bgr = cv2.resize(array, (200, 133))
self.last_image = array_bgr[67:, :, :]
array = array[:, :, ::-1]    # BGR => RGB
```

The `array` variable originally contains the image in BGR format, and `::-1` in NumPy reverses the order, so the last line of code effectively converts the image from BGR into RGB, before visualizing it.

Now, we can load the model in `game_loop()`, outside of the main loop:

```
model = keras.models.load_model('behave.h5')
```

Then, we can run the model in `game_loop()`, inside the main loop, and save the steering, as follows:

```
if world.camera_manager.last_image is not None:
    image_array = np.asarray(world.camera_manager.last_image)
    controller.self_driving_steer = model.predict(image_array[
        None, :, :, :], batch_size=1)[0][0].astype(float)
```

The last thing to do is just to use the steering that we computed, put a fix throttle, and limit the maximum speed, while we are at it:

```
if self.self_driving:
    self.player_max_speed = 0.3
    self.player_max_speed_fast = 0.3
    self._control.throttle = 0.3
    self._control.steer = self.self_driving_steer
    return
```

This is all nice and good, except that it might not work because of a GPU error. Let's see what it is and how to overcome it.

Making your GPU work

You might get an error similar to this one:

```
failed to create cublas handle: CUBLAS_STATUS_ALLOC_FAILED
```

My understanding of what's happening is that there is a conflict with some component of Carla, either the server or the client, which results in the GPU not having enough memory. In particular, it is TensorFlow creating the problem, as it tries to allocate all the memory in the GPU.

Luckily, this is easily fixable with a few lines of the following code:

```
import tensorflow
gpus = tensorflow.config.experimental.list_physical_devices('GPU')
if gpus:
    try:
        for gpu in gpus:
            tensorflow.config.experimental.set_memory_growth(gpu, True)
        print('TensorFlow allowed growth to ', len(gpus), ' GPUs')
    except RuntimeError as e:
        print(e)
```

The call to `set_memory_growth()` instructs TensorFlow to allocate only part of the GPU RAM, and eventually allocate more if required, solving our problem.

At this point, your car should be able to drive, so let's discuss a bit how it works.

Self-driving!

Now, you could start running `manual_control_drive.py`, maybe instructing it to use a lower resolution, using the `--res 480x320` parameter.

If you press the *D* key, the car should start to drive by itself. It's probably quite slow, but it should run, sometimes nicely, sometimes less nicely. It might not always take the turns that it is supposed to take. You can try to add images to the dataset or improve the architecture of the neural network – for example, by adding some dropout layers.

You could try to change the car or increase the speed. You might notice that at a higher speed, the car starts to move more erratically, as if the driver was drunk! This is due to the excessive latency between the car getting in the wrong position and the neural network reacting to it. I think this could be fixed partly with a computer fast enough to process many FPS. However, I think a real fix would be to also record higher speed runs, where the corrections would be stronger; this would require a better controller than the keyboard, and you should also insert the speed in the input, or have multiple neural networks and switch between them based on the speed.

Interestingly, sometimes it can somehow also drive even if we are using the outside camera, with the result that our car is part of the image! Of course, the result is not good, and you get the *drunk drive* effect even at low speed.

Just out of curiosity, let's check the saliency map. This is the image that we are sending to the network:

Figure 8.24 – Image from the back

Now, we can check the saliency map:

Figure 8.25 – Saliency maps: third convolution layer and output layer

The network is still able to recognize the lines and the road; however, it is very concerned about the car. My hypothesis is that the neural network *thinks* it is an obstacle and the road is ending.

If you want to teach the car how to drive well with this camera, or with any other one, you will need to train it with that specific camera. If you want the car to drive properly on another track, you will need to train it on that specific track. Eventually, if you train it on many tracks and on many conditions, it should be able to drive everywhere. But this means building a huge dataset, with millions of images. Eventually, if your dataset is too big, you will run out of memory.

In the next section, we will talk about generators, a technique that can help us overcome these problems.

Training bigger datasets using generators

When training big datasets, memory consumption can be an issue. In Keras, one way to solve this problem is by using Python generators. A Python generator is a function that can lazily return a potentially infinite stream of values, with a very low memory footprint as you only need memory for one object, plus, of course, all the supporting data that you might need; a generator can be used as if it were a list. A typical generator has a loop, and for every object that needs to be part of the stream, it will use the `yield` keyword.

In Keras, the generator needs to be aware of the batch size, because it needs to return a batch of samples and a batch of labels.

We will keep a list of the files to process, and we will write a generator that can use this list to return the image associated with it and the label.

We will write a generic generator that, hopefully, you can reuse on other cases, and it will accept four parameters:

- A list of IDs, which in our case are the filenames
- A function to retrieve the input (the image) from the ID
- A function to retrieve the label (the steering wheel) from the ID
- The batch size

To start, we need a function that can return an image given a file:

```
def extract_image(file_name):
    return cv2.imread(file_name)
```

We also need a function that, given a filename, can return the label, which in our case is the steering angle:

```
def extract_label(file_name):
    (seq, camera, steer, throttle, brake, img_type) =
      expand_name(file_name)
    return steer
```

We can now write the generator, as follows:

```
def generator(ids, fn_image, fn_label, batch_size=32):
    num_samples = len(ids)
    while 1: # The generator never terminates
        samples_ids = shuffle(ids) # New epoch

        for offset in range(0, num_samples, batch_size):
            batch_samples_ids = samples_ids[offset:offset + batch_size]
            batch_samples = [fn_image(x) for x in batch_samples_ids]
            batch_labels = [fn_label(x) for x in batch_samples_ids]

            yield np.array(batch_samples), np.array(batch_labels)
```

Every iteration in the `while` loop corresponds to an epoch, while the `for` loop generates all the batches required to complete each epoch; at the beginning of each epoch, we shuffle the IDs to improve the training.

In Keras, it used to be that you had to use the `fit_generator()` method, but nowadays, `fit()` is able to understand if the argument is a generator, but you still need to provide a couple of new parameters:

- `steps_per_epoch`: This gives how many batches there are in a single training epoch, which is the number of training samples divided by the batch size.
- `validation_steps`: This gives how many batches there are in a single validation epoch, which is the number of validation samples divided by the batch size.

This is the code that you need to use the `generator()` function that we just defined:

```
files = shuffle(files)
idx_split = int(len(files) * 0.8)
val_size = len(files) - idx_split
```

```
train_gen = generator(files[0:idx_split], extract_image,
   extract_label, batch_size)
valid_gen = generator(files[idx_split:], extract_image,
   extract_label, batch_size)
history_object = model.fit(train_gen, epochs=250,
   steps_per_epoch=idx_split/batch_size, validation_data=valid_
gen,
   validation_steps=val_size/batch_size, shuffle=False,
callbacks=
   [checkpoint, early_stopping])
```

Thanks to this code, you can now leverage very big datasets. However, there is also another application of generators: custom on-demand data augmentation. Let's say a few words about it.

Augmenting data the hard way

We already saw an easy way to perform data augmentation, using `ImageDataGenerator` in *Chapter 7, Detecting Pedestrians and Traffic Lights*. This could be appropriate for classifiers, because the transformations applied to the image do not alter its classification. However, in our case, some of these transformations would require a change in the prediction. In fact, Nvidia designed a custom data augmentation, where the image is randomly shifted and the steering wheel is updated accordingly. This could be done with a generator, where we take the original image, apply the transformation, and correct the steering wheel based on the amount of shifting.

But we are not limited to just replicating the same amount of images that we have in input, but we could create less (filtering) or more; for example, mirroring could be applied at runtime, and as a result, we duplicate the images in memory, without having to store double the amount of images and saving, as a consequence, half of the file access and the JPEG decompression; though of course, we would need some CPU to flip the image.

Summary

In this chapter, we went through many interesting topics.

We started by describing DAVE-2, an experiment of Nvidia with the goal to demonstrate that a neural network can learn how to drive on a road, and we decided to replicate the same experiment but on a much smaller scale. First, we collected the image from Carla, taking care of recording not only the main camera but also two additional side cameras, to teach the network how to correct errors.

Then, we created our neural network, copying the architecture of DAVE-2, and we trained it for regression, which requires some changes compared to the other training that we did so far. We learned how to generate saliency maps and get a better understanding of where the neural network is focusing its attention. Then, we integrated with Carla and used the network to *self-drive* the car!

At the end, we learned how to train a neural network using Python generators, and we discussed how this can be used to achieve more sophisticated data augmentations.

In the next chapter, we will explore a state-of-the-art technique that can be used to detect the road at a pixel level—semantic segmentation.

Questions

After reading the chapter, you should be able to answer the following questions:

1. What is the original name of the neural network that Nvidia trained for self-driving?
2. What is the difference between a classification and a regression task?
3. What is the Python keyword that you can use to create a generator?
4. What is a saliency map?
5. Why do we need to record three video streams?
6. Why are we running inference from the `game_loop()` method?

Further reading

- Nvidia DAVE-2: `https://devblogs.nvidia.com/deep-learning-self-driving-cars/`
- Notes related to Carla 0.9.0 API changes: `https://carla.org/2018/07/30/release-0.9.0/`
- Carla: `https://carla.org`
- `keras-vis`: `https://github.com/raghakot/keras-vis`

9
Semantic Segmentation

This is probably the most advanced chapter concerning deep learning, as we will go as far as classifying an image at a pixel level with a technique called semantic segmentation. We will use plenty of what we have learned so far, including data augmentation with generators.

We will study a very flexible and efficient neural network architecture called DenseNet in great detail, as well as its extension for semantic segmentation, FC-DenseNet, and then we will write it from scratch and train it with a dataset built with Carla.

I hope you will find this chapter inspiring and challenging. And be prepared for a long training session because our task can be quite demanding!

In this chapter, we will cover the following topics:

- Introducing semantic segmentation
- Understanding DenseNet for classification
- Semantic segmentation with CNN
- Adapting DenseNet for semantic segmentation
- Coding the blocks of FC-DenseNet
- Improving bad semantic segmentation

Technical requirements

To be able to use the code explained in this chapter, you will need to have the following tools and modules installed:

- The Carla simulator
- Python 3.7
- The NumPy module
- The TensorFlow module
- The Keras module
- The OpenCV-Python module
- A GPU (recommended)

The code for this chapter can be found at `https://github.com/PacktPublishing/Hands-On-Computer-Vision-for-Self-Driving-Cars`.

The Code in Action videos for this chapter can be found here:

`https://bit.ly/3jquo3v`

Introducing semantic segmentation

In the previous chapters, we implemented several classifiers, where we provided an image as input and the network said what it was. This can be excellent in many situations, but to be very useful, it usually needs to be combined with a method that can identify the region of interest. We did this in *Chapter 7, Detecting Pedestrians and Traffic Lights*, where we used SSD to identify a region of interest with a traffic light and then our neural network was able to tell the color. But even this would not be very useful to us, because the regions of interest produced by SSD are rectangles, and therefore a network telling us that there is a road basically as big as the image would not provide much information: is the road straight? Is there a turn? We cannot know. We need more precision.

If object detectors such as SSD brought classification to the next level, now we need to reach the level after that, and maybe more. In fact, we want to classify every pixel of the image, which is called **semantic segmentation**, and is quite a demanding task.

To understand this better, let's look at an example taken from Carla. The following is the original image:

Figure 9.1 – A frame from Carla

Now let's look at the same frame produced by the semantic segmentation camera:

Figure 9.2 – Semantic segmentation

This is simply great! Not only is the image very simplified, but every color has a specific meaning—the road is purple, the sidewalk is magenta, the trees are dark green, the lane lines are bright green, and so on. Just to set your expectations, we will not be able to achieve such a perfect result, and we will also work at a much lower resolution, but we will still achieve interesting results.

To be precise, this image is not the real output of the network, but it has been converted to show colors; **the raw semantic segmentation** output is a very dark image with some pixels set to low values, such as `rgb(7,0,0)`, where the 7 will then be converted to purple.

Carla's ability to create images with semantic segmentation is extremely helpful, and can allow you to experiment at will, without relying on premade and limited datasets.

Before we start to collect the dataset, let's discuss what the plan is in a bit more detail.

Defining our goal

Our goal is to use a dataset collected by us to train a neural network from scratch to perform semantic segmentation so that it can detect roads, sidewalks, pedestrians, traffic signs, and more at a pixel level.

The steps required for this are as follows:

1. **Creating the dataset**: We will use Carla to save the original image, the raw segmented image (black image with dark colors), and the converted image to use better colors for our convenience.

2. **Building the neural network**: We will study an architecture called **DenseNet** in great depth, and then we will see how networks performing semantic segmentations are usually structured. After this, we will look at an adaptation of DenseNet for semantic segmentation called **FC-DenseNet**, and we will implement it.

3. **Training the neural network**: Here, we will train the network and evaluate the result; the training could easily take several hours.

We will now see the changes required to collect the dataset.

Collecting the dataset

We have already seen how to record images from Carla and modify `manual_control.py` in *Chapter 8, Behavioral Cloning*, and you could do that, but we have an issue: we really want the RGB and raw cameras to be the exact same frame to avoid movements that would make our dataset less effective. This problem can be solved using synchronous mode, where Carla waits for all the sensors to be ready before sending them to the client, which ensures perfect correspondence between the three cameras that we are going to save: RGB, raw segmentation, and colored segmentation.

This time, we will modify another file, `synchronous_mode.py`, as it is more suitable for this task.

I will be specifying where each block of code is located in the file, but it is recommended that you go to GitHub and check out the full code there.

This file is much simpler than `manual_control.py`, and there are basically two interesting parts:

- `CarlaSyncMode`, a class that enables the synchronized mode
- `main()`, which initializes the world (the objects representing the track, the weather, and the vehicles) and the cameras, and then moves the car, drawing it on the screen

If you run it, you will see that this file self-drives the car, possibly at a very high speed, merging the RGB camera and semantic segmentation:

Figure 9.3 – Output of synchronous_mode.py

Don't be too impressed by the self-driving algorithm because, while very handy for us, it's also very limited.

Carla has a high number of **waypoints**, which are 3D-directed points. These points, which number in the thousands per track, follow the road and are taken from the OpenDRIVE map; OpenDRIVE is an open file format that Carla uses to describe the road. These points are oriented with the road, so if you move the car toward the points while also applying the orientations of these points, the car effectively moves as if it was self-driving. Brilliant! Until you add cars and walkers; then you start to get frames like these ones, because the car will move into other vehicles:

Figure 9.4 – Frames with a collision

This might be a bit surprising when you see it, but it is still fine for our task, so it is not a big problem.

Let's now see how we need to modify synchronous_mode.py.

Modifying synchronous_mode.py

All the following changes need to be made in the main() function:

- We will change the camera position to be the same one that we used with the behavioral cloning, although this is not required. This involves changing the two calls to carla.Transform() with this line (it's the same line for both the locations):

```
carla.Transform(carla.Location(x=1.6, z=1.7),
        carla.Rotation(pitch=-15))
```

- Just after moving the car, we can save the RGB camera and the raw semantic segmentation image:

  ```
  save_img(image_rgb, '_out/rgb/rgb_%08d.png' %
      image_rgb.frame)
  save_img(image_semseg, '_out/seg_raw/seg_raw_%08d.png' %
      image_rgb.frame)
  ```

- In the code, the line immediately after calls `image_semseg.convert()` to convert the raw image to the colored version, according to the CityScapes palette; now we can save the image with semantic segmentation so that it is properly colored:

  ```
  save_img(image_semseg, '_out/seg/seg_%08d.png' %
      image_rgb.frame)
  ```

- We are almost done. We just need to write the `save_img()` function:

  ```
  def save_img(image, path):
      array = np.frombuffer(image.raw_data, dtype=np.
  dtype("uint8"))
      array = np.reshape(array, (image.height, image.width,
  4))
      array = array[:, :, :3]
      img = cv2.resize(array, (160, 160),
          interpolation=cv2.INTER_NEAREST)
      cv2.imwrite(path, img)
  ```

The first lines of the preceding steps of code convert the image of Carla from a buffer to a NumPy array and select the first three channels, dropping the fourth one (the transparency channel). Then we resize the image to 160 X 160 using the INTER_NEAREST algorithm to avoid smoothing the image while resizing.

The last line saves the image.

> **Tip: Resize segmentation masks using the nearest-neighbor algorithm**
>
> Are you wondering why we resize using `INTER_NEAREST`, the nearest-neighbor algorithm, which is the most basic interpolation? The reason is that it does not interpolate the color but chooses the color of the pixel closer to the interpolated position, and this is important for the raw semantic segmentation. For example, let's say we are scaling four pixels down to one. Two of the pixels have a value of 7 (roads) and the other two pixels have a value of 9 (vegetation). We might be happy with the output being either 7 or 9, but we surely don't want it to be 8 (sidewalks)!
>
> But for RGB and colored segmentation, you can use more advanced interpolations.

This is everything that is required to collect images. The 160 X 160 resolution is the one I chose for my network, and we will discuss this choice later. If you use another resolution, please adjust the settings accordingly.

You can also save at full resolution, but then you have to either write a program to change it later or do this when you train the neural network, and since we will be using a generator, this means that we need to use this convention for every image and for every epoch—so more than 50,000 times in our case—plus it will make loading the JPEG slower, which also needs to be performed 50,000 times in our case.

Now that we have the dataset, we can build the neural network. Let's start with the architecture of DenseNet, which is the foundation of our model.

Understanding DenseNet for classification

DenseNet is a fascinating architecture of neural networks that is designed to be flexible, memory efficient, effective, and also relatively simple. There are really a lot of things to like about DenseNet.

The DenseNet architecture is designed to build very deep networks, solving the problem of the *vanishing gradient* with techniques derived from ResNet. Our implementation will reach 50 layers, but you can easily build a deeper network. In fact, Keras has three types of DenseNet trained on ImageNet, with 121, 169, and 201 layers, respectively. DenseNet also solves the problem of *dead neurons*, when you have neurons that are basically not active. The next section will show a high-level overview of DenseNet.

DenseNet from a bird's-eye view

For the moment, we will focus on DenseNet as a classifier, which is not what we are going to implement, but it is useful as a concept to start to understand it. The high-level architecture of DenseNet is illustrated in the following diagram:

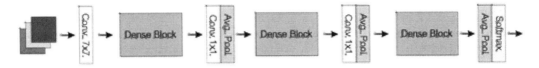

Figure 9.5 – High-level view of DenseNet as a classifier, with three dense blocks

The figure only shows three dense blocks, but there are usually a few more.

As you can see from the diagram, it is quite simple to understand the following:

- The input is an RGB image.
- There is an initial 7 X 7 convolution.
- There is a **dense block**, which contains some convolutions. We will describe this in depth soon.
- Every **dense block** is followed by a 1 X 1 convolution and an average pooling, which reduces the image size.
- The last **dense block** is followed directly by the average pooling.
- At the end, there is a dense (fully connected) layer with a **softmax**.

The 1 X 1 convolution can be used to reduce the number of channels to speed up the computations. The 1 X 1 convolution followed by the average pooling is called a **transition layer** by the DenseNet paper, and when the number of channels is reduced, they call the resulting network **DenseNet-C**, where the C means *compression* and the convolution layer is called the **compression layer**.

As a classifier, this high-level architecture is not particularly remarkable, but as you might have guessed, the innovation is in the dense blocks, which are the focus of the next section.

Understanding the dense blocks

The dense blocks give the name to the architecture and are the main part of DenseNet; they contain the convolutions, and you usually have several of them, depending on the resolution, the precision that you want to achieve, and the performance and training time. Please note that they are unrelated to the dense layers that we have already met.

The dense blocks are blocks that we can repeat to increase the depth of the network, and they achieve the following goals:

- They solve the *vanishing gradient* problem, allowing us to make very deep networks.
- They are very efficient, using a relatively small number of parameters.
- They solve the *dead neurons* problem, meaning that all the convolutions contribute to the final result, and we don't waste CPU and memory on neurons that are basically useless.

These are big goals, goals that many architectures struggle to achieve. So let's see how DenseNet can do what many other architectures cannot. The following is a dense block:

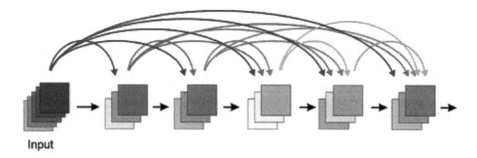

Figure 9.6 – Dense block with five convolutions, plus the input

This is indeed remarkable, and requires some explanation. Perhaps you remember **ResNet** from *Chapter 7, Detecting Pedestrians and Traffic Lights*, a neural network built by Microsoft that had a feature called *skip connections*, shortcuts that could allow a layer to skip other layers, helping to solve the vanishing gradient problem and therefore achieve deeper networks. In fact, some versions of ResNet can have more than 1,000 layers!

DenseNet brings this concept to the extreme, as inside every dense block, each convolutional layer is connected and concatenated to the other convolutional layers of the same block! This has two very important implications:

- The presence of the skip connections clearly achieves the same effect of the skip connections in ResNet, making deeper networks much easier to train.
- Thanks to the skip connections, the features of each layer can be reused by the following layers, making the network very efficient and greatly reducing the number of parameters compared to other architectures.

The feature's reuse can be better appreciated with the following diagram, which explains the effect of the dense block, focusing on the channels instead of the skip connections:

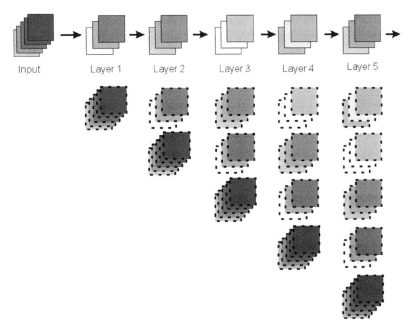

Figure 9.7 – Effects of the skip connections on a dense block with five layers and a growth rate of three

The first horizontal line shows the new features that are added by each convolution, while all the other horizontal lines are convolutions provided by the previous layers, and they are reused thanks to the skip connections.

Analyzing the diagram, where the content of each layer is a column, we can see the following:

- The input layer has 5 channels.
- Layer 1 adds 3 new channels and reuses the input, so it effectively has 8 channels.
- Layer 2 adds 3 new channels and reuses the input and layer 1, so it effectively has 11 channels.
- This continues until layer 5, which adds 3 new channels and reuses the input and layers 1, 2, 3, and 4, so it effectively has 20 channels.

This is very powerful, because the convolutions can reuse the previous layers, adding only some new channels, with the result that the network is compact and efficient. In addition, these new channels are going to provide new information because they have direct access to the previous layers, which means that they won't somehow replicate the same information or lose contact with what was already computed a few layers before. The number of new channels added on each layer is called the **growth rate**; it was **3** in our example, while in real life it will probably be 12, 16, or more.

For the dense blocks to work, all the convolution need to use padding with the value **same**, which, as we know, keeps the resolution unchanged.

Every dense block is followed by a transition layer with average pooling, which reduces the resolution; as skip connections require the resolution of the convolutions to be the same, this means that we can only have skip connections inside the same dense block.

Each layer of a dense block is composed of the following three components:

- A batch normalization layer
- A ReLU activation
- The convolution

The convolution block can therefore be written like this:

```
layer = BatchNormalization()(layer)
layer = ReLU()(layer)
layer = Conv2D(num_filters, kernel_size, padding="same",
    kernel_initializer='he_uniform')(layer)
```

This is a different style to writing Keras code, where instead of using the model object to describe the architecture, you build a chain of layers; this is the style to use with skip connections, as you need the flexibility to be able to use the same layer more than once.

In DenseNet, at the beginning of each dense block, you can add an optional 1 X 1 convolution, with the goal of reducing the number of channels of input and therefore improving performance; when this 1 X 1 convolution is present, we call it a **bottleneck layer** (because the number of channels is reduced), and the network is called **DenseNet-B**. When the network has both the bottleneck and the compression layer, it is called **DenseNet-BC**. As we already know, the ReLU activation will add nonlinearity, so having many layers can result in a network that can learn very complex functions, which we will definitely need for semantic segmentation.

If you are wondering about dropout, DenseNet can function well without it; one reason for this is the presence of normalization layers, which already provide a regularization effect, and so their combination with dropout is not particularly effective. In addition, the presence of dropout usually requires us to increase the size of the network, which is against the goals of DenseNet. That said, the original paper mentions using dropouts after the convolutional layers, when there is no data augmentation, and I think that, by extension, if there are not many samples, dropout can help.

Now that we have an understanding of how DenseNet works, let's learn how to make a neural network for semantic segmentation, which will pave the way to a later section about how to adapt DenseNet to perform semantic segmentation tasks.

Segmenting images with CNN

A typical semantic segmentation task receives as input an RGB image and needs to output an image with the raw segmentation, but this solution could be problematic. We already know that classifiers generate their results using *one-hot encoded* labels, and we can do the same for semantic segmentation: instead of generating a single image with the raw segmentation, the network can create a series of *one-hot encoded* images. In our case, as we need 13 classes, the network will output 13 RGB images, one per label, with the following features:

- One image describes only one label.
- The pixels belonging to the label have a value of 1 in the red channel, while all the other pixels are marked as 0.

Each given pixel can be 1 only in one image; it will be 0 in all the remaining images. This is a difficult task, but it does not necessarily require particular architectures: a series of convolutional layers with *same* padding can do it; however, their cost quickly becomes computationally expensive, and you might also have problems fitting the model in memory. As a consequence, there has been a push to improve this architecture.

As we already know, a typical way to solve this problem is to use a form of pooling to reduce the resolution while adding layers and channels. This works for classification, but as we need to generate an image with the same resolution as the input, we need a way to *go back* to that resolution. One way to do this is by using a **transposed convolution**, also called **deconvolution**, which is a transformation going in the opposite direction of a convolution that is able to increase the resolution of the output.

If you add a series of convolutions and a series of deconvolutions, the resulting network is U-shaped, with the left side starting from the input, adding convolutions and channels while reducing the resolution, and the right side having a series of deconvolutions that bring the resolution back to the original one. This can be more efficient than using only convolutions of the same size, but the resulting segmentation will effectively have a much lower resolution than the original input. To solve this problem, it's possible to introduce skip connections from the left side to the right to give the network enough information to restore the correct resolution not only formally, with the number of pixels, but also practically, at the mask level.

Now we can look at how to apply these ideas to DenseNet.

Adapting DenseNet for semantic segmentation

DenseNet is very suitable for semantic segmentation because of its efficiency, accuracy, and abundance of skip layers. In fact, using DenseNet for semantic segmentation proves to be effective even when the dataset is limited and when a label is underrepresented.

To use DenseNet for semantic segmentation, we need to be able to build the right side of the *U* network, which means that we need the following:

- A way to increase the resolution; if we call the transition layers of DenseNet *transition down*, then we need *transition-up* layers.
- We need to build the skip layers to join the left and right side of the *U* network.

Our reference network is FC-DenseNet, also known as one hundred layers tiramisu, but we are not trying to reach 100 layers.

In practice, we want to achieve an architecture similar to the following:

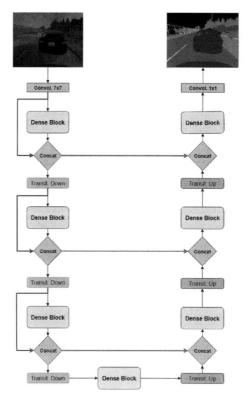

Figure 9.8 – Example of FC-DenseNet architecture

The horizontal red arrows connecting the concatenation layers in *Figure 9.8* are the skip connections used to improve the resolution of the output, and they can only work if the output of the corresponding dense block on the left is the same resolution as the input of the corresponding dense block on the right; this is achieved using the transition-up layers.

Let's now see how to implement FC-DenseNet.

Coding the blocks of FC-DenseNet

DenseNet is very flexible, so you can easily configure it in many ways. However, depending on the hardware of your computer, you might hit the limits of your GPU. The following are the values that I used on my computer, but feel free to change them to achieve better accuracy or to reduce the memory consumption or the time required to train the network:

- **Input and output resolution**: 160 X 160
- **Growth rate (number of channels added by each convolutional layer in a dense block)**: 12
- **Number of dense blocks**: 11: 5 down, 1 to transition between down and up, and 5 up
- **Number of convolutional blocks in each dense block**: 4
- **Batch size**: 4
- **Bottleneck layer in the dense blocks**: No
- **Compression factor**: 0.6
- **Dropout**: Yes, 0.2

    We will define some functions that you can use to build FC-DenseNet and, as usual, you are invited to check out the full code on GitHub.

    The first function just defines a convolution with batch normalization:

    ```
    def dn_conv(layer, num_filters, kernel_size,
        dropout=0.0):
            layer = BatchNormalization()(layer)
            layer = ReLU()(layer)
            layer = Conv2D(num_filters, kernel_size,
    padding="same", kernel_initializer='he_uniform')(layer)
            if dropout > 0.0:
    ```

```
        layer = Dropout(dropout)(layer)
    return layer
```

Nothing special—we had a batch normalization before the ReLU activation, followed by a convolutional layer and the optional dropout.

The next function defines a dense block using the previous method:

```
def dn_dense(layer, growth_rate, num_layers, add_
bottleneck_layer, dropout=0.0):
  block_layers = []
  for i in range(num_layers):
    new_layer = dn_conv(layer, 4 * growth_rate, (1, 1),
       dropout) if add_bottleneck_layer else layer
    new_layer = dn_conv(new_layer, growth_rate, (3, 3),
dropout)
    block_layers.append(new_layer)
    layer = Concatenate()([layer, new_layer])
  return layer, Concatenate()(block_layers)
```

There is a lot going on:

Convolutions method creates num_layers 3 X 3 convolutional layers, adding growth_rate channels every time. In addition, if add_bottleneck_layer is set, before each 3 X 3 convolutions it adds a 1 X 1 convolution to convert the number of channels in input to 4* growth_rate; I did not use the bottleneck layer in my configuration, but you can.

It returns two outputs, where the first output, layer, is the concatenation of all the outputs of each convolution, including the input, and the second output, derived from block_layers, is the concatenation of all the outputs of each convolution, excluding the input.

The reason why we need two outputs is because the down-sampling and the up-sampling path are a bit different. During down sampling, we include the input of the block, while during up sampling we don't; this is just to keep the size of the network and the computation time reasonable, as, in my case, without this change, the network would jump from 724 K parameters to 12 M!

The next function defines the transition layer that is used to reduce the resolution in the down-sampling path:

```
def dn_transition_down(layer, compression_factor=1.0,
dropout=0.0):
  num_filters_compressed = int(layer.shape[-1] *
    compression_factor)
```

```
    layer = dn_conv(layer, num_filters_compressed, (1, 1),
dropout)

    return AveragePooling2D(2, 2, padding='same')(layer)
```

It just creates a 1 X 1 convolution followed by an average pooling; if you choose to add a compression factor, then the number of channels will be reduced; I chose a compression factor of 0.6 because the network was too big without any compression and did not fit in the RAM of my GPU.

The next method is the transition layer used to increase the resolution in the up-sampling path:

```
def dn_transition_up(skip_connection, layer):
    num_filters = int(layer.shape[-1])
    layer = Conv2DTranspose(num_filters, kernel_size=3, strides=2,
        padding='same',                                   kernel_
initializer='he_uniform')(layer)

    return Concatenate()([layer, skip_connection])
```

It creates a deconvolution to increase the resolution, and it adds the skip connection, which is, of course, important in enabling us to also increase the effective resolution of the segmentation mask.

Now that we have all the building blocks, it is just a matter of assembling the full network.

Putting all the pieces together

First, a note on the resolution: I chose 160 X 160, as that was basically the maximum that my laptop could do, in combination with the other settings. You can try a different resolution, but you will see that not all the resolutions are possible. In fact, depending on the number of dense blocks, you might need to use multiples of 16, 32, or 64. Why is this? Simple. Let's take an example, assuming that we will use 160 X 160. If, during down sampling, you reduce the resolution 16 times (for example, you have 4 dense blocks, each one followed by a *transition-down* layer), then your intermediate resolution will be an integer number—in this case, 10 X 10.

When you up sample 4 times, your resolution will grow 16 fold, so your final resolution will still be 160 X 160. But if you start with 170 X 170, you will still end up with an intermediate resolution of 10 X 10, and up sampling it will produce a final resolution of 160 X 160! This is a problem, because you need to concatenate these outputs with the skip layers taken during down sampling, and if the two resolutions are different, then we cannot concatenate the layers and Keras will generate an error. As regards the ratio, it does not need to be a square and it does not need to match the ratio of your images.

The next thing that we need to do is create the input for the neural network and the first convolutional layer, as the dense blocks assume that there is a convolution before them:

```
input = Input(input_shape)
layer = Conv2D(36, 7, padding='same')(input)
```

I used a 7 X 7 convolution without max pooling, but feel free to experiment. You could use a bigger image and introduce a max pooling or an average pooling, or just create a bigger network, if you can train it at all.

Now we can generate the down-sampling path:

```
skip_connections = []

for idx in range(groups):
  (layer, _) = dn_dense(layer, growth_rate, 4,
    add_bottleneck_layer, dropout)
  skip_connections.append(layer)
  layer = dn_transition_down(layer, transition_compression_factor, dropout)
```

We simply create all the groups that we want, five in my configuration, and for each group we add a dense layer and a transition-down layer, and we also record the skip connections.

The following step builds the up-sampling path:

```
skip_connections.reverse()
(layer, block_layers) = dn_dense(layer, growth_rate, 4,
    add_bottleneck_layer, dropout)

for idx in range(groups):
  layer = dn_transition_up(skip_connections[idx], block_layers)
  (layer, block_layers) = dn_dense(layer, growth_rate, 4,
    add_bottleneck_layer, dropout)
```

We reverse the skip connections because when going up, we encounter the skip connections in the opposite order, and we add a dense layer that is not followed by a transition down. This is called a *bottleneck layer*, as it has a low amount of information. Then we simply create the transition-up and dense layer corresponding to the down-sampling path.

Now that we have the last part, let's generate the output:

```
layer = Conv2D(num_classes, kernel_size=1, padding='same',
    kernel_initializer='he_uniform')(layer)
output = Activation('softmax')(layer)

model = Model(input, output)
```

We simply add a 1 X 1 convolution and a softmax activation.

The difficult part is done, but we need to learn how to feed the input to the network.

Feeding the network

Feeding the neural network is not too difficult, but there are some practical complications because the network is quite demanding, and loading all the images in RAM might not be feasible, so we are going to use a generator. However, this time, we will also add a simple data augmentation—we will mirror half of the images.

But first, we will define a hierarchy where we have all the images in subdirectories of the `dataset` folder:

- `rgb` contains the images.
- `seg` contains the segmented and colored images.
- `seg_raw` contains the images in raw format (numeric labels in the red channel).

This means that when given an image in the `rgb` folder, we can get the corresponding raw segmentation by just changing the path to `seg_raw`. This is useful.

We will define a generic generator that is usable for data augmentation; our approach will be the following:

- The generator will receive a list of IDs—in our case, the paths of the rgb images.
- The generator will also receive two functions—one that, given an ID, can generate an image and another that, given an ID, can generate the corresponding label (changing the path to seg_raw).
- We will provide the index in the epoch to help with data augmentation.

This is the generic generator:

```
def generator(ids, fn_image, fn_label, augment, batch_size):
    num_samples = len(ids)
    while 1:  # Loop forever so the generator never terminates
        samples_ids = shuffle(ids)   # New epoch

        for offset in range(0, num_samples, batch_size):
            batch_samples_ids = samples_ids[offset:offset + batch_size]
            batch_samples = np.array([fn_image(x, augment, offset + idx) for idx, x in enumerate(batch_samples_ids)])
            batch_labels = np.array([fn_label(x, augment, offset + idx) for idx, x in enumerate(batch_samples_ids)])

            yield batch_samples, batch_labels
```

It is similar to what we have already seen in *Chapter 8, Behavioral Cloning*. It goes through all the IDs and obtains the images and labels for the batch; the main difference is that we pass two additional parameters to the functions, in addition to the current ID:

- A flag specifying whether we want to enable data augmentation
- The current index in the epoch to tell the function where we are

Now it will be relatively easy to write a function that returns the images:

```
def extract_image(file_name, augment, idx):
  img = cv2.resize(cv2.imread(file_name), size_cv,
      interpolation=cv2.INTER_NEAREST)

  if augment and (idx % 2 == 0):
```

```
        img = cv2.flip(img, 1)

    return img
```

We load the image and resize it using the nearest-neighbor algorithm, as already discussed. This way, half of the time the image will be flipped.

This is the function to extract the labels:

```
def extract_label(file_name, augment, idx):
    img = cv2.resize(cv2.imread(file_name.replace("rgb", "seg_raw",         2)), size_cv, interpolation=cv2.INTER_NEAREST)

    if augment and (idx % 2 == 0):
        img = cv2.flip(img, 1)

    return convert_to_segmentation_label(img, num_classes)
```

As expected, to get the label, we need to change the path from `rgb` to `seg_raw`, whereas when you augment the data in classifiers, the label does not change. In this case, the mask needs to be augmented in the same way, so we still need to mirror it when we also mirror the `rgb` image.

The trickier part is to generate the correct label because the raw format is not suitable. Normally, in a classifier, you provide a one-hot encoded label, meaning that if you have ten possible label values, every label will be converted to a vector of ten elements, where only one element is `1` and all the others are `0`. Here, we need to do the same, but for the whole image and at pixel level:

- Our label is not a single image but 13 images (as we have 13 possible label values).
- Each image is dedicated to a single label.
- The pixels of an image are `1` only where that label is present in the segmentation mask and `0` elsewhere.
- In practice, we apply one-hot encoding at pixel level.

This is the resulting code:

```
def convert_to_segmentation_label(image, num_classes):
    img_label = np.ndarray((image.shape[0], image.shape[1],
        num_classes), dtype=np.uint8)
```

```
    one_hot_encoding = []

    for i in range(num_classes):
        one_hot_encoding.append(to_categorical(i, num_classes))

    for i in range(image.shape[0]):
        for j in range(image.shape[1]):
            img_label[i, j] = one_hot_encoding[image[i, j, 2]]

    return img_label
```

At the beginning of the method, we create an image with 13 channels, and then we precompute the one-hot encoding (which contains 13 values) to speed up the computation. Then we simply apply the one-hot encoding to each pixel, based on the value of the red channel, which is where Carla stores the raw segmentation value.

Now you can start the training. You might consider running it overnight, as it might take a while, especially if you use dropout or if you decide to record additional images.

This is the graph with the training:

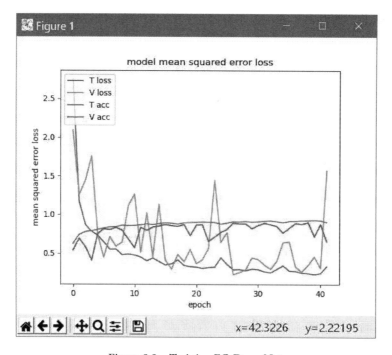

Figure 9.9 – Training FC-DenseNet

It's not great, because the validation loss has many spikes, which indicates that the training is unstable, and sometimes the loss increases quite a lot. Ideally, we would like a smooth, decreasing curve as this means that the loss decreases at every iteration. It would probably benefit from a bigger batch size.

But the overall performance is not bad:

```
Min Loss: 0.19355240797595402
Min Validation Loss: 0.14731630682945251
Max Accuracy: 0.9389197
Max Validation Accuracy: 0.9090136885643005
```

The validation accuracy is above 90%, which is promising.

Let's now see how it behaves with the test dataset.

Running the neural network

Running inference on the network is no different than the usual process, but we need to convert the output to a colored image that we can actually understand and use.

To do this, we need to define a palette of 13 colors that we are going to use to show the labels:

```
palette = [] # in rgb

palette.append([0, 0, 0])       # 0: None
palette.append([70, 70, 70])    # 1: Buildings
palette.append([190, 153, 153]) # 2: Fences
palette.append([192, 192, 192]) # 3: Other    (?)
palette.append([220, 20, 60])   # 4: Pedestrians
palette.append([153,153, 153])  # 5: Poles
palette.append([0, 255, 0])     # 6: RoadLines   ?
palette.append([128, 64, 128])  # 7: Roads
palette.append([244, 35,232])   # 8: Sidewalks
palette.append([107, 142, 35])  # 9: Vegetation
palette.append([0, 0, 142])     # 10: Vehicles
palette.append([102,102,156])   # 11: Walls
palette.append([220, 220, 0])   # 11: Traffic signs
```

And now we just need to derive two images using these colors—the raw segmentation and the colored segmentation. The following function does both:

```
def convert_from_segmentation_label(label):
    raw = np.zeros((label.shape[0], label.shape[1], 3), dtype=np.uint8)
    color = np.zeros((label.shape[0], label.shape[1], 3), dtype=np.uint8)

    for i in range(label.shape[0]):
        for j in range(label.shape[1]):
            color_label = int(np.argmax(label[i,j]))
            raw[i, j][2] = color_label
            # palette from rgb to bgr
            color[i, j][0] = palette[color_label][2]
            color[i, j][1] = palette[color_label][1]
            color[i, j][2] = palette[color_label][0]

    return (raw, color)
```

You might remember that our output is an image with 13 channels, one per label. So you can see that we get the label from these channels using `argmax`; this label is used directly for the raw image, where it is stored in the red channel, whereas for the colored segmentation image, we store the color from the palette, using `label` as index, exchanging the blue and the red channel because OpenCV is in BGR.

Let's see how it performs, bearing in mind that these images are very similar to the ones that the network saw during training.

The following is the result for one image, with other versions of the segmented picture:

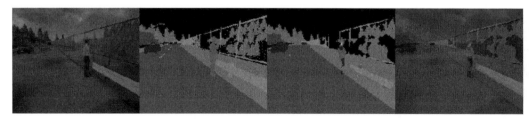

Figure 9.10 – From the left: RGB image, ground truth from Carla, colored segmentation mask, and segmentation in overlay

As you can see from the image, it is not perfect, but it does a good job: the road is detected properly and the guard rail and trees are kind of fine, and the pedestrian is detected, but not very well. Surely we can improve this.

Let's look at another problematic image:

Figure 9.11 – From the left: RGB image, ground truth from Carla, colored segmentation mask, and segmentation in overlay

The previous image is quite challenging, as the road is dark and the cars are also dark, but the network does a decent job of detecting the road and the car (though the shape is not great). It does not detect the lane line, but it is actually not visible in the road, so here the ground truth is too optimistic.

Let's see another example:

Figure 9.12 – From the left: RGB image, ground truth from Carla, colored segmentation mask, and segmentation in overlay

Here too, the result is not bad: the road and the trees are very well detected, and the traffic sign is decently detected, but it does not see the lane line, which is challenging but visible.

Just to be sure that it can indeed detect the lane line, let's look at a less challenging image:

Figure 9.13 – From the left: RGB image, colored segmentation mask, and segmentation in overlay

I don't have the ground truth for this image, which also means that although it is taken from the same batch as the training dataset, it might be a bit more different. Here, the network behaves very well: the road, lane line, sidewalk, and vegetation are all very well detected.

We have seen that the network performs decently, but surely we should add many more samples, both from the same track and also from other tracks, and with different kinds of weather. Unfortunately, this means that the training would be much more demanding.

Nevertheless, this kind of result with around a thousand images is, in my opinion, a good result. But what if you cannot get enough samples in the dataset? Let's learn a small trick.

Improving bad semantic segmentation

Sometimes things don't go as you hope. Maybe getting a lot of samples for the dataset is too expensive, or it takes too much time. Or perhaps there is no time because you need to try to impress some investors, or there is a technical issue or another type of problem, and you are stuck with a bad network and a few minutes to fix it. What can you do?

Well, there is a small trick that can help you; it will not transform a bad network into a good one, but it can nevertheless be better than nothing.

Let's look at an example from a bad network:

Figure 9.14 – Badly trained network

It has a validation accuracy of around 80%, and it has been trained with around 500 images. It's quite bad, but it looks even worse than what it really is because of the areas that are full of dots, where the network seems to not be able to decide what it is looking at. Can we fix this with some postprocessing? Yes, we can. You might remember from *Chapter 1, OpenCV Basics and Camera Calibration*, that OpenCV has several algorithms for blurring, and one in particular, the median blur, has a very interesting characteristic: it selects the median of the colors encountered, so it emits only colors that are already present in the few pixels that it analyzes, and it is very effective at reducing *salt and pepper* noise, which is what we are experiencing. So, let's see the result of applying this to the previous image:

Figure 9.15 – Badly trained network, from the left: RGB image, colored segmentation, segmentation corrected with media blur (three pixels), and segmentation in overlay

As you can see, while far from perfect, it makes the image more usable. And it is only one line of code:

```
median = cv2.medianBlur(color, 3)
```

I used three pixels, but you can use more, if required. I hope you don't find yourself in a position where your network underperforms, but if you do, then this will surely be worth a try.

Summary

Congratulations! You completed the final chapter on deep learning.

We started this chapter by discussing what semantic segmentation means, then we talked extensively about DenseNet and why it is such a great architecture. We quickly talked about using a stack of convolutional layers to implement semantic segmentation, but we focused on a more efficient way, which is using DenseNet after adapting it to this task. In particular, we developed an architecture similar to FC-DenseNet. We collected a dataset with the ground truth for semantic segmentation, using Carla, and then we trained our neural network on it and saw how it performed and when detecting roads and other objects, such as pedestrians and sidewalks. We even discussed a trick to improve the output of a bad semantic segmentation.

This chapter was quite advanced, and it required a good understanding of all the previous chapters about deep learning. It has been quite a ride, and I think it is fair to say that this has been a *dense* chapter. Now that you have a good knowledge of how to train a network to recognize what is present in front of a car, it is time to take control of the car and make it steer.

Questions

After reading this chapter, you will be able to answer the following questions:

1. What is a distinguished characteristic of DenseNet?
2. What is the name of the family architecture such as inspired the authors of DenseNet?
3. What is FC-DenseNet?
4. Why do we say that FC-DenseNet is U-shaped?
5. Do you need a fancy architecture like DenseNet to perform semantic segmentation?
6. If you have a neural network that performs poorly at semantic segmentation, is there a quick fix that you can use sometimes, if you have no other options?
7. What are skip connections used for in FC-DenseNet and other U-shaped architectures?

Further reading

- DenseNet paper (https://arxiv.org/abs/1608.06993)
- FC-DenseNet paper (https://arxiv.org/abs/1611.09326)

Section 3: Mapping and Controls

Here, we will learn about mapping and localizing ourselves so that we can control and navigate our car in the real world!

In this section, we have the following chapters:

- *Chapter 10, Steering, Throttle, and Brake Control*
- *Chapter 11, Mapping Our Environments*

10
Steering, Throttle, and Brake Control

In this chapter, you will learn about more methods for controlling the steering, throttle, and brake using techniques from the field of control systems. If you recall *Chapter 8, Behavioral Cloning*, you learned how to steer a car using a neural network and camera images. While this most closely mimics how a human drives a car, it can be resource-intensive due to the computational needs of neural networks.

There are more traditional and less resource-intensive methods for controlling a vehicle. The most widely used of these is the **PID** (short for **Proportional, Integral, Derivative**) controller, which you will implement in CARLA to drive your car around the simulated town.

There is also another method that is widely used in self-driving cars, called the **MPC** (short for **Model Predictive Controller**). The MPC focuses on simulating trajectories, calculating the cost of each trajectory, and selecting the trajectory with the minimum cost. We will walk through some example code that you could implement in place of the PID you will learn.

In this chapter, you will learn the following topics:

- Why do you need controls?
- Types of controllers

- Implementing a PID in CARLA
- An example MPC in C++

By the end of the chapter, you will have gained knowledge of why we need controls, and the skills to select a controller for a given application. You will also know how to implement a PID controller in Python and get exposure to an MPC controller example written in C++.

Technical requirements

In this chapter, we will require the following software and libraries:

- Python 3.7, available at `https://www.python.org/downloads/`.
- CARLA Simulator 0.9.9, available at `https://carla.readthedocs.io/en/latest/start_quickstart/#carla-installation`.
- The NumPy module, which can be installed with the `pip3 install numpy` command.
- A GPU is highly recommended.

The code for the chapter can be found here:

`https://github.com/PacktPublishing/Hands-On-Vision-and-Behavior-for-Self-Driving-Cars/tree/master/Chapter10`

The Code in Action videos for this chapter can be found here:

`https://bit.ly/2T7WnKo`

Why do you need controls?

This may seem completely obvious since you are trying to build a self-driving car, but let's cover it quickly.

When you build a self-driving car, what are you trying to achieve? The ultimate goal is to get the vehicle to move from a start position to a destination by commanding actuators such as the steering, throttle, and brakes. Historically, the commands to these actuators have been provided by you, the human driver, via the steering wheel, and the throttle and brake pedals. Now you are trying to remove yourself as the thing responsible for primary driving tasks. So, what do you put in place of yourself? A controller!

What is a controller?

A controller is simply an algorithm that takes some type of error signal and transforms it into an actuation signal to achieve a desired setpoint for a given process. Let's define some of these terms as follows:

- The **Control Variable** (**CV**) or process variable is the variable that you would like to control.
- The **setpoint** is the desired value of the CV.
- The **error** is the difference between the current state of the CV and the **setpoint**.
- The **actuation** is the signal sent to the process to influence the reduction of the error.
- The **process** is the system being controlled.
- You may see the **process** sometimes called the *plant* or the *transfer function*.

For example, let's say that you are trying to maintain your self-driving car within the bounds of the lane it is driving in. The center of the lane would be the **setpoint**. You first need to know the **error**, or how far you are away from the lane center – let's call this your **Cross-Track Error** (**CTE**). You then need to determine what **actuation** command you need to safely return the car (aka the **process**) to the center of the lane, thereby minimizing the car's CTE. Ultimately, think of the controller as a function that is continually trying to minimize the car's **error** for a given CV relative to the **setpoint** of that variable.

So to achieve this, let's review the types of controllers available.

Types of controllers

There is a vast multitude of controllers that have been invented and implemented in control systems. The following is a sample of the different types of controllers:

- The PID controller and its offshoots
- Optimal control
- Robust control
- State-space control
- Vector control
- The MPC
- Linear-quadratic control

Controllers can also be categorized by the types of systems they are used in, such as the following examples:

- Linear versus nonlinear
- Analog (continuous) versus digital (discrete)
- **Single Input, Single Output (SISO)** versus **Multiple Input, Multiple Output (MIMO)**

By far the most common and widely used controllers in self-driving cars are the PID and MPC. PID controllers are used in SISO systems, while MPCs can be used in MIMO systems. This will be useful to remember when you consider which type of controller to select for your self-driving car. For example, if you only want to control the speed of the vehicle by implementing cruise control, you may want to select a SISO controller such as the PID. Conversely, if you want to control multiple outputs, such as the steering angle and speed in a single controller, you may choose to implement a MIMO controller such as the MPC.

In the following section, you will be introduced to the basics of PIDs in preparation to understand the code you will learn.

PID

The PID controller is the most ubiquitous form of control system, and has more than a century of research and implementation behind it. It has many flavors and subtle tweaks that can be made for specific applications. Here you will focus on learning the basics and implementing a simple controller for both the lateral and longitudinal control of your self-driving car. You will need both longitudinal and lateral PID controllers since PID is a SISO controller. Refer to the following figure which shows a typical PID block diagram:

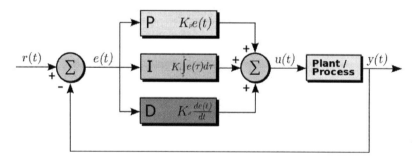

Figure 10.1 – PID block diagram

Let's look at a simple example of controlling the temperature in your home using *Figure 10.1*. Your home likely has a thermostat that allows you to set the temperature you would like. We will call the temperature you have chosen the **setpoint** or *r(t)*. The instantaneous temperature in your home is the **CV** or *y(t)*. Now your thermostat's job is to use the heater/cooler in your home to drive the temperature (the CV) in your home to the **setpoint**. The CV, *y(t)*, is fed back to a subtraction block to determine the **error**, $e(t) = r(t) - y(t)$, between the temperature you want in the home and the current temperature. The **error** is then passed to the P, I, and D control terms, which will each be multiplied by a **gain** value (usually represented by *K*), which are in turn summed together to produce the control input into your heater/cooler. Your heater/cooler has a certain power capacity, and your home has a certain volume of air. The combination of the heater/cooler capacity and the volume of your home determines how quickly your home will heat up or cool down when a new **setpoint** is chosen. This is known as the **process**, plant, or *transfer function* of your home. The process represents how a system's CV will respond to a change in **setpoint**, also known as the *step response*.

The following graph shows an example step response for a system. At time *t=0*, the **setpoint** (shown by the dotted line) is stepped from 0 to 0.95. The response of the system is illustrated in the following figure:

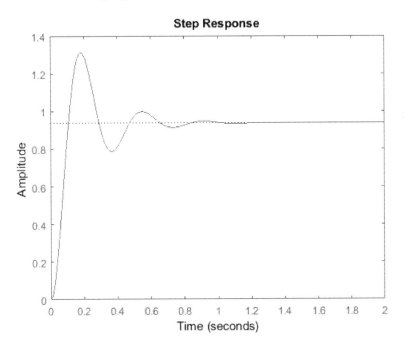

Figure 10.2 – Step response example

We can see that this system and controller combined have created a response that will overshoot the setpoint and oscillate around it unil the response eventually settles on the setpoint value.

Another example of a control system that is more relevant to this book would be the cruise control system in a self-driving car. In this case, the car's current speed is the CV, the desired speed is the setpoint, and the physical dynamics of the car and motor are the process. You will see later how to implement a cruise controller as well as a steering controller.

For now, let's understand what the proportional, integral, and derivative control terms of PID mean.

> **Pedal to the metal!**
>
> Have you ever thought about how you decide how much to press the throttle pedal when you are driving?
>
> What factors determine how much you mash the pedal?
>
> –Is it how fast you are going versus how much faster you want to go?
>
> –Does it have to do with how quickly you are approaching your target speed?
>
> –Do you continually check your speed to make sure you haven't drifted from your target speed?
>
> Think about all of these as we race through the next few sections.

Before we start discussing the P, I, and D control terms, we need to define what the **gain** is.

The **gain** is a scaling factor used to weight a control term more or less heavily in the total control input to the **process**.

Understanding what proportional means

In the cruise control example, you are trying to match your car's speed to a setpoint speed. The difference between the setpoint speed and your car's current speed is called the **error**. When the car's speed is below the setpoint, the error is positive, and when it is above the setpoint, the error is negative:

$$error_{speed} = setpoint_{speed} - current_{speed}$$

The proportional control term simply takes $error_{speed}$ and multiplies it by a scaling factor known as the proportional **gain**:

$$K_P * error_{speed}$$

What this means is that the larger the **error**, the larger the control input to the process, or in the case of cruise control, the larger the throttle input. This makes sense, right?

Let's check this with some actual numbers. First, let's define the throttle as going from 0 to 100%. Next, let's map that to the acceleration of a car, say, that of the Tesla Model X, at 37 m/s2. *Ludicrous Mode*! So, 100% of the throttle gives an acceleration of 37 m/s2.

If your setpoint speed is 100 km/h and you start from 0 km/h, then your current error is 100 km/h. Then, if you want maximum acceleration with an error of 100 km/h, you could set your proportional gain to be 1:

$$Throttle = K_P * error_{speed} = 1 * 100 = 100\%$$

As your error in speed decreases, the throttle would also decrease until you reach a throttle input of zero at the point when the error is zero.

Wait! Zero throttle means we are coasting. This would work great if there was no friction, air resistance, and so on, but we all know that isn't the case. This means that you would never really stay at the target speed and would rather oscillate just below our target speed, leaving us with a steady-state bias:

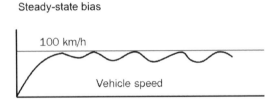

Figure 10.3 – Steady-state bias in a proportional controller

Oh no – how do we maintain our target speed? No fear, we have the mighty integrator that can help bring us up to speed.

Understanding the integral term

Introducing the mighty integrator! The integrator term in PID seeks to address any steady-state bias in the system. It does this by integrating all the past errors in the system. Really, this just means that it is summing up all the errors we have seen at each time step:

$$total\_error_{speed} = total\_error_{speed} + current\_error_{speed}$$

We then take the total error and scale it with a gain, K_P, like we did with the proportional term. Then, we use this result as a control input to the system as follows:

$$K_I \cdot total\_error_{speed} \cdot dt$$

In your cruise control example, the Model X's speed only briefly achieved the setpoint speed and then quickly dipped back down below as the proportional input became zero and the air resistance slowed it down. This means that if you summed up all the errors over time you would find that they are always positive and continue to grow.

So, the further we go in time, the larger the integrator term, $\texttt{total\_error}_{speed}$, becomes. This means that if you choose K_I appropriately, the throttle commanded will be greater than zero even when the instantaneous error is zero. Remember, we sum all the control terms to get the total throttle input. So far, we have the P and I terms, which give us the following:

$$Throttle = K_P \cdot error_{speed} + K_I \cdot total\_error_{speed}$$

Nice! Now you are oscillating around the setpoint instead of being biased below it. But you may ask, *how can we prevent the constant overshooting and undershooting of the speed setpoint, and instead stabilize at a nice smooth throttle application?* I thought you would never ask!

Derivative control to the rescue!

Derivative term

The last trouble you must overcome is adjusting your throttle as you approach the setpoint without overshooting it. The derivative term helps with this by adjusting the throttle based on how quickly you are approaching the setpoint. In terms of the error, this means the rate of change of the error, as follows:

$$K_p * (current\_error_{speed} - previous\_error_{speed}) / (time_{current} - time_{previous})$$

When the preceding formula is simplified, we get the following, where d denotes change:

$$K_p * error_{speed} * d/dt$$

If the error is decreasing – meaning you are approaching the setpoint – the derivative term will be negative. This means that the derivative term will aim to reduce your total throttle since the throttle is now given by the sum of all the P, I, and D control terms. The following equation shows this:

$$Throttle = K_p * error_{speed} + K_I * total_{error\ speed} * dt + K_D * error_{speed}) d/dt$$

Okay, you now know what each part of PID means in real terms. The real trick is tuning your K_p, K_I, and K_D gains to make the car's speed and acceleration act as you want them to. That is beyond the scope of this book, but there are some great references at the end of the chapter for learning more about this.

Next, you will learn about a more modern form of controller that is very popular in self-driving cars today – the MPC.

> **Pump the brakes!**
> What would you call a negative throttle?

MPC

The **MPC** is a modern and very versatile controller that is used in MIMO systems. This is perfect for your self-driving car, since you have multiple inputs such as the throttle, brake, and steering torque. You also have multiple outputs such as the lateral position relative to the lane and the car's speed. As you learned previously, PID would require two separate controllers (lateral and longitudinal) to control the car. With MPC you can do this all in one beautiful controller.

MPC has become popular in recent years due to the increase in computing speed, which allows for the *online* optimization that is required to perform real-time driving tasks.

Before you can learn what the MPC does, let's first contemplate what your magical brain does when you drive a car:

1. You select a destination.
2. You plan your route (waypoints).
3. You execute your route within the bounds of the traffic laws, your car's dynamics and performance (*Ludicrous Mode, engage!*), your time constraints (*I'm late for a life-changing interview!*), and the traffic around you.

MPC works like you

If you really think about how you drive, you are continually assessing the state of the cars around you, your car, the time until your destination, your position in the lane, your distance from the car in front of yours, the traffic signs and signals, your speed, your throttle position, your steering torque, your brake position, and so much more! At the same time, you are continually simulating various maneuvers you can execute based on the current state of traffic – for instance, *there is a car in the lane to my left so I can't go there, the car in front of me is going really slow, there isn't a car in the lane to my right but one is approaching quickly,* and *I need to get to this interview and I am running late*.

You are also constantly weighing the cost of each maneuver if executed, based on the following cost considerations:

- The cost of being late to the interview: high!
- The cost of breaking the law: high!
- The cost of causing an accident: unfathomable!
- The cost of using Ludicrous Mode: medium!
- The cost of damaging your car: *is there something higher than infinity? Let's pick that!*

You then quickly estimate the cost of any of your possible maneuvers:

- *Passing in the left lane means I could crash into the car next to me and potentially cause an accident or damage my car, and still probably miss my interview.* The cost: astronomical!
- *I could continue in my lane behind this sloth of a car. This will make me late.* The cost: high!
- *Passing in the right lane will require Ludicrous Mode acceleration to make sure the approaching car doesn't hit me.* The cost: medium!

You choose the last of the preceding options, since it has the lowest cost of the simulated maneuvers based on the costs you have ascribed to each consideration.

Great, you have chosen a maneuver! Now you need to execute it.

You smash the Ludicrous Mode button for 5 seconds while you cinch your seatbelt until it feels like a boa constrictor and you chop your blinker on as if you were the *Karate Kid*! You grip the steering wheel with white-knuckle fury and then put the pedal to the metal as you visualize the power and majesty of the extra 35 horses that thrust you back into your seat. You simultaneously crank the steering wheel to rail you into the right lane and fly by the sloth with adrenaline and a smug grin plastered on your face as you watch the previously approaching car fading into oblivion behind you!

Now that you are blissfully satisfied with your maneuver, you start the entire process over for the next maneuver and repeat until you arrive safely and on time for your interview! You did it!

MPC pipeline

MPC takes a similar approach to dynamic driving tasks that humans do. MPC simply formalizes the driving tasks into mathematics and physics (with less thrill and excitement). The steps are very similar.

Establish constraints such as the following:

1. The vehicle's dynamic model for estimating its state in the next time step:

- The minimum turn radius
- The maximum steering angle
- The maximum throttle
- The maximum brake
- The maximum lateral jerk (a derivative of acceleration)
- The maximum longitudinal acceleration

2. Establish the cost functions, including the following:

- The cost of not being at the desired state
- The cost of using actuators
- The cost of sequential actuations
- The cost of using the throttle with steering
- The cost of crossing lane lines
- The cost of collisions

3. Next, simulate possible trajectories and the associated control inputs that obey the mathematical cost and constraints for the next N time steps.
4. Use an optimization algorithm to select the simulated trajectory with the lowest cost.
5. Execute the control inputs for one time step.
6. Measure the state of the system at the new time step.
7. Repeat *steps 3–6*.

There is a lot more detail in each of these steps and you are encouraged to learn more by following the links in the *Further reading* section at the end of the chapter. For now, here are some quick guidelines to think about.

Sample time, TS:

- This is the discrete time step at which you repeat *steps 3–7* of the MPC pipeline.
- Usually, TS is selected so that there are at least 10 time steps in the open-loop rise time.

Prediction horizon, N:

- This is the number of time steps into the future for which you will simulate the car state and control inputs.
- Usually, 20 time steps are used to cover the open-loop response of the car.

You can also examine the following figure, which illustrates many of the concepts and parameters you've learned that constitute the MPC problem:

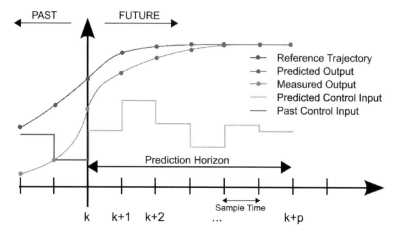

Figure 10.4 – Concepts and parameters that constitute the MPC problem

Here is a quick description of each of the parameters shown in the preceding graph:

- The **Reference Trajectory** is the desired trajectory of the controlled variable; for example, the lateral position of the vehicle in the lane.
- The **Predicted Output** is the prediction of the controlled variable state after the predicted control input has been applied. It is informed by the dynamic model of the system, the constraints, and the previously measured output.
- The **Measured Output** is the measured past state of the controlled variable.
- The **Predicted Control Input** is the system's prediction of the control actuations that must be performed to achieve the predicted output.
- The **Past Control Input** is the actual control actuations that were performed in the past, leading up to the current state.

MPC is a powerful though resource-intensive control algorithm that can sometimes simplify your architecture by allowing MIMO to fit into a single module.

This is a lot to take in at once, but if you have made it this far, you are in luck! In the next section, we will dive into the real code that you can use to control your self-driving car in CARLA using PID!

Implementing PID in CARLA

Congratulations on making it to the truly fun and hands-on portion of this chapter. You have learned a lot so far about PIDs and MPCs. Now it is time to put that knowledge to use!

In this section, we will walk through all the relevant code that is available on GitHub for this chapter:

https://github.com/PacktPublishing/Hands-On-Vision-and-Behavior-for-Self-Driving-Cars

You will learn how to apply the equations and concepts of PID in Python and then interface with CARLA.

First, you will need to install CARLA.

Installing CARLA

The CARLA project has a Linux and Windows Quick Start guide available at https://carla.readthedocs.io/en/latest/start_quickstart/.

For Linux, the CARLA files will be located here:

```
/opt/carla-simulator/
```

Inside this folder you will find a `/bin/` folder that contains the executable simulator script, which you can run with the following command:

```
$ /opt/carla-simulator/bin/CarlaUE4.sh -opengl
```

The -opengl tag runs the simulator using OpenGL instead of Vulkan. Depending on your system setup and GPU, you may drop -opengl. You should see a simulator environment window pop up that looks like this:

Figure 10.5 – CARLA simulator environment opening

For this chapter, you will be primarily working from the examples folders located at the following destinations:

- Linux: /opt/carla-simulator/PythonAPI/examples
- Windows: WindowsNoEditor\PythonAPI\examples

This folder contains all the example CARLA scripts that teach you the basics of the CARLA API. In this folder, you will find a script called automatic_control.py, which is the basis of the script you will be working with throughout the rest of this chapter.

Now that you have installed and successfully run the simulator, you will clone the Packt-Town04-PID.py script that contains the PID controller.

Cloning Packt-Town04-PID.py

You can find the repository for this chapter under Chapter10 at https://github.com/PacktPublishing/Hands-On-Vision-and-Behavior-for-Self-Driving-Cars.

You can clone the entire repo to any location on your machine.

You will then need to link the `Packt-Town04-PID.py` script into the `examples` folder previously discussed. You can use this command in Linux:

```
$ ln -s /full/path/to/Packt-Town04-PID.py /opt/carla-simulator/PythonAPI/examples/
```

Now that you have the script and have linked it to the correct location within CARLA, let's walk through the code and what it does.

Walking through your Packt-Town04-PID.py control script

Your `Packt-Town04-PID.py` code is based on the `automatic_control.py` example script and is pieced together from the relevant snippets of code located in the `/opt/carla-simulator/PythonAPI/carla/agents` subfolders, namely, the following scripts:

- `behavior_agent.py`
- `local_planner.py`
- `controller.py`
- `agent.py`

This is a very good way to learn how to interact with the CARLA simulator and learn the API without having to write everything from scratch.

Finding the CARLA module

If you now look at `Packt-Town04-PID.py`, the first thing that you might notice after the usual imports is this block of code:

```
try:
    sys.path.append(glob.glob('../carla/dist/carla-*%d.%d-%s.egg' % (
        sys.version_info.major,
        sys.version_info.minor,
        'win-amd64' if os.name == 'nt' else 'linux-x86_64'))[0])
except IndexError:
    pass
```

This block loads an egg file containing the code for CARLA, which is in the `/opt/carla-simulator/PythonAPI/carla/dist/` folder.

Classes of interest

After this, you will probably notice that the code is organized into the following classes:

- `World`: The virtual world where our vehicle moves, including the map and all the actors (such as vehicles, pedestrians, and sensors).
- `KeyboardControl`: This reacts to the keys pressed by the user and has some logic to convert the binary on/off keys for steering, braking, and accelerating to a wider range of values, based on how much time they are pressed, making the car much easier to control.
- `HUD`: This renders all the information related to the simulation including the speed, steering, and throttle. It manages the notifications that can show some information to the user for a few seconds.
- `FadingText`: This class is used by the `HUD` class to show notifications that disappear after a few seconds.
- `HelpText`: This class displays some text using `pygame`, a gaming library used by CARLA.
- `CollisionSensor`: This is a sensor that can detect collisions.
- `LaneInvasionSensor`: This is a sensor that can detect that you crossed a lane line.
- `GnssSensor`: This is a GPS/GNSS sensor that provides the GNSS position inside the OpenDRIVE map.
- `CameraManager`: This is a class that manages the camera and prints it.
- `Agent`: This is the base class to define an agent in the game.
- `AgentState`: This is a class to represent the possible states of the agent.
- `BehaviorAgent`: This class implements an agent that navigates the world to reach a destination by computing the shortest possible path to it.
- `LocalPlanner`: This class implements a trajectory to follow by generating waypoints on the fly. It also calls the `VehiclePIDController` class with the appropriate gains. This is where the magic happens for this chapter.
- `VehiclePIDController`: This class calls the lateral and longitudinal controllers.

- **PIDLongitudinalController**: This class holds the PID math that you have been learning about for cruise control.
- **PIDLateralController**: This class holds the PID math for steering control to keep your car following the waypoints generated by the `LocalPlanner` class.

There are also a couple of other notable methods:

- `main()`: This is mostly dedicated to parsing the arguments received by the OS.
- `game_loop()`: This mostly initializes pygame, the CARLA client, and all the related objects. It also implements the game loop where, 60 times per second, the keys are analyzed and the most updated image is shown on the screen.

Setting the world

Inside the `game_loop()` method you will find where to set the world map. It is currently set to `Town04`:

```
selected_world = client.load_world("Town04")
```

Car personalization

If you are a car enthusiast who would like to choose your car model and color, you can do so with this code inside the `World()` class:

```
blueprint=self.world.get_blueprint_library().filter('vehicle.lincoln.mkz2017')[0]
        blueprint.set_attribute('role_name', 'hero')
        if blueprint.has_attribute('color'):
            color = '236,102,17'
            blueprint.set_attribute('color', color)
```

Spawn point

The next thing you may want to change is the spawn point of the vehicle in the map. You can do this by picking a different index for `spawn_points[0]`:

```
spawn_point = spawn_points[0] if spawn_points else carla.Transform()
```

Now that you have gone through your customization and understand the layout of the classes and what they do, we will now dive into the meat of this chapter's code – the PID controllers!

PIDLongitudinalController

This is your cruise control and is responsible for actuating the throttle and brake. Do you remember earlier when we tickled your brain and asked what a negative throttle would be called? Well, the answer here is the brake. So any time the controller calculates a negative throttle input, it will actuate the brake with the control value.

Gains

This gains class is initialized with the PID gains that have been tuned by the CARLA team:

```
self._k_p = K_P
self._k_d = K_D
self._k_i = K_I
```

The values are set back in the `LocalPlanner` class in the following code:

```
self.args_long_hw_dict = {
    'K_P': 0.37,
    'K_D': 0.024,
    'K_I': 0.032,
    'dt': 1.0 / self.FPS}
self.args_long_city_dict = {
    'K_P': 0.15,
    'K_D': 0.05,
    'K_I': 0.07,
    'dt': 1.0 / self.FPS}
```

Gain scheduling

Notice that there are different gains based on highway versus city driving. The gains are scheduled in `LocalPlanner` based on the current speed of the car:

```
if target_speed > 50:
    args_lat = self.args_lat_hw_dict
    args_long = self.args_long_hw_dict
else:
    args_lat = self.args_lat_city_dict
    args_long = self.args_long_city_dict
```

PID math

And now for the PID implementation math you have been waiting for! The `_pid_control()` method contains the heart of the PID controller and the calculations that you learned in the *PID* subsection of the *Types of controllers* section:

1. First, we calculate the error in the speed:

    ```
    error = target_speed - current_speed
    ```

2. Next, we add the current error to the error buffer so we can use it later to calculate the integral and derivative terms:

    ```
    self._error_buffer.append(error)
    ```

3. Then, if the error buffer has at least two values in it, we calculate the integral and derivative terms:

    ```
    if len(self._error_buffer) >= 2:
    ```

4. Next, we calculate the derivative term by subtracting the previous error value from the current error value and divide that by the **sampling time**:

    ```
    _de = (self._error_buffer[-1] - self._error_buffer[-2]) / self._dt
    ```

5. Next, we calculate the integral term by summing all the errors we have seen and multiplying by the **sampling time**:

    ```
    _ie = sum(self._error_buffer) * self._dt
    ```

    If we don't have enough in the buffer, we simply set our integral and derivative terms to zero:

    ```
    else:
        _de = 0.0
        _ie = 0.0
    ```

6. Finally, we calculate the control input by summing all the gain-weighted PID terms and returning the value clipped to ±1.0. Recall the math for this is as follows:

$$Throttle\ or\ Brake = K_p * error_{speed} + K_I * total\_error_{speed} * dt + K_D * error_{speed} * d/dt$$

The throttle is commanded if the value is positive, otherwise, the brake is commanded:

```
return np.clip((self._k_p * error) + (self._k_d * _de) + (self._k_i * _ie), -1.0, 1.0)
```

Now that you know the basic math for a PID, you will now see how to implement this in the lateral PID controller.

PIDLateralController

This is your steering control and is responsible for actuating the steering angle.

Gains

This class is initialized with the PID gains that have been tuned by the CARLA team:

```
self._k_p = K_P
self._k_d = K_D
self._k_i = K_I
```

The values set back in the `LocalPlanner` class are in the following code:

```
self.args_lat_hw_dict = {
    'K_P': 0.75,
    'K_D': 0.02,
    'K_I': 0.4,
    'dt': 1.0 / self.FPS}
self.args_lat_city_dict = {
    'K_P': 0.58,
    'K_D': 0.02,
    'K_I': 0.5,
    'dt': 1.0 / self.FPS}
```

Gain scheduling

Notice that there are different gains based on highway versus city driving just as there were for the longitudinal control. The gains are scheduled in `LocalPlanner` based on the current speed of the car:

```
if target_speed > 50:
    args_lat = self.args_lat_hw_dict
```

```
            args_long = self.args_long_hw_dict
    else:
            args_lat = self.args_lat_city_dict
            args_long = self.args_long_city_dict
```

PID math

The math for the lateral control is a little different but has the same basic principle. Again, the math is in the `_pid_control()` method. Let's see how to go about it:

1. First, we find the starting point of our vehicle vector in global coordinates:

   ```
   v_begin = vehicle_transform.location
   ```

2. Next, we find the end of our vehicle vector in global coordinates using the yaw angle of the vehicle:

   ```
   v_end = v_begin + carla.Location(x=math.cos(math.radians(vehicle_transform.rotation.yaw)),
                                    y=math.sin(math.radians(vehicle_transform.rotation.yaw)))
   ```

3. Next, we create the vehicle vector, which is the direction our vehicle is pointing in global coordinates:

   ```
   v_vec = np.array([v_end.x - v_begin.x, v_end.y - v_begin.y, 0.0])
   ```

4. Next, we calculate the vector from the vehicle's position to the next waypoint:

   ```
   w_vec = np.array([waypoint.transform.location.x - v_begin.x, waypoint.transform.location.y - v_begin.y, 0.0])
   ```

5. Next, we find the angle between the vehicle vector and the vector pointing from the vehicle location to the waypoint. This is essentially our steering error:

   ```
   _dot = math.acos(np.clip(np.dot(w_vec, v_vec) / (np.linalg.norm(w_vec) * np.linalg.norm(v_vec)), -1.0, 1.0))
   ```

6. Next, we find the cross product of the two vectors to determine which side of the waypoint we are on:

```
_cross = np.cross(v_vec, w_vec)
```

7. Next, we adjust the angle _dot value to be negative if the cross product was negative:

```
if _cross[2] < 0:
    _dot *= -1.0
```

8. Next, we append the current steering error to our error buffer:

```
self._e_buffer.append(_dot)
```

9. Next, if the error buffer has at least two values in it, we calculate the integral and derivative terms:

```
if len(self._e_buffer) >= 2:
```

10. Next, we calculate the derivative term by subtracting the previous error value from the current error value and divide by the **sampling time**:

```
_de = (self._e_buffer[-1] - self._e_buffer[-2]) / self._dt
```

11. Next, we calculate the integral term by summing all the errors we have seen and multiplying by the sampling time:

```
_ie = sum(self._e_buffer) * self._dt
```

If we don't have enough in the buffer, we simply set our integral and derivative terms to zero:

```
else:
    _de = 0.0
    _ie = 0.0
```

12. Finally, we calculate the control input by summing all the gain-weighted PID terms and returning the value clipped to ±1.0. We haven't seen this yet for steering, but it works the same as for speed:

$$Steering_{angle} = K_p \cdot error_{speed} + K_I \cdot total\_error_{speed} \cdot dt + K_D \cdot error_{speed} \cdot \frac{d}{dt}$$

A negative steering angle simply means *turn left* while positive means *turn right*:

```
            return np.clip((self._k_p * _dot) + (self._k_d * _de) + (self._k_i * _ie), -1.0, 1.0)
```

Now that you have learned how to implement the PID control in Python, it is time to see it working!

Running the script

You should first ensure that you have started the CARLA simulator by running the following code:

```
$ /opt/carla-simulator/bin/CarlaUE4.sh -opengl
```

Then in a new Terminal window, you can run the `Packt-Town04-PID.py` script and watch the magic unfold. The command to run the script is as follows:

```
$ python3 /opt/carla-simulator/PythonAPI/examples/Packt-Town04-PID.py
```

You should see a new window pop up that looks like the following screenshot:

Figure 10.6 – Packt-Town04-PID.py runtime window

Congratulations! You made a car steer and accelerate itself using nothing but a keyboard and your newfound knowledge! In the next section, you will learn how to apply an MPC controller using C++.

An example MPC in C++

A full implementation of MPC is beyond the scope of this chapter but you can review this example implementation written in C++ at https://github.com/Krishtof-Korda/CarND-MPC-Project-Submission/blob/master/src/MPC.cpp.

The following example will walk you through the implementation of an MPC module that you can use in place of a PID controller for both lateral and longitudinal control. Recall that MPC is a MIMO system, meaning you can control multiple outputs.

The following example shows all the basic components and code you'll need to build an MPC controller:

1. First, use the following code to fit a polynomial to your **prediction horizon** waypoints:

   ```
   Main.cpp --> polyfit()
   ```

   Use the following code to calculate cross-tracking errors:

   ```
   Main.cpp --> polyeval()
   double cte = polyeval(coeffs, px) - py;
   ```

   Use the following code to calculate orientation errors:

   ```
   double epsi = psi - atan(coeffs[1] + 2*coeffs[2]*px + 3*coeffs[3]*px*px) ;
   ```

2. Now, we use `MPC.cpp` to structure the vector so that it can be passed to an optimizer. The optimizer takes all the state and actuator variables in a single vector. So, here, you will establish the start index of each variable in the vector:

   ```
   size_t x_start = 0;
   size_t y_start = x_start + N;
   size_t psi_start = y_start + N;
   size_t v_start = psi_start + N;
   size_t cte_start = v_start + N;
   size_t epsi_start = cte_start + N;
   size_t delta_start = epsi_start + N;
   size_t a_start = delta_start + N - 1;
   ```

3. Next, assign all the adjustable weights for your costs:

```
const double w_cte = 1;
const double w_epsi = 100;
const double w_v = 1;
const double w_delta = 10000;
const double w_a = 7;
const double w_delta_smooth = 1000;
const double w_a_smooth = 1;
const double w_throttle_steer = 10;
```

4. After that, you can establish your cost functions based on those weights.

For this, you must add a cost, if you are at the relative state compared to the reference state. In other words, add a cost for not being on the desired path, heading, or velocity, as follows:

```
for (int t = 0; t < N; t++) {
    fg[0] += w_cte * CppAD::pow(vars[cte_start + t], 2);
    fg[0] += w_epsi * CppAD::pow(vars[epsi_start + t], 2);
    fg[0] += w_v * CppAD::pow(vars[v_start + t] - ref_v, 2);
}
```

Then, you need to add a cost for the use of actuators. This helps minimize the actuations if they are not needed. Think of this as the car likes to be lazy and will only command an actuation if the cost is low enough:

```
for (int t = 0; t < N - 1; t++) {
    fg[0] += w_delta * CppAD::pow(vars[delta_start + t], 2);
    fg[0] += w_a * CppAD::pow(vars[a_start + t], 2);
}
```

5. Next, you need to add a cost for sequential use of the actuators. This will help minimize oscillatory use of the actuators, such as when a new driver jumps between the throttle and the brake clumsily:

```
for (int t = 0; t < N - 2; t++) {
    fg[0] += w_delta_smooth * CppAD::pow(vars[delta_start + t + 1] - vars[delta_start + t], 2);
    fg[0] += w_a_smooth * CppAD::pow(vars[a_start + t + 1] - vars[a_start + t], 2);
}
```

6. Next, it's a good idea to add a cost for using the throttle while at high steering angles. You don't want to mash the throttle in the middle of a turn and spin out of control:

```
for (int t = 0; t < N - 1; t++) {
    fg[0] += w_throttle_steer * CppAD::pow(vars[delta_start + t] / vars[a_start + t], 2);
}
```

7. Now, establish the initial constraints:

```
fg[1 + x_start]    = vars[x_start];
fg[1 + y_start]    = vars[y_start];
fg[1 + psi_start]  = vars[psi_start];
fg[1 + v_start]    = vars[v_start];
fg[1 + cte_start]  = vars[cte_start];
fg[1 + epsi_start] = vars[epsi_start];
```

8. Now that we've done this, we can establish the vehicle model constraints based on the state variable and the **prediction horizon** waypoints.

For this, create variables for the state at time t+1; that is, the current time step:

```
for (int t = 1; t < N; t++) {
    AD<double> x1 = vars[x_start + t];
    AD<double> y1 = vars[y_start + t];
```

```
            AD<double> psi1 = vars[psi_start + t];
            AD<double> v1 = vars[v_start + t];
            AD<double> cte1 = vars[cte_start + t];
            AD<double> epsi1 = vars[epsi_start + t];
```

9. Then, create the variables for the state at time t; that is, the previous time step:

```
            AD<double> x0 = vars[x_start + t - 1];
            AD<double> y0 = vars[y_start + t - 1];
            AD<double> psi0 = vars[psi_start + t - 1];
            AD<double> v0 = vars[v_start + t - 1];
            AD<double> cte0 = vars[cte_start + t - 1];
            AD<double> epsi0 = vars[epsi_start + t - 1];
```

10. Now, you need to ensure you only consider the actuation at time t. So, here, we only consider the steering (delta0) and the acceleration (a0) at time t:

```
            AD<double> delta0 = vars[delta_start + t - 1];
            AD<double> a0 = vars[a_start + t - 1];
```

11. Next, you need the constraint of the waypoint line you are trying to follow. This is done by creating a polynomial that's fitted to the waypoints. This is dependent on the number of coefficients. For example, a second-order polynomial will have three coefficients:

```
AD<double> f0 = 0.0;
for (int i=0; i<coeffs.size(); i++){
f0 += coeffs[i] * CppAD::pow(x0, i);
}
```

Using the same coefficients, you can establish the constraint for the desired heading of the car:

```
            AD<double> psides0 = 0.0;
                for (int i=1; i<coeffs.size(); i++){
    psides0 += i * coeffs[i] * pow(x0, i-1);
                }
            psides0 = CppAD::atan(psides0);
```

12. Finally, you need to create constraints for the vehicle model. In this case, a simplified vehicle model known as the bicycle model can be used:

```
        fg[1 + x_start + t] = x1 - (x0 + v0 *
CppAD::cos(psi0) * dt);
        fg[1 + y_start + t] = y1 - (y0 + v0 *
CppAD::sin(psi0) * dt);
        fg[1 + psi_start + t] = psi1 - (psi0 + v0 * delta0
* dt / Lf);
        fg[1 + v_start + t] = v1 - (v0 + a0 * dt);
        fg[1 + cte_start + t] = cte1 - ((f0 - y0) + (v0 *
CppAD::sin(epsi0) * dt));
        fg[1 + epsi_start + t] = epsi1 - ((psi0 - psides0)
+ v0 * delta0 / Lf * dt);

}
```

Great! You now have at least an example of how to code an MPC in C++. You can take this basic example and translate it to any language that you need for your control application. You have another weapon in your arsenal of control knowledge!

Summary

Congratulations! You now have a lateral and longitudinal controller for a self-driving car! You should be proud of what you have learned and applied in this chapter.

You have learned about the two most ubiquitous controllers, namely, the PID and MPC. You learned that PIDs are well suited for SISO systems and are very efficient, but require several controllers to control multiple outputs. Meanwhile, you also learned that MPCs are suited for MIMO systems with enough resources to continually optimize in real time at each time step.

With this, you have trudged through the minutia of the mathematics and models and emerged with your very own PID controller implemented in CARLA and Python.

In the next chapter, you are going to learn how to build maps and localize your self-driving car so you always know where you are in the world!

Questions

Having read this chapter, you should be able to answer the following questions:

1. What controller type is best suited for a vehicle with lower computing resources?
2. What does the integral term of a PID controller correct for?
3. What does the derivative term of a PID controller correct for?
4. What is the difference between a cost and a constraint in an MPC?

Further reading

- Control theory: https://en.wikipedia.org/wiki/Control_theory#Main_control_strategies
- *Self-Tuning PID Controller for Autonomous Car Tracking in Urban Traffic*: http://oa.upm.es/30015/1/INVE_MEM_2013_165545.pdf
- The Twiddle algorithm for tuning PID controllers: https://martin-thoma.com/twiddle/
- *Lateral Tracking Control for the Intelligent Vehicle Based on Adaptive PID Neural Network*: https://www.ncbi.nlm.nih.gov/pmc/articles/PMC5492364/
- *MPC-Based Approach to Active Steering for Autonomous Vehicle Systems*: https://borrelli.me.berkeley.edu/pdfpub/pub-6.pdf
- *Kinematic and Dynamic Vehicle Models for Autonomous Driving Control Design*: https://borrelli.me.berkeley.edu/pdfpub/IV_KinematicMPC_jason.pdf

11
Mapping Our Environments

There are a few fundamental things that your self-driving car needs to navigate the world.

First of all, you need to have a map of your environment. This map is very similar to the map you use on your phone for getting to your favorite restaurant.

Secondly, you need a way to localize your position on that map in the real world. On your phone, this is the blue dot localized by the GPS.

In this chapter, you will learn about various ways for your self-driving car to map and localize through its environment, so it knows where it is in the world. You can imagine why this is important since the entire reason for making a self-driving car is to go places!

You will learn the following topics to help you build a self-driving car worthy of being called Magellan:

- Why you need maps and localization
- Types of mapping and localization
- Open source mapping tools
- SLAM with an Ouster lidar and Google Cartographer

Technical requirements

The chapter requires the following software:

- Linux
- ROS Melodic: `http://wiki.ros.org/melodic/Installation/Ubuntu`
- Python 3.7: `https://www.python.org/downloads/release/python-370/`
- C++
- Google Cartographer ROS: `https://github.com/cartographer-project/cartographer_ros`
- `ouster_example_cartographer`: `https://github.com/Krishtof-Korda/ouster_example_cartographer`

The code for the chapter can be found at the following link:

`https://github.com/PacktPublishing/Hands-On-Vision-and-Behavior-for-Self-Driving-Cars`

The code in Action videos for the chapter can be found here:

`https://bit.ly/2IVkJVZ`

Why you need maps and localization

In this chapter, you will learn the importance of maps and localization, and the combination of them. Maps and localization are things we often take for granted in the modern world, but as you will see, they are very important, especially for self-driving cars, where the amazing human brain is not utilized.

Maps

Take a moment and imagine a world without cell phones, without MapQuest (yup, I'm an elder millennial), without paper maps, and without Anaximander of Greece!

How well do you think you could navigate from your home to a city you have never been to, let alone the new Trader Joe's that just opened a few cities away? I am sure you could do it, but you would probably stop every few kilometers and ask a local for the next few directions to get you closer to that bold and earthy Two Buck Chuck. But you can see why maps really make our lives easier and open up possibilities to venture to new places with little fear of getting lost and ending up at Walley World.

Now, you are very fortunate that companies such as Google and Apple have painstakingly mapped every street, alleyway, and side street you can think of. That is a huge task and we benefit from it every day. Hooray maps!

Localization

Okay, now imagine that you are teleported here:

Figure 11.1 – Monkey Face in Russia. Image source: `http://bit.ly/6547672-17351141`

You have been given a map of the area and need to find your way to the nearest body of water. The first thing you need to do – after you stop shaking from being teleported – is figure out where in the world you are on the map you have. You would likely look around you to pick out landmarks nearby, and then try to find those landmarks on your map. *Monkey Face, I'm right in the middle of the Monkey Face!* Congratulations, you just localized yourself in the map and can use it to find the elixir of life!

Now you see why both a map and localization are necessary for navigating the world and environments.

Now, you say, *But wait, what if something has changed in the world since the map was generated?!*

Surely you have been driving along, following the sweet voice of navigation from your phone when *wham!* You just rolled up to some road construction that has closed the road and is forcing you to take a 30-minute detour. You blurt out to your phone, *Curse you, nav voice from oblivion! How did you not know that there was construction?*

The truth is that your dear navigator voice, no matter how up to date, will always miss real-time information about the world. Just imagine some ducks crossing the road; the voice will never warn you about that. In the next section, you will learn the many ways to save the ducks with various types of mapping and localization.

Types of mapping and localization

The field of localization and mapping is absolutely full of amazing research and is continually growing. The advancement of GPUs and computer processing speeds has led to the development of some very exciting algorithms.

Quickly, let's get back to saving our ducks! Recall in the previous section that our dear sat-nav voice did not see the ducks crossing the road in front of us. A map will never be completely accurate since the world is ever-changing and morphing. Therefore, we must have a way to not only localize using a pre-built map but also build a map in real time so that we can see when new obstacles appear in our map and navigate around them. Introducing SLAM for the ducks (not dunks).

Although there are independent methods for mapping and localization, in this chapter, we will focus on **Simultaneous Localization and Mapping (SLAM)**. If you are curious, though, the following is a quick breakdown of the most commonly used algorithms for independent localization and mapping:

- Particle filters
- Markov localization
- Grid localization
- Extended Kalman filters for range-bearing localization
- Kalman filters for dead reckoning (odometry)

> **Note**
>
> You can read more about localization here:
>
> `https://www.cs.cmu.edu/~motionplanning/lecture/Chap8-Kalman-Mapping_howie.pdf`
>
> `http://robots.stanford.edu/papers/thrun.pf-in-robotics-uai02.pdf`
>
> `https://www.ri.cmu.edu/pub_files/pub1/fox_dieter_1999_3/fox_dieter_1999_3.pdf`

Some example types of mapping are as follows:

- Occupancy grid
- Feature-based (landmark)
- Topological (graph-based)
- Visual teach and repeat

> **Note**
> To read more about mapping, refer to the following links:
> `https://www.cs.cmu.edu/~motionplanning/lecture/Chap8-Kalman-Mapping_howie.pdf`
> `https://www.ri.cmu.edu/pub_files/pub1/thrun_sebastian_1996_8/thrun_sebastian_1996_8.pdf`

There is a lot of great information on these algorithms and implementations, but for this book, we will focus on the most widely used form of localization and mapping, the simultaneous kind: SLAM.

Simultaneous localization and mapping (SLAM)

Let's jump back into our imagination for a moment.

Imagine you suddenly woke up one night and there was absolutely no light, no moon, no glow worms – just pitch black! Fear not, you will use the magic of SLAM to navigate from your bed to get that tasty midnight snack!

You fumble your left hand around until you feel the edge of your bed. Boom, you just localized yourself on the bed and have mapped the left edge of the bed in your mind. You make the assumption that you didn't flip vertically in bed while sleeping, so this really is the left side of your bed.

Next, you swing your legs over the edge of the bed, slowly lowering yourself until you feel the floor. Blam, you just mapped a portion of your floor. Now, you carefully stand up and put your arms out in front of you. You sway your arms in a Lissajous curve in front of you, like Helen Keller searching for a spider's web. Simultaneously, you carefully sweep your feet across the floor, like a modern interpretive dancer looking for any steps, transitions, edges, and pitfalls, so you don't trip.

Each time you move forward, you carefully keep track in your mind which direction you are facing and how far you have stepped (**odometry**). All the time, you are building a mental map of the room and using your hands and feet as range sensors, giving you a sense of where you are in the room (**localizing**). Each time you find an obstacle, you store that in your mental map and navigate gingerly around it. You are SLAMing!

SLAM typically uses some kind of range-finding sensor, such as a lidar sensor:

Figure 11.2 – OS1-128 digital lidar sensor, courtesy of Ouster, Inc.

When you were navigating your room, your arms and legs were acting as your range finders. Lidar sensors use laser light, which illuminates the environment and bounces off objects. The time of flight between the light leaving and returning is used to estimate the range to the object using the speed of light. Lidar sensors, such as the OS1-128, produce rich and dense point clouds with highly accurate distance information:

Figure 11.3 – Lidar point cloud in an urban setting, courtesy of Ouster, Inc.

This distance information is what SLAM algorithms use to localize and map the world.

An **Inertial Measurement Unit (IMU)** is also needed to help estimate the pose of the vehicle and estimate the distance traveled between successive measurements. One reason that Ouster lidar sensors are popular for map creation is that they come with an IMU built in, which lets you start mapping with a single device. Later in the chapter, you will learn how to map with an Ouster lidar sensor and Google Cartographer.

SLAM is the concept of building a map on the fly with no *a priori* information and simultaneously localizing in the map as it is being built. You can imagine that this is very difficult and is a bit of a *chicken or egg* problem. To localize, you need a map (the egg) to localize from, but at the same time, in order to build your map on the fly, you need to localize (the chicken) and know where you are on the map you are trying to build. This is like a problem from a time travel movie: surviving to live long enough to go back in time to save yourself in the first place. Does your head hurt yet?

The good news is that this field has been studied for over 30 years and has borne beautiful fruit in the form of algorithms for robotics and self-driving cars. Let's see what lies ahead!

Types of SLAM

The following is a brief list of some state-of-the-art algorithms used throughout robotics, drone mapping, and self-driving industries. Each of these algorithms has different applications. RGB-D SLAM, for example, is used for camera-based SLAM, while LIO SAM is specific to lidar sensors. Kinetic fusion is another interesting form of SLAM used to map complex objects indoors. A more complete list can be found on the KITTI website at http://www.cvlibs.net/datasets/kitti/eval_odometry.php:

- **LIO SAM**: https://arxiv.org/pdf/2007.00258.pdf
- **LOAM**: https://ri.cmu.edu/pub_files/2014/7/Ji_LidarMapping_RSS2014_v8.pdf
- **RGB-D SLAM**: https://felixendres.github.io/rgbdslam_v2/
- **Kinetic fusion**: https://www.microsoft.com/en-us/research/wp-content/uploads/2016/02/ismar2011.pdf

Next, you will learn about a very important method of reducing error in a SLAM algorithm.

Loop closure in SLAM

One thing to consider with mapping and localization is that nothing is perfect. You will never find a sensor that is perfectly accurate. All sensors are probabilistic with some distribution containing a mean and variance of a measurement. These are determined empirically at the factory during the calibration process and then provided in the datasheet. You may ask, *Why do I care?*

Good question! The fact that the sensors always have some error means the longer you navigate using these sensors, the more your map and the estimation of your position within that map will drift from reality.

SLAM algorithms almost universally have a trick up their sleeve to combat this drift: **loop closure**! Loop closure works like this. Let's say you pass by the Aldar building on your trip to Abu Dhabi:

Figure 11.4 – The Aldar headquarters building, Abu Dhabi, UAE

You register this magnificent circular building into your map and continue on your way. Then, sometime later, perhaps after you grabbed lunch at Li Beirut, you drive back, passing the Aldar building a second time. Now when you pass it, you measure your distance from it and compare that to where you think you are relative to when you first registered it on your map. You realize that you are not where you expect to be relative to it. Snap! The algorithm takes this information and iteratively corrects the entire map to represent where you really are in the world.

SLAM is constantly doing this with every feature it maps and returns to later. You will see this in action when you play with the open source SLAM in the next few sections. Before that, let's quickly show you some of the available open source mapping tools available to you for your mapping pleasure.

Open source mapping tools

SLAM is quite complicated to implement and understand, but fortunately, there are plenty of open source solutions that you can use in your self-driving car. The website *Awesome Open Source* (https://awesomeopensource.com/projects/slam) has a treasure trove of SLAM algorithms that you can use.

Here is a curated selection to whet your appetite:

- **Cartographer by Google** (https://github.com/cartographer-project/cartographer)
- **LIO-SAM by TixiaoShan** (https://github.com/TixiaoShan/LIO-SAM)
- **LeGO-LOAM by RobustFieldAutonomy** (https://github.com/RobustFieldAutonomyLab/LeGO-LOAM)

Since Cartographer is by far the most popular and supported, you will get to play with and experience all it has to offer in the next section.

SLAM with an Ouster lidar and Google Cartographer

This is the moment you have been waiting for: building maps with hands-on experience using Cartographer and an Ouster lidar sensor!

An Ouster lidar was chosen for this hands-on example because it has a built-in **IMU**, which is needed to perform SLAM. This means that you don't need to purchase another sensor to provide the inertial data.

The example you will see is the offline processing of data collected from an Ouster sensor and is adapted from the work of Wil Selby. Please visit Wil Selby's website home page for more cool projects and ideas: https://www.wilselby.com/.

Selby also has a related project that performs the SLAM online (in real time) for a DIY driverless car in ROS: https://github.com/wilselby/diy_driverless_car_ROS.

Ouster sensor

You can learn more about the Ouster data format and usage of the sensor from the OS1 user guide:

https://github.com/PacktPublishing/Hands-On-Vision-and-Behavior-for-Self-Driving-Cars/blob/master/Chapter11/OS1-User-Guide-v1.14.0-beta.12.pdf

Don't worry, you don't need to buy a sensor to get your hands dirty in this chapter. We have provided you with some sample data collected from an OS1-128 for you to use. You will see later how to download the data.

The repo

You will find the code for this chapter in the `ouster_example_cartographer` submodule at the following link:

https://github.com/PacktPublishing/Hands-On-Vision-and-Behavior-for-Self-Driving-Cars/tree/master/Chapter11

To ensure that you have the latest code in the submodule, you can run the following command from within the `Chapter11` folder:

```
$ git submodule update --remote ouster_example_cartographer
```

Getting started with cartographer_ros

Before we dive into the code, you are encouraged to learn the basics of Cartographer by reading the algorithm walkthrough:

https://google-cartographer-ros.readthedocs.io/en/latest/algo_walkthrough.html

Let's begin with a quick overview of the Cartographer configuration files needed to make it work using your sensor.

Cartographer_ros configuration

Cartographer needs the following configuration files to understand about your sensor, robot, transforms, and so on. The files can be found in the `ouster_example_cartographer/cartographer_ros/` folder:

- `configuration_files/demo_3d.rviz`
- `configuration_files/cart_3d.lua`

- `urdf/os_sensor.urdf`
- `launch/offline_cart_3d.launch`
- `configuration_files/assets_writer_cart_3d.lua`
- `configuration_files/transform.lua`

The files referenced here are for performing offline SLAM on a bag collected from an Ouster sensor.

Now, let's step through each file and explain how it contributes to making SLAM work inside ROS.

demo_3d.rviz

This file sets the configuration of the `rviz` GUI window. It's based on the example file provided in the `cartographer_ros` source files:

`https://github.com/cartographer-project/cartographer_ros/blob/master/cartographer_ros/configuration_files/demo_3d.rviz`

It specifies the frames of reference. The details of the various reference frames are available at the following link:

`https://www.ros.org/reps/rep-0105.html`

The following code snippet is where you will add your frame names based on the sensor you are using for your project:

```
Frames:
    All Enabled: true
    base_link:
      Value: true
    map:
      Value: true
    odom:
      Value: true
    os:
      Value: true
    os_imu:
      Value: true
```

The following are the definitions of each frame from the preceding code:

- `base_link` is the coordinate frame of your robot.
- `map` is the fixed coordinate frame of the world.
- `odom` is a world-fixed frame that is computed based on odometry from the IMU, wheel encoders, visual odometry, and so on. This can drift over time, but can be useful in maintaining continuous smooth position information without discrete jumps. Cartographer uses this frame to publish non-loop-closing local SLAM results.
- `os` is the coordinate frame of the Ouster sensor or any other lidar sensor you have chosen for your project. This is used to transform lidar range readings to the `base_link` frame.
- `os_imu` is the coordinate frame of the IMU in the Ouster sensor or any other IMU you have chosen for your project. This is the frame that Cartographer will track during SLAM. It will also be transformed back to the `base_link` frame.

Next, the hierarchy `tf` transform tree of frames is defined so that you can transform between any of the frames:

```
Tree:
    map:
        odom:
            base_link:
                os:
                    {}
                os_imu:
                    {}
```

You can see that the `os` and `os_imu` frames are both related to `base_link` (the vehicle frame). This means you cannot directly transform from `os` (the lidar frame) to `os_imu` (the IMU frame). Instead, you would transform both into the `base_link` frame. From there, you can transform up the `tf` tree all the way to the map frame. This is what Cartographer will do when building the map using the lidar range measurements and IMU pose measurements.

Next, `RobotModel` is configured to display the links (meaning sensors, arms, or anything that has a coordinate frame on the robot that you want to track) in their correct pose according to the `tf` transform tree previously defined.

The following code snippet shows you where to put your link names previously defined in the `Frames` section:

```
Class: rviz/RobotModel
    Collision Enabled: false
    Enabled: true
    Links:
      All Links Enabled: true
      Expand Joint Details: false
      Expand Link Details: false
      Expand Tree: false
      Link Tree Style: Links in Alphabetic Order
      base_link:
        Alpha: 1
        Show Axes: false
        Show Trail: false
      os:
        Alpha: 1
        Show Axes: false
        Show Trail: false
        Value: true
      os_imu:
        Alpha: 1
        Show Axes: false
        Show Trail: false
        Value: true
```

You can see `base_link`, the `os` lidar, and `os_imu` links are added here.

Next, `rviz/PointCloud2` is mapped to the topic for the `PointCloud2` lidar points data, which for an Ouster lidar sensor bag file is stored in the `/os_cloud_node/points` topic. If you are using any other lidar sensor, you would place that lidar's topic name in the `Topic:` field:

```
Name: PointCloud2
Position Transformer: XYZ
Queue Size: 200
Selectable: true
```

```
            Size (Pixels): 3
            Size (m): 0.029999999329447746
            Style: Flat Squares
            Topic: /os_cloud_node/points
```

You can see that the topic from the lidar is mapped as a `PointCloud2` type.

That wraps up the specific configurations for the lidar and IMU sensors in `rviz`. Next, you will see how the `cart_3d.lua` file is modified to match your robot-specific layout.

cart_3d.lua

This file sets the configuration of the robot SLAM tuning parameters. A `.lua` file should be robot-specific, rather than bag-specific. It is based on the example file provided in the `cartographer_ros` source files:

https://github.com/cartographer-project/cartographer_ros/blob/master/cartographer_ros/configuration_files/backpack_3d.lua

You are encouraged to tune the parameters in the `.lua` file based on your specific application. A guide for tuning is available at the following link:

https://google-cartographer-ros.readthedocs.io/en/latest/algo_walkthrough.html

Here, we will touch quickly on some options that you can configure for your self-driving car:

```
options = {
  map_builder = MAP_BUILDER,
  trajectory_builder = TRAJECTORY_BUILDER,
  map_frame = "map",
  tracking_frame = "os_imu",
  published_frame = "base_link",
  odom_frame = "base_link",
  provide_odom_frame = false,
  publish_frame_projected_to_2d = false,
  use_odometry = false,
  use_nav_sat = false,
  use_landmarks = false,
  num_laser_scans = 0,
  num_multi_echo_laser_scans = 0,
```

```
    num_subdivisions_per_laser_scan = 1,
    num_point_clouds = 1,
    lookup_transform_timeout_sec = 0.2,
    submap_publish_period_sec = 0.3,
    pose_publish_period_sec = 5e-3,
    trajectory_publish_period_sec = 30e-3,
    rangefinder_sampling_ratio = 1.,
    odometry_sampling_ratio = 1.,
    fixed_frame_pose_sampling_ratio = 1.,
    imu_sampling_ratio = 1.,
    landmarks_sampling_ratio = 1.,
}
```

The preceding options are configured for offline SLAM from the bag file provided on the Ouster website at the following link:

https://data.ouster.io/downloads/os1_townhomes_cartographer.zip

https://data.ouster.io/downloads/os1_townhomes_cartographer.zip

You will need to modify the highlighted ones if you are doing online (real-time) SLAM on your self-driving car:

- odom_frame = "base_link": This should be set to odom so that Cartographer publishes the non-loop-closing continuous pose as odom_frame.
- provide_odom_frame = false: This should be set to true so that Cartographer knows that the odom_frame is published.
- num_laser_scans = 0: This should be set to 1 so that the lidar sensor's scan data is used straight from the sensor, rather than from point clouds from a bag file.
- num_point_clouds = 1: This should be set to 0 if not using a bag file and you are instead using a live lidar scan.

Next, you will see how the sensor urd file is configured.

os_sensor.urdf

This file is used to configure the physical transforms of your self-driving car. Each sensor you mount on the vehicle will be a link. Think of links as rigid bodies, like links in a chain. Each link is rigid in a chain, but the links can move relative to each other and each have their own coordinate frames.

In this file, you will see that we have set up the Ouster sensor as the robot, `<robot name="os_sensor">`.

We added links that represent the lidar coordinate frame, `<link name="os_lidar">`, and the IMU coordinate frame, `<link name="os_imu">`, of the sensor.

The following code shows how we provide the transforms from each frame back to the `base_link` frame:

```xml
<joint name="sensor_link_joint" type="fixed">
    <parent link="base_link" />
    <child link="os_sensor" />
    <origin xyz="0 0 0" rpy="0 0 0" />
</joint>

<joint name="imu_link_joint" type="fixed">
    <parent link="os_sensor" />
    <child link="os_imu" />
    <origin xyz="0.006253 -0.011775 0.007645" rpy="0 0 0" />
</joint>

<joint name="os1_link_joint" type="fixed">
    <parent link="os_sensor" />
    <child link="os_lidar" />
    <origin xyz="0.0 0.0 0.03618" rpy="0 0 3.14159" />
</joint>
```

You can see that `os_sensor` is placed at the center of the `base_link` coordinate frame, while `os_imu` and `os_lidar` are given their respective translations and rotations relative to `os_sensor`. These translations and rotations are provided in the Ouster sensor user guide under *Section 8*:

https://github.com/Krishtof-Korda/ouster_example_cartographer/blob/master/OS1-User-Guide-v1.14.0-beta.12.pdf

Next, you will learn how the launch file is configured to call all the previous configuration files and launch the SLAM process.

offline_cart_3d.launch

This file is used to call all the configuration files previously discussed.

It also remaps the `points2` and `imu` topics to the bag file Ouster `os_cloud_node` topics. If you are using another type of lidar sensor, simply use the topic name of that sensor in place:

```
<remap from="points2" to="/os_cloud_node/points" />
<remap from="imu" to="/os_cloud_node/imu" />
```

Next, you will learn how the `assets_writer_cart_3d.lua` file is used to save the map data.

assets_writer_cart_3d.lua

This file is used to configure the options for generating the fully aggregated point cloud that will be output in `.ply` format.

You can set the VOXEL_SIZE value that should be used to downsample the points and only take the centroid. This is important since without down sampling, you would need tremendous processing cycles.

VOXEL_SIZE = 5e-2

You also set `min_max_range_filter`, which only keeps points that are within a specified range from the lidar sensor. This is usually based on the specs in the datasheet of the lidar sensor. The Ouster OS1 datasheet can be found on the Ouster (https://outser.com/) website.

The following code snippet shows where you can configure the range filter options:

```
tracking_frame = "os_imu",
pipeline = {
  {
    action = "min_max_range_filter",
    min_range = 1.,
    max_range = 60.,
  },
```

Finally, you will learn how the `transform.lua` file is used to do 2D projections.

The transform.lua file

This file is a generic file for performing transforms and is used in the previous file to create the 2D map x-ray and probability grid images.

Fantastic, now that you understand what each configuration file does, it's time for you to see it in action! The next section will guide you through running SLAM using a prebuilt Docker image. This will hopefully get you SLAMing quicker than you can say *The cars of the future will drive us!*

Docker image

A Docker image has been created for you to download. This will help to ensure that all the required packages are installed and minimizes the time you need to get everything working.

If you are running on a Linux operating system, you can simply run `install-docker.sh`, located in the `ouster_example_cartographer` submodule, with the following command:

```
$ ./install-docker.sh
```

If you are on another operating system (Windows 10 or macOS), you can download and install Docker directly from their website:

`https://docs.docker.com/get-docker/`

You can verify that Docker was installed correctly with the following command:

```
$ docker -version
```

Great! Hopefully, things have gone smoothly, and you are ready to run the Docker image in a container. It is highly recommended to use a Linux machine with an Nvidia graphics card in order to make the code and Docker image work. The `run-docker.sh` script is provided to help start Docker with the correct options for your graphics processor. It is highly recommended to use a Nvidia GPU to process the SLAM efficiently. You can use other GPUs but the support for them is low.

The following section will provide you some troubleshooting steps for connecting Docker with your Nvidia GPU.

Docker Nvidia troubleshooting

Depending on the Nvidia setup on your Linux machine, you may need to perform the following commands before connecting to your Docker container:

```
# Stop docker before running 'sudo dockerd --add-
runtime=nvidia=/usr/bin/nvidia-container-runtime'
$ sudo systemctl stop docker

# Change mode of docker.sock if you have a permission issue
$ sudo chmod 666 /var/run/docker.sock

# Add the nvidia runtime to allow docker to use nvidia GPU
# This needs to be run in a separate shell from run-docker.sh
$ sudo dockerd --add-runtime=nvidia=/usr/bin/nvidia-container-
runtime
```

Now, you can run Docker and connect it to your GPU with the following command:

```
$ ./run-docker.sh
```

This script will pull the latest Docker image from Docker Hub and run the image either with the Nvidia runtime, if available, or simply on the CPU.

This file also has many useful commands in the comments for running Cartographer in 2D or 3D mode. You will learn about 3D mode here.

The next few sections will walk you through the steps of performing SLAM on the data you will download from Ouster.

Getting the sample data

The sample data that you will be SLAMing is available from the Ouster website.

Download it with the following commands:

```
$ mkdir /root/bags
$ cd /root/bags
$ curl -O https://data.ouster.io/downloads/os1_townhomes_
cartographer.zip
$ unzip /root/bags/os1_townhomes_cartographer.zip -d /root/
bags/
```

Sourcing the workspace

You will need to source the `catkin` workspace to ensure it is set up with ROS:

```
$ source /root/catkin_ws/devel/setup.bash
```

Validating rosbag

It is a good idea to validate `rosbag` using the built-in cartographer bag validation tool. This will ensure that the bag has continuous data and will produce results:

```
$ rosrun cartographer_ros cartographer_rosbag_validate -bag_filename /root/bags/os1_townhomes_cartographer.bag
```

Preparing to launch

To run your offline SLAM on the bag, you first need to get to the launchpad:

```
$ cd /root/catkin_ws/src/ouster_example_cartographer/cartographer_ros/launch
```

Launching offline on the bag

Now, you are ready to launch the offline SLAM. This will create a `.pbstream` file that will be used later to write your assets, such as the following:

- `.ply`, the point cloud file
- A 2D x-ray image of the mapped space
- A 2D probability grid image of an open versus an occupied area

The following command will launch the offline SLAM process on your bag file:

```
$ roslaunch offline_cart_3d.launch bag_filenames:=/root/bags/os1_townhomes_cartographer.bag
```

You should see an `rviz` window open that looks something like that in the following figure:

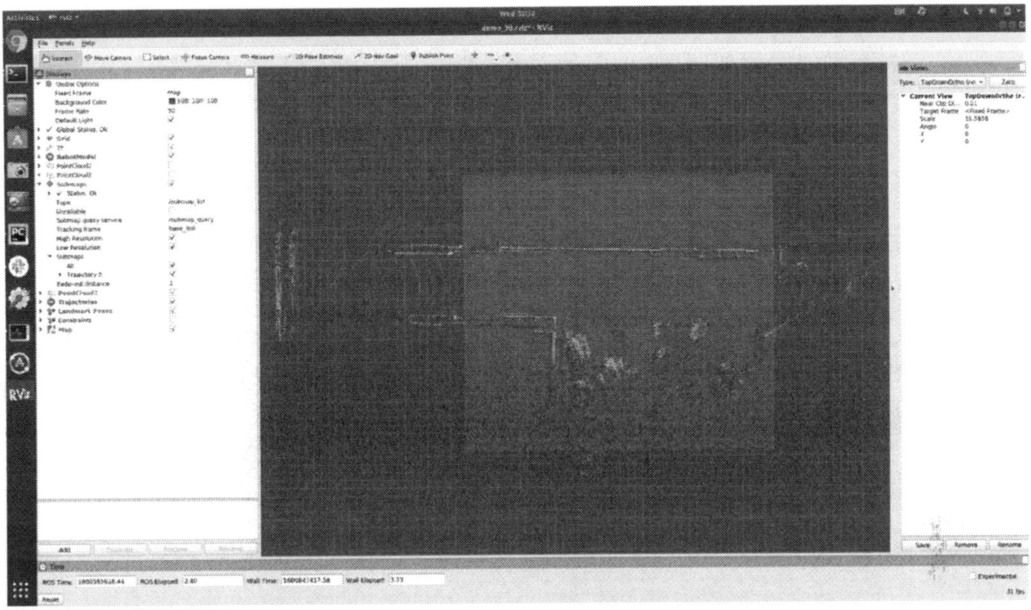

Figure 11.5 – The rviz window Cartographer launch

Now, you can sit back and watch in wonder as Cartographer meticulously performs SLAM.

First, it will make smaller local submaps. Then, it will scan match the submap to the global map. You will notice that it snaps the point cloud every few seconds when it has collected enough data to match the global map.

When the process is complete, you will have a file in the `/root/bags` folder named `os1_townhomes_cartographer.bag.pbstream`. You will use this file to write your assets.

Writing your sweet, sweet assets

I hope you are ready because you are about to get the final product from SLAM – a map of some random street you have never seen before. Just what you dreamed of, right?

Run the following command to collect your prize!

```
$ roslaunch assets_writer_cart_3d.launch bag_filenames:=/root/bags/os1_townhomes_cartographer.bag  pose_graph_filename:=/root/bags/os1_townhomes_cartographer.bag.pbstream
```

This will take a while; go grab a bite of your favorite comfort food. We will see you back here in an hour.

Welcome back! Feast your eyes on your prizes!

Opening your first prize

Voila! Your very own x-ray 2D map!

```
$ xdg-open os1_townhomes_cartographer.bag_xray_xy_all.png
```

This is how the output appears:

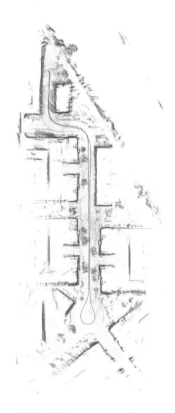

Figure 11.6 – 2D x-ray map of townhomes

Opening your second prize

Shazam! Your very own probability grid 2D map!

```
$ xdg-open os1_townhomes_cartographer.bag_probability_grid.png
```

This is how the output appears:

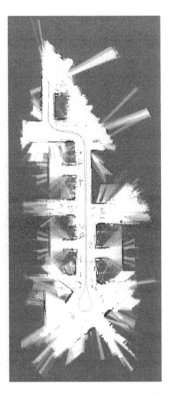

Figure 11.7 – 2D probability grid map of townhomes

Your final prize

You will find a file in the `/root/bags` folder that is named `os1_townhomes_cartographer.bag_points.ply`. This prize will take a little more effort to truly appreciate.

You can use any tool that is capable of opening a `.ply` file. CloudCompare is a **FOSS** (that is, a **free open source software**) tool for this and can be downloaded from the following link:

`https://www.danielgm.net/cc/`

You can also use CloudCompare to save your `.ply` file into other formats, such as XYZ, XYZRGB, CGO, ASC, CATIA ASC, PLY, LAS, PTS, or PCD.

`unitycoder` has good instructions for making the conversion available at the following link:

`https://github.com/unitycoder/UnityPointCloudViewer/wiki/Converting-Points-Clouds-with-CloudCompare`

This is how the output appears:

Figure 11.8 – Point cloud 3D map viewed in CloudCompare

Have a look at *Figure 11.8* and *Figure 11.9*, which show what the 3D map of points looks like using the CloudCompare viewer:

Figure 11.9 – Point cloud 3D map viewed in CloudCompare, top-view

Congratulations on making your first of what we hope are many maps! This is just the beginning of your journey and we can't wait to see what you make with your newfound skills! Next, we will summarize everything you learned.

Summary

Wow, you have come a long way in this chapter and book. You began with nothing but a mobile phone and a blue GPS dot. You traveled across the globe to Russia and found the life-juice at the Monkey Face. You grabbed some snacks by SLAMing your way through your Cimmerian dark home. You learned the difference between maps and localization, and the various types of each. You picked up some open source tools and lashed them to your adventure belt for future use.

You also learned how to apply the open source Cartographer on Ouster OS1-128 lidar sensor data, coupled with the built-in IMU to generate dense and tangible maps of some really nice townhomes that you manipulated using CloudCompare. Now you know how to create maps and can go out and map your own spaces and localize within them! The world is your Ouster (pardon me, oyster)! We can't wait to see what you build next with your creativity and knowhow!

We really hope that you enjoyed learning with us; we certainly enjoyed sharing this knowledge with you and hope you are inspired to build the future!

Questions

You should be able to answer the following questions now:

1. What is the difference between mapping and localization?
2. What frame does Cartographer typically use as the tracking frame?
3. Why is SLAM needed?
4. In which file do you set `min_max_range_filter`?

Further reading

- W. Hess, D. Kohler, H. Rapp, and D. Andor, *Real-Time Loop Closure in 2D LIDAR SLAM*: https://opensource.googleblog.com/2016/10/introducing-cartographer.html (https://research.google/pubs/pub45466/), in *Robotics and Automation (ICRA)*, 2016 IEEE International Conference on. IEEE, 2016. pp. 1271–1278.

- Cartographer: https://github.com/cartographer-project/cartographer_ros
- More on Cartographer: https://google-cartographer-ros.readthedocs.io/en/latest/compilation.html
- Localization types: https://www.cpp.edu/~ftang/courses/CS521/notes/Localization.pdf
- RGB-D SLAM: https://felixendres.github.io/rgbdslam_v2/
- Probabilistic algorithms in robotics: http://robots.stanford.edu/papers/thrun.probrob.pdf

Assessments

Chapter 1

1. Yes, though in some cases, you might need a custom build.
2. Usually `bilateralFilter()`.
3. The HOG detector.
4. Using `VideoCapture()`.
5. A bigger aperture increases the amount of light available to the sensor, but reduces the depth of field.
6. You need a higher ISO when there is not enough light for your required shutter speed and aperture settings.
7. Yes, sub-pixel precision improves the calibration in a noticeable way.

Chapter 2

1. For **UART**: **Single-ended**: Two wires (data and ground). There is no clock line needed since it is asynchronous and devices keep their own time and agree ahead of time on the baud rate. **Differential**: Two wires (data high and data low). The differential voltage is measured instead of voltage versus ground.

   I2C: Two wires, **serial clock (SCL)** and **serial data (SDA)**, using a bus architecture with master and slave devices.

   SPI: $3 + 1n$ wires, where n is the number of slave devices. Three primary wires: **signal clock (SCLK), master out slave in (MOSI)**, and **master in slave out (MISO)**; and one **slave select (SS)** wire for each slave device.

   CAN: Two wires, CAN-HI and CAN-LO, using a bus architecture with CAN-HI and CAN-LO acting as a differential pair.

2. Noise can be reduced by using a differential pair where noise affects both signals similarly. The wires are twisted around each other to cancel any induced currents.
3. Serial transmission sends all bits across a single wire one after the other, serially. Parallel transmission sends each bit on its own wire simultaneously. So, for an 8-bit word, parallel transmission will be 8x faster.
4. I2C, SPI, CAN, and Ethernet.
5. I2C and SPI.
6. UART.

Chapter 3

1. HLS, HSV, LAB, and YcbCr.
2. To get a bird's-eye view of the lanes, so that they are parallel also in the image.
3. Using a histogram.
4. Sliding window.
5. Using `polyfit()`, and then using the coefficients to draw the line.
6. `Scharr()` works well.
7. The **exponentially weighted moving average** is simple and effective.

Chapter 4

1. It is a neuron in a neural network.
2. Adam.
3. It is an operation that applies a kernel to some pixels, obtaining a new pixel as a result.
4. It is a neural network with at least one convolutional layer.
5. It is a layer connecting all the neurons of one layer to all the neurons of the previous layer.
6. It linearizes the 2D output of a convolutional layer, to make it possible to use the output with a dense layer.
7. TensorFlow.
8. LeNet.

Chapter 5

1. You do what you have to do... but ideally, you want to use it only once, in order to avoid bias in your choice of model.
2. It is the process of generating more data out of the initial dataset, to increase its size and improve the generalization of the network.
3. Not exactly: Keras replaces the original images with the ones coming from data augmentation.
4. In general, the dense layers tend to be the ones with the most parameters; in particular, the first one after the last convolutional layer is usually by far the biggest.
5. While the line of the training loss goes down with the number of epochs, the validation loss goes up.
6. Not always: you can use a strategy to first overfit the network (to properly learn the training dataset), and then to improve generalization and remove the overfitting.

Chapter 6

1. To increase the number of non-linear activations and let the network learn more complex functions.
2. Not necessarily. In fact, a well-crafted deep network can be faster and more precise.
3. When the training accuracy increases but the validation accuracy decreases.
4. Early stopping.
5. With batch normalization.
6. Using data augmentation.
7. Because it learns not to rely on only a few channels.
8. The training will probably be slower.
9. The training will probably be slower.

Chapter 7

1. SSD is a neural network able to find multiple objects in an image, and its output includes the position of the object detected. It can work in real time.
2. Inception is an influential and precise neural network created by Google.
3. A layer that has been frozen cannot be trained.

4. No, it cannot. It can only detect traffic lights, but not their color.
5. Transfer learning is the process of taking a neural network trained on a task and adapting it to solve a new, related task.
6. Adding dropout, increasing the size of the dataset, increasing the variety of data augmentation, and adding batch normalization.
7. Given the variety of images in ImageNet, it's difficult to choose the kernel size of the convolutional layers, so they used kernels of multiple sizes in parallel.

Chapter 8

1. DAVE-2, but it can also be called DriveNet.
2. In a classification task, the image is classified according to some pre-defined categories, while in a regression task we generate a continuous prediction; in our case, for example, a steering angle between −1 and 1.
3. You can use the `yield` keyword.
4. It is a visualization tool that can help us understand where the neural network is focusing its attention.
5. We need three video streams to help the neural network understand how to correct wrong positions, as the side cameras are effectively corrections from positions far from the center of the car.
6. For performance reasons, and to be sure that all the code is running only on the client.

Chapter 9

1. The dense blocks, where each layer is connected to all the output of the previous layers, including the input.
2. ResNet.
3. It is an adaptation of DenseNet for performing semantic segmentation.
4. Because it can be visualized like a U, with the left side downsampling and the right side upsampling.
5. No, you can just stack a series of convolutions. However, due to the high resolution, achieving a good result will be challenging, and most likely would use a lot of memory and be quite slow.

6. You can use a median blur to remove the *salt and pepper* noise that can be present in the segmentation masks of poorly trained networks.

7. They are used to propagate high-resolution channels and help the network achieve a good real resolution.

Chapter 10

1. PID, since only simple algebraic equations are being solved. Recall that MPC needs to solve a multivariate optimization in real time, which requires very high levels of processing power to ensure a low enough latency for driving.

2. The integral term in PID corrects for any steady-state bias in the system by applying a control input based on the accumulated errors of the system.

3. The derivative term in PID corrects for overshooting the setpoint by adjusting the control input based on the time rate of change of the error.

4. A cost is used to assign a value to a trajectory where that value is minimized. Example costs are the cost of collisions, the cost of sequential actuations, the cost of using actuators, and the cost of not being at the destination.

   A constraint is a physical limit of the system, such as turn radius, maximum lateral and longitudinal acceleration, vehicle dynamics, and maximum steering angle.

Chapter 11

1. Mapping seeks to store information about navigable space in the environment, whereas localization seeks to determine where a robot is within the environment.

2. `odom_frame`.

3. SLAM is needed because a map will never have fully current information about the environment. Therefore, you need to constantly be creating a map of navigable space as you go. SLAM also provides a method for mapping environments without expensive high-accuracy IMU equipment.

4. `assets_writer_cart_3d.lua`.

Other Books You May Enjoy

If you enjoyed this book, you may be interested in these other books by Packt:

Learning OpenCV 4 Computer Vision with Python 3 – Third Edition
Joseph Howse, Joe Minichino
ISBN: 978-1-78953-161-9

- Install and familiarize yourself with OpenCV 4's Python 3 bindings
- Understand image processing and video analysis basics
- Use a depth camera to distinguish foreground and background regions
- Detect and identify objects, and track their motion in videos
- Train and use your own models to match images and classify objects
- Detect and recognize faces, and classify their gender and age
- Build an augmented reality application to track an image in 3D
- Work with machine learning models, including SVMs, artificial neural networks (ANNs), and deep neural networks (DNNs)

Hands-On Computer Vision with TensorFlow 2

Benjamin Planche, Eliot Andres

ISBN: 978-1-78883-064-5

- Create your own neural networks from scratch
- Classify images with modern architectures including Inception and ResNet
- Detect and segment objects in images with YOLO, Mask R-CNN, and U-Net
- Tackle problems in developing self-driving cars and facial emotion recognition systems
- Boost your application's performance with transfer learning, GANs, and domain adaptation
- Use recurrent neural networks for video analysis
- Optimize and deploy your networks on mobile devices and in the browser

Leave a review - let other readers know what you think

Please share your thoughts on this book with others by leaving a review on the site that you bought it from. If you purchased the book from Amazon, please leave us an honest review on this book's Amazon page. This is vital so that other potential readers can see and use your unbiased opinion to make purchasing decisions, we can understand what our customers think about our products, and our authors can see your feedback on the title that they have worked with Packt to create. It will only take a few minutes of your time, but is valuable to other potential customers, our authors, and Packt. Thank you!

Index

A

activation function 93
activations
  visualizing 141-145
actuation 283
AlexNet
  discovering 197
Amplitude Modulation (AM) 34
analog signal
  versus digital signal 34-36
aperture 20
assets
  writing 331, 332

B

batch normalization
  about 160
  batch size 164
  used, for building network 160-164
bias 93
binaries, for Linux and Windows
  reference link 179
blueprints 241
bottleneck layer 262

C

C++
  MPC, example 304-308
calibration
  generating 30, 31
camera
  about 18
  benefits 27
  considerations, selecting 26, 27
  drawbacks 28
  primary factors 26
camera calibration
  about 85
  with OpenCV 28, 29
camera components
  about 25
  aperture 25
  lens 26
  light-sensitive array 25
camera terminology
  about 18
  aperture 20
  Depth of Field (DoF) 21
  dynamic range 22
  Field of View (FoV) 18

focal length 20
Frame rate (FPS) 24
f-stop 20
ISO sensitivity 23
lens distortion 25
lens flare 24
resolution 19
CAN bus protocol
  cons 55
  pros 54
Carla
  installation link 179
  neural network, integrating
    with 239-243
  reference link 122
  used, for collecting images 179-185
CARLA
  Packt-Town04-PID.py script,
    executing 304
cartographer_ros
  about 320
  configuring 320
catkin workspace
  setting up 330
CIFAR-10
  using 111-116
classifiers
  about 125
  data augmentation 127-129
  real-world dataset, creating 126
CloudCompare
  download link 333
CMOS active-pixel sensor 25
CMOS sensor 25
CNN
  used, for segmenting images 263
combined threshold 77, 78

Common Objects in Context
    (COCO) 186
compression layer 259
configuration files, cartographer_ros
  assets_writer_cart_3d.lua 327
  cart_3d.lua 324, 325
  demo_3d.rviz 321-323
  offline_cart_3d.launch 327
  os_sensor.urf 325, 326
  transform.lua file 328
  VOXEL_SIZE 327
controller
  about 283
  need for 282
  types of systems 284
Controller Area Network (CAN)
  about 51, 52
  features 51
  message format 53
controller types
  about 283, 284
  Model Predictive Control (MPC) 289
  Proportional, Integral,
    Derivative (PID) 284-286
Control Variable (CV) 283
convergence 137
convolutional layers
  tuning 131-134
Convolutional Neural Network
  (CNN) 95, 194, 232
convolutions
  about 95-97
  advantages 97
Coordinated Universal Time (UTC) 38
cost function 136
Cross-Track Error (CTE) 283
custom dataset 123

D

data augmentation
  about 127-129
  used, for improving dataset 165-168
dataset
  defining 123, 124
  existing 121
  feeding, to Inception 204
  improving, with data
    augmentation 165-168
  in Keras module 121
  obtaining 120
  preprocessing 227, 228
  recording 226, 227
  splitting 124, 125
  synthetic datasets 122
  testing 123
  training 123
  validating 123
DAVE-2 215, 216
deconvolution 263
deep learning
  about 91
  success 94
dense block 259-262
dense layer
  neural network, training 136
  tuning 135, 136
DenseNet
  about 258
  adapting, for semantic
    segmentation 264, 265
  as classifier 259
  for classification 258
DenseNet architecture 254
DenseNet-B 262
DenseNet-BC 262

Depth of Field (DoF) 20, 21
derivative 137
derivative term 288, 289
differential line
  versus single-ended line 41-44
digital signal
  versus analog signal 34-36
distortion detection 29, 30
Docker
  connection, troubleshooting
    with Nvidia 329
  reference link 328
Docker image 328
dropout
  about 168
  used, for improving validation
    accuracy 168-174
dynamic range 22
Dynamic Vision Sensor (DVS) 184

E

edge detection
  about 74-76
  combined threshold 77, 78
  interpolated threshold 76
Electronic Control Units (ECUs) 51
error 283
Ethernet 55, 56
exponentially weighted
    moving average 84

F

FC-DenseNet
  about 254
  coding blocks 265-267
  network, assembling 267, 269

neural network, executing 273-276
neural network, feeding 269-273
semantic segmentation,
    improving 276, 277
feature 92
feedforward neural networks 92
Field of View (FoV) 18, 26
focal length 20
FoV calculators
  reference link 27
framed-based serial protocols
  about 50
  Controller Area Network (CAN) 51-53
  Ethernet 55, 56
  internet protocols 55, 56
  Transmission Control
      Protocol (TCP) 59-61
  User Datagram Protocol (UDP) 56-59
Frames Per Second (FPS) 24, 224
f-stop 20

G

gain 286
Google Cartographer
  SLAM, using with 319
GoogLeNet 197
GPU
  working 244
growth rate 261

H

High Dynamic Range (HDR) 22
Histogram of Oriented Gradients (HOG)
  about 15
  camera 18
  camera, benefits 27, 28

camera components 25
camera, considerations selecting 26, 27
camera, drawbacks 27, 28
camera terminology 18
sliding window mechanism 16
used, for pedestrian detection 15
using, with OpenCV 16, 17
histograms
  used, for searching lanes 78, 79
HLS color space
  thresholding, working on 69
HSV color space
  thresholding, working on 70

I

image
  blurring 11, 12
  brightness, modifying 13, 14
  contrast, modifying 13, 14
  flipping 10, 11
  gamma, modifying 13, 14
  manipulating 10
  rectangle and text, drawing 15
image classification
  Inception, using 200, 201
image files
  working with 7, 8, 9
ImageNet 195, 196
ImageNet Large-Scale Visual Recognition
    Challenge (ILSVRC) 195
images
  annotating 190, 191
  collecting, with Carla 179-185
  segmenting, with CNN 263
Inception
  about 197-200
  dataset, feeding 204

using, for image classification 200, 201
using, for transfer learning 201-204
Inception v3 179
Inertial Measurement Unit
    (IMU) 317, 319
inference 145, 146
integral term 287
Inter-Integrated Circuit (I2C)
    about 44-46
    benefits 47
    disadvantages 47
International Organization for
    Standardization (ISO) sensitivity 23
internet protocols 55, 56
interpolated threshold 76

K

Keras
    installing 98
Keras module
    dataset in 121
kernel 95

L

LAB color space
    thresholding, working on 70
lanes
    searching, with histograms 78, 79
LeNet
    about 103
    layers 103
lens distortion 25
lens flare 24
localization
    about 313
    need for 312

reference link 314
types 314, 315
localizing 316
local minimum 137
loop closure 318
loss function 136

M

machine learning 90
manual_control.py 216-218
maps
    about 312
    need for 312
    reference link 315
    types 314, 315
Master In Slave Out (MISO) 48
Master Out Slave In (MOSI) 48
MaxPooling
    tuning 134, 135
mean squared error (MSE) 136
megapixels (MP) 19
MNIST hand-written digits
    detecting 99
    labels 101
    load_data() method 100
    one-hot encoding 102
    testing dataset 102
    training dataset 102
    training samples 100
MNIST model
    applying 174
model
    building 129-131
    convolutional layers, tuning 131-134
    dense layer, tuning 135, 136
    MaxPooling, tuning 134, 135

neural network, initializing 138
neural network, training 137, 138
model, of neural network
  architecture 105-107
  code 104
  defining 103
  training 107-110
Model Predictive Control (MPC)
  about 289
  example, in C++ 304-308
  pipeline 290, 291
  working 289, 290
Multiple Input, Multiple
    Output (MIMO) 284

N

naïve 199
naïve Inception block 198
network
  building, with batch
    normalization 160-164
neural network
  backward pass 137
  driving, with behavioral
    cloning 214, 215
  forward pass 137
  initializing 138
  integrating, with Carla 239-243
  layers, adding 153-155
  modeling 228, 229
  overfitting 139-141
  training 136-175
  training accuracy 151
  training efficiency 156-159
  training, for regression 229-231
  training speed 152, 153
  underfitting 139-141

validation error 164, 165
neural networks 91
neuron 91-93
NumPy
  about 4
  grayscale image 5, 6
  image size 5

O

odometry
  about 316
  reference link 317
offline SLAM
  launching 330, 331
  launch, preparing 330
one-hot encoding 102
one video stream
  recording 219-221
OpenCV
  about 4
  distortion detection 30
  HOG, using 16, 17
  RGB images 6, 7
  used, for camera calibration 28, 29
  used, for distortion detection 29
  used, for generating calibration 30, 31
open source mapping tools
  about 319
  reference link 319
Open Systems Interconnection (OSI) 55
Ouster
  URL 327
Ouster lidar
  SLAM, using with 319
Ouster sensor 320
overfitting 139

P

parallel data
  versus serial data 36, 37
parameters 94
pedestrian detection
  with HOG 15
perspective
  correcting 72-74
point cloud 3D map 333-335
Printed Circuit Board (PCB) 44
probability grid 2D map 332
process 283
Proportional, Integral,
    Derivative (PID) 284-286
proportional term 286, 287

R

raw semantic segmentation 254
real-world dataset
  creating 126
Recommended Standard 232 (RS-232) 41
Recommended Standard 422 (RS-422) 41
Rectified Linear Unit (ReLU) 93
Region Of Interest (ROI) 6
regression
  neural network, training for 229-231
repo 320
ResNet50 187
resolution 19
RGB/BGR
  thresholding, working on 67-69
rosbag
  validating 330

S

saliency maps
  visualizing 232-239
samples
  retraining 146
self-driving
  about 244-246
  bigger datasets, training with
      generators 246, 247
  data, augmenting 248
semantic segmentation
  about 252, 254
  dataset, collecting 255, 256
  goal, defining 254
  synchronous_mode.py,
      modifying 256, 257
  used, for adapting DenseNet 264, 265
Serial Clock Wire (SCL) 45
serial data
  versus parallel data 36, 37
Serial Data Wire (SDA) 45
Serial Peripheral Interface (SPI)
  about 48, 49
  cons 50
  pros 50
setpoint 283
signal types 34
Simultaneous Localization and
    Mapping (SLAM)
  about 314-317
  loop closure 318
  performing, on data 329
  types 317
  with Google Cartographer 319
  with Ouster lidar 319

single-ended line
    versus differential line 41-44
Single Input, Single Output (SISO) 284
Single Shot MultiBox Detector (SSD)
    downloading 187, 188
    executing 188-190
    implementing 185
    loading 187, 188
    used, for detecting pedestrians 178, 179
    used, for detecting traffic lights 179
    used, for detecting vehicles 178, 179
sliding window algorithm
    about 79, 80
    coordinates of 81, 82
    initializing 80, 81
    polynomial fitting 82-84
sub-pixel precision 31
Support Vector Machine (SVM) 17
synthetic datasets 122

T

TCP header fields 61
Temps Universel Coordonné (TUC) 38
TensorFlow
    installing 98
TensorFlow detection model zoo
    discovering 186
three video streams
    recording 221-225
thresholding
    performing 66
    working, on different color spaces 67
    working, on HLS color space 69
    working, on HSV color space 70
    working, on LAB color space 70
    working, on RGB/BGR 67-69
    working, on YCbCr color space 71

traffic light
    color, detecting 191, 192
    color, recognizing 209-211
    dataset, creating 192-194
    recognizing 209-211
transfer function 93
transfer learning
    about 192, 194
    Inception, using 201-204
    performance 205-208
transition layer 259
Transmission Control Protocol
        (TCP) 59, 60
transposed convolution 263

U

underfitting 139
Universal Asynchronous Receive
        and Transmit (UART)
    about 38
    cons 40
    example 39
    packet structure 38
    pros 40
User Datagram Protocol (UDP) 56-59

V

validation accuracy
    improving, with dropout 168-174
video
    average, rolling 84
    enhancing 84
    partial histogram 84
video files
    working with 9, 10

W

weak reference 218
webcams
   working with 10
Wil Selby's
   reference link 319
WordNet 195

X

x-ray 2D map 332

Y

YCbCr color space
   thresholding, working on 71

Printed in Poland
by Amazon Fulfillment
Poland Sp. z o.o., Wrocław